LIKE A NATURAL WOMAN

LIKE A NATURAL WOMAN

Spectacular Female Performance in Classical Hollywood

KIRSTEN PULLEN

RUTGERS UNIVERSITY PRESS
NEW BRUNSWICK, NEW JERSEY, AND LONDON

Library of Congress Cataloging-in-Publication Data

Pullen, Kirsten.

Like a natural woman : spectacular female performance in classical Hollywood / Kirsten Pullen.

     pages   cm

Includes bibliographical references and index.

ISBN 978–0–8135–6265–0 (hardback) — ISBN 978–0–8135–6264–3 (pbk.) — ISBN 978–0–8135–6266–7 (e-book)

1. Women in motion pictures. 2. Motion picture actors and actresses—California—Los Angeles. I. Title.

PN1995.9.W6.P85 2014

791.4302'809252—dc23

                                                                    2013040629

A British Cataloging-in-Publication record for this book is available from the British Library.

Visit our website: http://rutgerspress.rutgers.edu

Manufactured in the United States of America

For Ivy, my own spectacular female

CONTENTS

PREFACE

I began working on what finally became this book in 2004. Over the next ten years, I moved from the University of Calgary in Canada to Texas A&M University in College Station. My husband and I bought and sold a house, and bought another. I got tenure. We had a wonderful baby girl who is now a wonderful first grader. I helped start two different graduate programs in performance studies. I took research trips to Dallas and Los Angeles. We fell in love with the Texas heat if not always the Texas politics. I got the incredible opportunity to direct the Academy for the Visual and Performing Arts at Texas A&M University. And I watched a lot of old movies and television programs; read a lot of books, magazines, and gossip columns; and wrote lots of conference papers about film and television performance in the 1930s–1960s. It took a long time to get here, but I've enjoyed nearly every part of the process.

When I began working on what finally became this book, all of my subjects were still alive, except for Carmen Miranda, who died in 1955. All of the subjects except Zsa Zsa Gabor (who may outlive us all!) have since died. My world is smaller with their passing, and I wish they knew how important, inspiring, challenging, and entertaining I found their lives and work. They are all spectacular women, and I want to first thank them for living such interesting lives and producing such indelible personae. Every time there's a movie sold with the image of a buxom babe, we should thank Jane Russell—and every time we hear of another Hollywood starlet starting her own production company because she's been pigeonholed by Hollywood, we should remember that Russell was one of the first to leverage her celebrity this way. The Aqualillies are reviving Esther Williams's classic water ballet style for a new generation, combining athleticism and eroticism much as she did three generations before. After Lena Horne's death in 2010, hundreds mourned at her funeral, and the contemporary mixed-race actress Halle Berry gave her a tribute at that year's Academy Awards, the only performer singled out for an Oscar memorial. Carmen Miranda's be-turbaned silhouette is nearly as recognizable today as it was in the 1940s, not least because it's been reappropriated by drag queens who admire her parodic cita-tions of femininity. Zsa Zsa Gabor is still referenced when contemporary female celebrities self-promote themselves into a fortune or marry someone they barely know. Though most of my students stare blankly when I mention their names and their films, Russell, Williams, Horne, Miranda, and Gabor continue to reso-nate in contemporary popular culture. I am grateful to each of them, and I insist they are worthy of prolonged academic scrutiny.

A decade is a long time, and so there are many other people to whom I am grateful. The staffs at the UCLA Film and Television Archive and the Southern Methodist University DeGolyer Library's Ronald Davis Oral History Collection on the Performing Arts reconfirmed my joy in archival research. Leslie Mitchner at Rutgers University Press is a patient, positive, and generous editor who encour-aged instead of bullied and made me feel good about this project when I feared I'd never see the end. Adrienne McLean's reviewer comments strengthened the book in important ways, and India Cooper is a dream of a copy editor. Both the University of Calgary (with a Starter Research Grant) and Texas A&M Univer-sity (with a Melbern G. Glasscock Stipendiary Faculty Fellowship, a Program to Enhance Scholarly and Creative Activities Award, and especially the Ray A. Rothrock '77 Research Fellowship) provided the financial support necessary to conduct archival research; upgrade computers; purchase films, magazines, and database subscriptions; pay for images; and hire research assistants. I worked with terrific graduate students on this project: the brilliant Canadian feminist Erin Wunker at Calgary and the proud Texas Aggie performance scholars Han-nah Adamy, Bridget Liddell, the incomparable Emily Piepenbrink, and espe-cially the smart, brave Evleen Nasir. Many colleagues read and talked through this project, especially TAMU Writing Accountability Group members Jayson Beaster-Jones, Joshua Barbour, Tasha Dubriwny, Jennifer Jones Barbour, Kristan Poirot, Srivi Ramasubramanian, and Cara Wallis. My smart and sexy fellow Wis-consin PhD and ASTR roommate, Jessica Berson, has listened to me talk about these women for at least ten years. Kim Solga and Roberta Barker helped shape the project when they put me on their "Unsafe Realisms" ATHE panel and then kept inviting me to share my work on the naturalist paradigm at conferences and in print. I have had two of the best mentors an Iowa girl could hope for in Susan Bennett at the University of Calgary and Judith Hamera at Texas A&M Univer-sity. Both have offered unflagging personal and professional support and always know exactly what to say and when to say it. If I'm good at my job, it's largely thanks to their models of feminist scholarship, pedagogy, and administration.

As a scholar, my personal and professional lives merge in ways that are impos-sible to untangle. Facebook became a key motivator late in my writing process, especially when I struggled with administrative overload. Thanks for liking my posts, far-flung colleagues, TAMU students and faculty, family, and high school classmates! My in-laws, John and Rachel Heuman, always remember to ask questions about my book, and always have something nice to say when I answer. My sister, Heidi Pullen, and brother-in-law, Clark Stroupe, always tell me that they're proud of me already, and Heidi sent me a Lainey Gossip shout-out when I needed it most. My parents, Carl and Norma, are remarkable (they helped with my tenure dossier) and read every word of the manuscript before anyone else. Ivy helped by listening to bedtime stories of Hollywood stars and repeating fun facts about them at the dinner table. Josh Heuman is an amazing father, a brilliant scholar, and the love of my life. I owe him everything and can never thank him enough.

LIKE A NATURAL WOMAN

PLAYING HERSELF

THE NATURALIST PARADIGM AND THE
SPECTACLE OF FEMALE SEXUALITY

In the 1954 Twentieth Century–Fox film *There's No Business like Show Business*, the ambitious vaudevillian Vicky (Marilyn Monroe) cha-chas, struts, can-cans, and bump-and-grinds her way through "Heat Wave," delivering a weather forecast of "hot and humid nights."[1] She sings that she "started this heat wave," undulating her hips and thrusting her pelvis, "in such a way that the customers say that I certainly can . . . can-can." It's a showstopper among showstoppers. In addition to Monroe's sexy number, Ethel Merman (as vaudeville matriarch Molly Donahue) sings the title song, already her standard; Johnnie Ray (playing performer-turned-priest Steve Donahue) inspires all with the gospel-tinged "If You Believe"; and Donald O'Connor tap-dances his love for Monroe's Vicky with a group of Greek-goddess statues come to life. In "Heat Wave," however, Monroe is so provocatively sexual that patriarch Terry Donahue (Dan Dailey) tells his wife that "you can certainly see why" the producer gave Vicky the number, passing over the Donahue family version.

    There's No Business like Show Business is a backstage musical. Rick Altman's influential *The American Film Musical* defines the genre as "primarily concerned with putting on a show." Altman further clarifies that the focus is not on the show-within-a-show itself, but rather how the show is produced and performed. At the same time, the show's success is linked to the romance between the leads. For Altman, either the show leads to love between the two leads ("hero and heroine are thrown together by their common profession; their make-believe love" becomes real), or love creates the show ("only by the joint efforts of a romantic couple can the show be brought to a successful conclusion"). Further, for Altman this link between romance and theatrical/cinematic production "endows the coupling process with the magical qualities" to justify "an American popular mythology" that suggests American society succeeds on the "foundation of marriage for love." The energy and excitement of the song-and-dance sequences underscore the inevitability of the romantic narrative, making it seem natural.[2]

Altman's exegesis is important precisely because he persuasively and thoroughly links Hollywood film musicals to an ideology of heterosexual romance leading inevitably to marriage and family. Altman also gestures toward the capitalist narratives on which the film musical is built. Other scholars, such as Jane Feuer, explicitly focus their attention on economic and class ideologies and the consumerist/capitalist thrust of the movie musical. Still others, such as Richard Dyer, illustrate how Hollywood musicals forcefully construct American identity and utopic community. In short, several American popular mythologies—of true love, hard work leading inevitably to financial success, disparate groups united in paradisiacal unity—are encapsulated by this midcentury genre. In important and previously overlooked ways, however, the movie musical also participates in a midcentury project to solidify understandings of film acting as simultaneously rooted in performers' biographies and a specific technique that can be learned and perfected. This paradox defines the naturalist paradigm that structures film performance and reception across genres from the so-called Golden Age to today.

There's No Business like Show Business is a particularly rich text for analysis. Multiple shows are being made, and a family narrative doubles the romance narrative. Tim Donahue (O'Connor) must resolve his conflicts with his family and Vicky in order to participate in the finale, a benefit performance for the closing of the legendary Hippodrome. Tim and his sister, Katy (Mitzi Gaynor), had earlier been featured in *Manhattan Parade*, a Broadway revue built around Vicky's singular talents. Love blooms between Vicky and Tim during rehearsals, but Tim is a drinker with a jealous streak. He and Vicky argue when she's late because of a meeting with Lew Harris, the producer.

> VICKY: It's different with me. I've been on my own since I was fifteen. This show is my big chance. It's make or break.
>
> TIM: Don't worry, honey, you'll make it. You've got what it takes, and you know how to use it.
>
> VICKY: I don't have to take that from you, Tim. Why should I? I don't owe you a thing.
>
> TIM: That's right, you don't. You only owe Lew Harris. You owe him everything. And let it not be said that you're a girl who welches on her debts.

Vicky angrily sends him away, and the drunken Tim gets in a minor car accident and then runs off to join the navy. Molly takes over his role in the revue, which does indeed make Vicky a major star, though Molly continues to blame her for Tim's absence. The finale resolves everything, with both sons (Steve is an army chaplain on leave for the day) appearing backstage, Molly forgiving Vicky, Terry returning from his search for Tim, and Katy announcing her pregnancy (she'd earlier married Charlie Gibbs, the lyricist for *Manhattan Parade*).

Figure 1: The stars and a cast of hundreds for the finale of *There's No Business like Show Business*, 1954, Twentieth Century–Fox.

The finale begins with a reprise of the Donahues' signature "Alexander's Ragtime Band" and segues into "There's No Business like Show Business." A cast of thousands (or at least scores), costumed to represent particular geographic regions and dancing in a variety of concert, folk, and Broadway styles, backs up the five Donahues and Vicky. The women are dressed in red, white, and blue evening gowns; the boys are in uniform, and father Terry is in his traveling suit (see figure 1).

As is always the case with finales during the so-called Golden Age of the movie musical, much ideological work—about nation, family, heterosexual love, consumption, gender, and race—is finessed through jaunty tunes, dizzying camera work, energetically dancing bodies, and spectacular costumes and stage sets. The project of this book is at least in part to explain how naturalism as a performance technique and a set of aesthetic principles helps mask this ideological focus. At the same time, however, it demonstrates how naturalist performance can also reveal contradictions inherent in movie musical narratives and spectacle, as well as other Classical Hollywood films. Finally, *There's No Business like Show Business* stars Marilyn Monroe, perhaps the most spectacular 1950s performer but also a serious acting student, therefore crystallizing the ambivalent position of female performers and gendered performance in Classical Hollywood film.

In this book, I follow David Bordwell, Janet Staiger, and Kristin Thompson to define Classical Hollywood cinema as a film style that privileges storytelling above all other elements; develops a clear and unambiguous narrative; offers a realistic and natural representation of people, places, and events; hides its production processes through the use of continuity editing; and presents a universal emotional appeal that transcends individual audience differences.[3] Naturalist performance sustains all other elements of the filmic illusion because of its promise of authenticity and coherence. The everydayness of the performers (contrasted, with, for example, the theatricality of silent film or the deliberate strangeness of midcentury artistic experiments such as *Rules of the Game*) supports the everyday plots and their seemingly reasonable ideologies. Though Classical Hollywood cinema isn't synonymous with the studio system, it not coincidentally flourished during the period when the eight major studios (MGM, Warner Bros., Twentieth Century–Fox, Paramount, Universal, Columbia, RKO, and United Artists) exercised enormous control over the content, casting, publicity, design, direction, and distribution of US film.

I define naturalism as an acting technique that seeks close correspondence between performer and character to present motivated actions and genuine emotion. Though not synonymous with Method acting, it generally corresponds to the teachings of Lee Strasberg, Stella Adler, and Sanford Meisner, all of whom worked with the Group Theatre before developing their own careers as performers, directors, and teachers. There are key differences between US schools of naturalist acting, but all take Konstantin Stanislavsky's System as their foundation. Here, I develop a history of the naturalist paradigm in US film, arguing that naturalist acting as developed by the Group Theatre and made famous as Strasberg's Method structures all Classical Hollywood film performance, regardless of studio, performer, or genre. The naturalist paradigm is a particular acting style with concrete methods and techniques, but it is also a discursive construction that masks its specific strategy and subsumes performers' labor under the guise of playing oneself.

In particular, I focus on how naturalist performance in popular forms (most especially movie musicals but also film noir, television sitcoms, and cabaret acts) presents and makes performative ideals of femininity. My project recovers the performance techniques of Jane Russell (1921–2011), Esther Williams (1921–2013), Lena Horne (1917–2010), Carmen Miranda (1909–1955), and Zsa Zsa Gabor (1921?–), indicating multiple, ambivalent representations of femininity. For these actresses, and in general, a female star's greatest asset was her face and figure; film studios and audiences were assumed to be interested in exceptionally beautiful women rather than subtleties of acting. According to studio narratives, female performers were little more than pretty mannequins manipulated by offscreen directors, their performances pieced together by talented editors. Therefore, my research also recovers these actresses' labor and agency. Traditional constructions of popular performance styles (such as those required to sing, dance, and swim, or balance fruit-filled turbans, or chat on a variety show) erases the agency of actors laboring to develop nuanced, consistent, believable characters and personae through the use of voice, gesture, stance, and action.

Though movie musicals may seem divorced from naturalist acting, the spectacular performances at their core are influenced by naturalist discourses. *There's No Business like Show Business*, for example, is a backstage musical, and the musical numbers are performances from a vaudeville show rather than musically scored expressions of plot, theme, or character. Even so, the musical numbers in this and most other backstage musicals are indicative of character; more importantly, they indicate star persona. For example, the former vaudevillian Ethel Merman plays the vaudeville matriarch Molly Donahue, mugging and belting her way through the film. She also sings the title song to introduce the finale. Though "There's No Business like Show Business" was originally written for the stage musical *Annie Get Your Gun*, she reprises it here, and in fact, this is Merman's only *film* performance of her standard. Linked to her persona as well as the film's narrative, Merman's standard thus reinforces one of the film's themes, that "the show" is more important to "show people" than anything else, except, of course, for love.

There's No Business like Show Business actively circulates Merman's star persona as well as Monroe's, a common strategy for Golden Age movie musicals. Steven Cohan explains that not only characters but also musical numbers "were tailored to suit the star's special abilities, with plots designed primarily to offer ready excuses for a song or dance number in the distinct style associated with the star."[4] Further, because these films were relatively shallow, with more attention paid to spectacular musical sequences than to plot or character, star persona was a kind of shorthand for audiences, guiding their expectations and providing narrative and character logic. This strategy is obvious in Marilyn Monroe's impersonation of Vicky, a sexy blonde who uses her pretty face, breathy voice, and phenomenal body (rather than her talent) to steal the spotlight from the hardworking Donahue family. Though Monroe and Vicky did work hard, and did possess considerable dramatic, vocal, and dance talent, they were both accused of trading on their sexuality for their success. Further, as Vicky's reminder to Tim points out, she'd been on her own since she was fifteen, which references Monroe's own biography as a ward of the state who married at sixteen rather than return to foster care.

More importantly, however, Monroe's three major musical numbers ("After You Get What You Want," "Heat Wave," and "Lazy") circulate her star persona as a sex goddess. Her languid sensuality is the hallmark of this and most of her other Fox musical performances. She enters the stage on a sledge for "Heat Wave," her skirt pulled open to showcase her long white legs and wearing a tiny black bandeau top, a white hat with colorful flowers, a split black-and-white skirt with hot pink underskirt, and towering black platform shoes. Her skirt, which recalls the *baiana* Carmen Miranda popularized a decade before, is especially risqué. Monroe's navel is covered by a black sequined pasty above a triangular cutout that reveals her bare skin and mirrors the small black sequined triangle covering her pubis (see figure 2).

After the visibly sweating male dancers sing about how hot it is, she steps down and joins them. The black bandeau and skirt highlight her slender, soft belly, which undulates like a snake charmer. All her movements are fluid: sinuous arms curve inward as hips effortlessly weave circles and figure eights. It seems as though she's responding with her body to the music rather than executing

Figure 2: Marilyn Monroe generating her own "Heat Wave" in *There's No Business like Show Business*, 1954, Twentieth Century–Fox.

precise choreography (a typical illusion for female dancers in particular, where they labor to make complicated steps appear spontaneous). The apparent naturalness of her movements is underscored about halfway through the number when she takes a newspaper and plops down on the stage floor to read the weather report. Her legs akimbo, she leans forward on her elbows and begins reading about the terrific heat about to envelop the audience, looking like a little girl with the Sunday funnies. After the weather report, Monroe's movements become more intensely sexual, and she spreads her thighs and bends her knees as she wraps her arms around a pillar while grinding against it. She takes a wide stride across the stage, and when she stops to twist her hips, her thighs are spread wide open. She purrs the words of the song (her singing is never especially virtuosic, particularly when compared to Merman's, Ray's, or Dailey's, but it is more than competent), interrupting the lyrics to learn the backup dancers' names and flirt with the audience. "Heat Wave" is the kind of seriously sexy number that reminds contemporary audiences that wholesome 1950s movie musicals often included thinly veiled references to sexual pleasure. It's so sexy, in fact, that Ed Sullivan described Monroe's performance as "one of the most flagrant violations of good taste" he had witnessed.[5] Whether it violates good taste is a matter of opinion, but it does clearly identify Vicky/Monroe as a sexually experienced, spectacular commodity who exists for her own and the audience's pleasure.

During the filming of *There's No Business like Show Business*, Monroe met Paula and Susan Strasberg, the acting guru's wife and daughter. A year later, after leaving Joe DiMaggio during the filming of *The Seven-Year Itch*, Monroe abandoned Hollywood. She fled to New York to become a serious actress, because "if I thought I had to keep on wiggling in crummy movies, I wouldn't want to work in movies anymore."[6] Though Monroe had previously studied acting with Stanislavsky's student Michael Chekhov and the UCLA acting coach Natasha Lytess, she worked primarily in musical comedies or romantic farces that solidified her dumb blonde persona. In 1955, she began meeting privately with Lee Strasberg and seeing a psychotherapist in a dual effort to work through some of her psychological issues and become a serious dramatic actress. According to Susan Strasberg, her father "believed that Marilyn's work as an actress held the greatest hope of integration for her"; if she could control her emotions, she'd be a "genius" onstage and happy offstage, rather than a dangerously depressed and drug-dependent woman. Ultimately, Monroe began taking classes at the Actors Studio, where Strasberg pronounced her *Golden Boy* scene excellent, and her scene from *Anna Christie* was met with applause from the other students, a relatively rare occurrence.[7]

Monroe developed a strong personal relationship with the Strasbergs, staying in their New York apartment (sometimes in the youngest child Johnny's room, banishing him to the sofa), sharing meals with the family, and spending long hours in private lessons with Lee. Paula eventually replaced Natasha Lytess as her on-set acting coach. Monroe and Susan were good friends, and she extravagantly gifted the Strasbergs, giving Johnny her '56 Thunderbird and Paula the pearls DiMaggio bought her on their honeymoon. In her memoir *Marilyn and Me: Sisters, Rivals, Friends*, Susan Strasberg describes her relationship with Monroe as well as Monroe's relationship with Lee Strasberg, Method acting, and the Actors Studio. Strasberg especially remembered her parents' insistence on personal truth in acting: "My parents believed that the most difficult thing to be was yourself. Most people are trained from childhood to hide behind a thousand masks, lying, pretending, ignoring. An actor has to be capable of the full range of human expression—emotionally free and spontaneous, yet self aware, revealing the wonderful and terrible things that make us truly human and unique."[8] For Lee Strasberg and adherents of his Method, truthfully playing oneself was the goal of every actor. Performers revealed their "natural" psychology and "true" emotions while playing fictional characters.

The Naturalist Paradigm and the Naturalist Paradox

Susan Strasberg's description neatly summarizes the central paradox of Method (and by extension naturalist) acting. Through specific exercises, rigorous study, and sustained development of craft, actors will get better, and their representation of emotional truth and character psychology will become more authentic. At the same time, the only real tools actors have are their own personal memories and experiences, their psychological makeup, and their imaginative ability to place themselves in another's position. In short, actors do "work," but that work is internal, self-reflexive, and meant to develop emotional authenticity. By the time Monroe performed "Heat Wave," most US film audience members were at least passingly familiar with this articulation of film acting. And, as I demonstrate through the following case studies, most US film actors had access to training that drew upon this definitional paradox. Rather than belonging solely to those who were "taught and encouraged to mumble, grumble, slouch, spit, bite, scratch, ride motorcycles, wear sweatshirts and blue jeans, be so carried away by their emotions that they forget themselves,"[9] naturalism was taught to all actors working in Hollywood studios, encouraging them to merge their personalities and biographies with the characters they played. At the same time, the Hollywood apparatus consciously promoted this view of acting and actors, through official publicity, its own films (such as the backstage musical), and studio-sanctioned gossip. In short, actors and audiences were especially aware of the specifics of naturalist and Method acting at the height of Monroe's career, in no small part because of that career itself.

Cynthia Baron locates "the public's sudden interest in acting in the 1950s . . . [as] in part an effect of the work of actors such as Marlon Brando." Brando's performances in 1950s films (many directed by Elia Kazan) "captured public imagination so completely" that they defined Method acting for audiences.[10] Further, as many critics note, Method acting is particularly well suited to the demands of cinematic performance. According to Sharon Marie Carnicke, Strasberg's Method gives actors "concrete tools with which to compensate for the practical conditions of film making" such as filming scenes out of narrative sequence, working without an audience, and the spatial relationships between camera and performer.[11] Defining a specific *method* by which performers can construct performances, especially cinematic performances, meant that its details could be communicated to and understood by a general audience. Thus, Strasberg's insistence on naming his training and technique Method acting gave his "teachings an aura of scientific validity."[12] Further, as Bruce McConachie points out, actors embraced the Method in "the hope of raising their professional status" during "the early cold war."[13]

The Method also merged with studio discourse about the professionalization of acting. The same celebrity enterprise that fed public curiosity about actors' lives offered details about actors' labor and increasingly highlighted actors' actual work, especially after World War II. Obvious changes to the national workforce in terms of gender, class, and ethnicity had occurred, and narratives of ambition, sacrifice, and success dominated representations of physical and intellectual labor in the postwar economy. Hollywood participated in those representations by telling particular stories in films and television programs as well as highlighting different facets of performers' jobs. According to Cynthia Baron, studio publicity informed audiences that "actors exerted psychic labor to break down personal inhibitions and call forth private, often painful memories."[14] Thus, publicity about naturalist acting, whether generated by Strasberg, the film studios, or actors themselves, continued to focus on the "private" lives of stars, corresponding to earlier star narratives that promised to reveal performers' authentic selves to their audiences. The difference, however, lay in emphasis. Where previous exposés of private lives focused on home furnishings, hobbies, and accounts of actorly physical transformation, they now also included the mental labor and memorable experiences necessary to effect a psychological transformation.

Other critics, such as Michael Trask, focus less on the appropriateness of Method acting for film performance or particularly virtuosic naturalist actors in order to investigate "American culture's fixation on performance in the first decade or so of the Cold War."[15] Colin Counsell, for example, suggests US citizens understood their "inner, essential self [as] under threat of suppression from a socialised other," a struggle that Method acting made manifest; further, Lee Strasberg's emphasis on unblocking suppressed emotion in order "to present audiences with their own individual and genuine 'truth'" links naturalist acting techniques to the rise of psychoanalysis and psychological explanations for human behavior.[16] Trask points out that "for postwar sociologists, the dramaturgic approach to society" provided compelling explanations for the seeming split between the authentic self and "the understanding that persons were already attuned to the fictive or rehearsed qualities of their identities." Even more importantly for Trask, Method actors and teachers' "notions of the 'real, live, and human' relied on a model of naturalness borrowed from the field of physiology," especially the work of the behavioralist B. F. Skinner.[17] Finally, Bruce McConachie explains that "the model of the self embedded in Method performance conformed to the contained, psychologized self of cold war culture."[18] Thus, not only psychology but also significant cultural forces shaped by the politics and economy of the US ideological battle against communism entwined with popular understandings of naturalist acting, especially the Method. In short, audiences understood and cared deeply about naturalist acting. Lee Strasberg's complaint "that general people—the barbershop and beauty parlor attendants—are discussing the work of the Actors Studio" demonstrates how completely Method acting captured popular imagination, allowing the naturalist paradigm to dominate film and even television performance.[19]

Despite the dominance of the naturalist paradigm and the popularity of Method acting, some critics decried naturalism. In 1946, the film critic Alexander Knox complained that "behaving" was "much admired in Hollywood and elsewhere, mainly on the grounds that it holds the mirror up to nature. It is natural." Instead, he demanded that actors act, and defined acting as *behaving plus interpretation.*" In an essay published a year later, he explained that even film, which offered "pageantry and mechanical tricks" undreamed of by previous stage directors, designers, and performers, needed strong acting in order to allow audiences to suspend their disbelief and enjoy a film.[20] Representing a Cold War, middle-class inability to communicate, suggested Fredric Jameson, the "agonies and exhalations of method acting were perfectly calculated to render [an] asphyxiation of the spirit that cannot complete its sentence."[21] For the film critic Theodore Hoffman, Method actors have "a tautness to their voices which makes them inaudible or gratingly monotonous. . . . They like to scratch themselves, rub their arms, brush their hair, count their buttons. . . . One gets the impression that a great deal is happening to the characters, but one isn't always sure just what. And in the end, one gets a kind of cheated feeling, as if the actors were going through all that rigmarole for their own pleasure and really weren't the least bit interested in communicating anything to the audience."[22] These critiques of Method acting, then, demonstrate that too much naturalness, too slavish a reliance on personal authenticity, and too copious a re-creation of inner emotional states was off-putting to some audiences, whether on film, television, or the stage.

In spite of these and similar criticisms, the naturalist paradigm governed film performance and film reception in the Classical Hollywood era. Though naturalism is generally understood to refer to "serious" drama and "serious" actors, I attempt to demonstrate here how naturalism structures all performance, including musical, television, and variety performance, as well as audience expectations about the kinds of characters particular performers might portray. Naturalism is therefore also a set of discursive structures that shape on- and offscreen performances of sex, race, class, and gender. Naturalism doesn't dominate Classical Hollywood film and other media during this era because it is the "best" style; rather it emerges from a web of studio school training, film narratives, production processes, publicity, and gossip.

Jane Russell, Esther Williams, Carmen Miranda, Lena Horne, and Zsa Zsa Gabor are part of a cohort of television, film, and cabaret performers, often appearing with each other and with the same supporting actors who share training and technique. This cohort reinforces naturalism's normative status. At the same time, these five actresses demonstrate how the embodied nature of performance undermines the assumed conservativism of naturalism, and the

Classical narratives within which it is mobilized. Their case studies illuminate links between cinematic performance and the performativity of gender. They mark the limits of performative vocabularies of femininity, offering their audiences new repertoires of self-fashioning. As spectacular performers best known for their physical bodies rather than their bodies of work, these strategic case studies offer general insights because their roles, celebrity status, and biographies parallel many Classical Hollywood female stars. At the same time, they offer unique perspectives on celebrity, race and ethnicity, performance traditions, physique, and sexuality.

Like a Natural Woman examines assumptions about film performance in general and naturalism in particular that marginalize the contributions of actors, especially female actors. Though most recognize that acting is at least partly under the control of particular actors, film scholars have also defined performance as specific, aggregate technique; as one component of mise-en-scène; or as an element of star persona, focusing on the ideological meanings of the actor as movie star.[23] At the same time, naturalist discourses of acting suggest that authentic performance is easy for audiences to identify and understand: actor and character merge through a genuinely experienced emotional response to other characters, narrative, and setting while drawing on their own psychology to enrich that response. This apparent transparency masks a highly selective and fairly restricting set of discourses that structure how film performance is produced (in particular, the concerted labor and specific techniques through which actors develop "authentic" personae and performances) as well as received (in particular, how the reification of "natural" performance facilitates a cinematic illusion that the events as well as the ideology of a film are inevitable and true). Feminist critics, following from Laura Mulvey,[24] have decried naturalism for encouraging audiences to wallow in emotion rather than activate critical thought: the "authenticity" of the onscreen representation—and the pleasure it produces—invite audiences to identify with and even aspire to conservative ideologies of sex, race, class, and gender.

At the same time, there's a great deal at stake in terms of aesthetics and value in nominating some performances as "naturalist" and others as "natural." Not surprisingly, those distinctions tend to privilege male actors and genres (like dramas, thrillers, and biographies) directed to male audiences. Theorizing acting as a political, economic, and social institution as well as an aesthetic practice, I suggest that performance supports dominant constructions but also exploits contradictions within conventional representations of sex and gender. Though Russell's, Williams's, Horne's, Miranda's, and Gabor's film and television appearances may seem less representations of naturalist acting than simply examples of acting "naturally," I demonstrate how naturalist discourse regulates how those performances were produced and received, as well as how these women were trained in naturalist technique.

A decade ago, Sue Harper reviewed several then-current film histories and posited that popular films are used to "provide [film scholars] with valuable information about the taste-communities of a particular period," while independent, avant-garde films "provide [film scholars] with a sort of fossilized version of artistic consciousness."[25] At that point, she suggests, films tell us about historical and aesthetic context, but not about performance style and technique, nor the histories of acting and training. Her criticism was echoed by other scholars in the early 2000s. Paul McDonald explains that "film studies has developed an intellectual agenda with lines of inquiry that have firmly encouraged a disregard for acting";[26] in general, films are read as texts about ideology and aesthetics rather than records of performance. In their interventionist Screen Acting (2000), Peter Krämer and Alan Lovell first excuse film scholars by reminding readers that "acting is an elusive art" and therefore difficult to analyze.[27] Then they sum up general arguments against acting analysis. First, as a discipline film studies has historically focused on authorship and the figure of the director. Mise-en-scène is the analytic frame of auteur theory, and it subordinates acting along with costumes, lighting, and set to the overall visual impact of the film as determined by the director. In addition, they suggest that evaluations of theatrical performance are enabled by multiple productions of a central core of texts; Kenneth Branagh's Hamlet can be compared to Laurence Olivier's and even David Garrick's in order to critique what each actor brings to the role. Cinematic performances do not offer similar comparative strategies because the repertoire is much less repeatable. Film acting is often dismissed as unskilled and therefore unimportant rather than evaluated as a distinct mode of performance with its own objectives, methods, and techniques. As early as the 1990s, Barry King offered another explanation for film acting's low status: most actors, "even . . . those whose main professional activities have been confined to the screen," agree that "stage acting provides a yardstick against which to evaluate acting on screen."[28] Stage acting seems to require more of the actor and has therefore been examined more closely; further, as a much longer tradition, its practices have been relatively thoroughly historicized.

The first scholarly examinations of cinematic performance generally coincided with the late-1980s interest in star studies. Richard Dyer decried the "tradition in film theory [that] has tended to deny that performance has any expressive value: what you read into the performer, you read in by virtue of signs other than performance signs,"[29] though even his focus remains less on the agency of the performer than on the audience. As James Naremore pointed out at about the same time, critics traditionally assumed that "a performer does not have to invent anything or master a discipline so long as he or she is embedded in a story": narrative, not acting, makes meaning. But Naremore insists that "the very technique of film acting has ideological importance" and develops a system for analyzing "how the basic formal structure [of film performance] can be mapped onto history, technology, and the politics of the spectacle."[30] Though often linking performance and ideology, and focusing on both film texts and star personae as a text itself, some did explore the questions of agency, embodiment, and performance I take up here.

In the past ten years, several film and theater historians (often through the rubrics of performance studies) have recovered film acting techniques and theories, establishing links between stage and screen; *Like a Natural Woman* participates in that project. Sharon Marie Carnicke, for example, develops a history of Method acting, which includes several articles and monographs, that carefully considers its different applications in film and theater. *Reframing Screen Performance*, cowritten with Cynthia Baron, reconsiders the elements of film performance and is an important touchstone for my own work. Baron's anthology (coedited with Diane Carson and Frank P. Tomasulo) *More than a Method* not surprisingly "challenges the idea that reference to training or working method is the best or only way to categorize performances" and offers new rubrics for post-studio-system acting.[31] Carole Zucker's introduction to the anthology *Making Visible the Invisible* notes that the modes for examining film acting vary from semiotics to star studies to "socio-historical interpretation[s] of performer/spectator/industry relationships" to feminist analyses of the images of women. She asserts that "this polyvalence of critical positions is both salutary and commendable" and indicates that the field is vigorous, enthusiastic, and open in its "inaugural stage."[32] Thus, there are several suggestions for confronting the disciplinary and methodological challenges of evaluating film performance, many of which draw on performance studies theories of embodiment. I'm particularly invested in how the body in/as performance offers its own especial challenges to the narrative closure and hegemonic ideologies presumably endemic to Classical Hollywood film.

The frequent disavowal of embodiment and agency in film performance is especially notable given the importance placed on casting. Lev Kuleshov, one of cinema's early director-theorists, argued that "because film needs real material and not a pretense of reality . . . people who, in themselves, as they were born, present some kind of interest for cinematic treatment" are best for film.[33] This assertion, however, elides an industry emphasis placed on particular bodies and particular body types, ignoring the assumptions about appropriate class, race, and gender those omissions ought to foreground. Martin Barker asks, "What could be wrong with the notion that the primary distinguishing feature of stars is simply that they are exceptionally *beautiful*?"[34] The answers seem self-evident: if critics focus on surface appearances, then it seems they're ignoring both the innate talent and concerted labor that constitute successful film performance. At the same time, "exceptional beauty" is bounded by ideologies of sex and gender, physical ability, and race. Therefore, physical attractiveness—beauty, sex appeal, charm, glamour—is, as Lovell and Krämer point out, "an area of acting which has hardly been touched by film scholars," though it is a noteworthy element of many star performances. Generally, of course, actresses' bodies and sexualities are the most scrutinized components of their personae, and Lovell and Krämer suggest that feminists "have quite rightly objected to the limitations" of equating appearance with acting.[35] At the same time, physical appearance both suggests meaning and can be manipulated by performers; as my case studies on Esther Williams and Lena Horne especially demonstrate, physical appearance can produce ambivalent meanings and enable counteranalysis of seemingly conservative film texts.

When physical appearance is included in analyses of film acting, it joins the already multiple and contradictory definitions of cinematic performance. Jeremy Butler, for example, determines two "not altogether exclusive" approaches to film performance. One is "performance as the work of the actor. The actor creates a performance from the materials of body movement and speech, and/or by 'reliving' the role. This performance is then recorded." The other is "performance as the work of the entire apparatus of film. . . . The 'performance' occurs when the film or program is screened in a theater. . . . The spectator then views or 'reads' that performance—gathering meaning or pleasure not only from the speech and body movements of the actors but also from the lighting, set design, editing, and so forth."[36] Performance, then, may be simultaneously understood as acting or as the viewing of a complete text.

Richard de Cordova offers another understanding of performance. Reading "performance" as separate from acting, de Cordova suggests that performance "incorporates a specific mode of address . . . has an identifiable beginning and end," intervenes within the overarching narrative, "has an institutional or ideological function," and is an expression of "the inner emotional states of the characters." Performance, then, stands outside of narrative or character, calling attention to itself as performance, as when a character sings a song, does a cheer, or even virtuosically cooks an evening meal. The musical, of course, is filled with examples of performance under this definition, and de Cordova's larger project is to assess how "performance is structured within particular films and particular genres" and to call for more comparative analysis of performance between genres.[37] Understanding performance as "extra" to narrative seems especially foreign to performance studies scholars, who tend to view "performance" on a continuum from everyday life to spectacle; I'm focusing here on developing a theory of film performance that understands naturalism across genres and at different moments in the narrative.

Golden Age musicals are usually understood as following two conventions in regard to de Cordova's definition of performance. Unintegrated (also called aggregate) musicals, such as the backstage spectacular *There's No Business like Show Business*, add musical numbers without any reference to narrative or character continuity. In integrated musicals, as Jerome A. Delamater explains, "song and dance numbers gr[o]w 'naturally' from the narrative." Not coincidentally, as I detail below, integrated musicals are generally understood as the pinnacle of the genre. For Delamater, who compares performance in integrated and unintegrated musicals, "singing and dancing become part of acting in the musical," and thus *performance* rather than *acting* should be the term used to analyze these texts. "Acting in the musical," Delamater insists, "includes a kind of performance that is not just an impersonation of fictional characters but is a presentation of the performer's singing and dancing abilities."[38] For the women I consider, these abilities are predicated on their spectacular bodies and those bodies' "natural" response to the exigencies of character and narrative but also illuminate their labor and talent as they sing, dance, and swim.

I respond to all these discussions of film performance by focusing on the historical moment when the naturalist paradigm first dominates film performance and reception. In the case studies that follow, I work through the ways in which the naturalist paradigm intersects with film publicity, the spectacular female body, histories of racial representation, non-naturalist performance, and the performance of self. Each case study illuminates a particular crisis in naturalism and suggests how Russell, Williams, Horne, Miranda, and Gabor negotiated that crisis. Ultimately, I suggest that naturalism, rather than being an always already restrictive force, might enable feminist meanings, narratives, and characters.

The Limits of Naturalism; or, The Problem of Lindsay Lohan

Marilyn Monroe casts a long shadow for film scholars, film audiences, and film actors. When she was alive, her tremendous popularity drove other Hollywood studios to try to create a blond bombshell of their own: Jayne Mansfield, Mamie Van Doren, and even Zsa Zsa and Eva Gabor were touted as her rivals. After her death, hundreds of biographies, memoirs, and novelizations about her life, loves, and career were written by scholars, close friends, and acquaintances: Google Books, for example, lists about six hundred separate titles, and eleven new titles were published in the first three months of 2013 alone. She's appeared on the cover of *Vanity Fair*, a magazine about contemporary US culture, politics, and entertainment, three times since 2008. In 2011, *My Week with Marilyn* was a critical success, and Michelle Williams (playing Monroe) was nominated for an Academy Award for her performance; though she lost to Meryl Streep, she did win a Golden Globe and a clutch of other prizes for her portrayal. In 2012, NBC began airing *Smash*, a musical drama about the production of a new Broadway version of Monroe's life, *Bombshell*, charting the trials and tribulations of two aspiring actresses vying to play the titular blonde. Not only these two fictional actresses but many others have desperately tried to fill her kitten heels; the most famous, perhaps, is Lindsay Lohan.

In a disparaging article for the *Huffington Post*, Cavan Sieczkowski asserts that Lohan has "long cited Marilyn Monroe as her personal icon."[39] In fact, Lohan has embodied the star on film more than once: a 2008 photo essay for *New York* magazine, shot by Bert Stern, who had previously lensed "The Last Sitting" of Monroe, on which the photos were based; the March 2009 cover of Spanish *Vogue* magazine; the January/February 2012 *Playboy* cover and editorial, where she and the photographer Yu Tsai re-created Monroe's 1953 shoot for *Playboy*'s inaugural issue; and a cameo in the 2013 film *InAPPropriate Comedy* (which the *New York Times* judged "awfully awful").[40] But Lohan's embodiment goes further than these appearances. She, like her fellow notorious celebrities Jessica Alba, Christina Aguilera, Pamela Anderson, Mischa Barton, Carmen Electra, Megan Fox, Paris Hilton, the Kardashian sisters, Bai Ling, Tara Reid, Denise Richards, Rihanna, Jessica Simpson, Britney Spears, and the dozens of other female performers who are better known for their bodies than their bodies of work, are the descendants of the women I consider here. Their messy personal lives, hypersexualized bodies, and struggle to be taken seriously as hardworking, talented singers, dancers, and actors are intelligible through the lives, bodies, and work of Russell, Williams, Horne, Miranda, Monroe, and Gabor. For all these women, the naturalist paradigm defining acting as a technique to be learned but also rooted in a performer's psychology partially determines how audiences receive their performances. Further, now as in Classical Hollywood, celebrity gossip and celebrity images suture performers to particular personae, determining their reception in both narrative and real-world contexts. Clearly, Lohan is not alone in her citation of Monroe and other midcentury spectacular performers. Even so, her case study illuminates how naturalism continues to influence performance and audience response. Further, though I argue that in the cases of Russell, Williams, Horne, Miranda, and Gabor naturalism enables subversive readings and transgressive portrayals of femininity, the naturalist paradigm seems to increasingly trap actresses inside a hypersexualized image only partly of their own making.

Lindsay Dee Lohan was born July 2, 1986, the oldest child of Dina and Michael Lohan. Her parents separated when she was three, reuniting and reseparating several times during her childhood and adolescence, finally divorcing in 2005. Michael was "a former Wall Street trader who spent years in jail for criminal contempt in a securities case, attempted assault, and D.U.I."; Dina raised the children on Long Island while also acting as Lohan's manager for much of her career.[41] Lohan began working in commercials at three and catapulted to fame in the 1998 film *The Parent Trap*, playing twins Hallie and Annie opposite Dennis Quaid and Natasha Richardson as the parents whose divorce separated the sisters at birth. Janet Maslin's review praised Lohan's "apparent[ly] effortless" performance, suggesting that it "easily makes" the film's many coincidences "credible."[42] Several retrospective articles about Lohan's promise versus her tabloid-worthy arrests, physical altercations, and public romances note her early talent: "She was thoroughly natural even in her first movies," Caryn James reminds us, for example.[43]

As a teenage girl Lohan played several teenage girls, often struggling to fit into their high school societies: Anna in another Disney remake, *Freaky Friday* (2003); Mary Elizabeth and her alter ego, Lola, in *Confessions of a Teenage Drama Queen* (2004); Cady in the critically and commercially successful *Mean Girls* (2004); and Maggie in her third Disney remake, *Herbie: Fully Loaded* (2005). She released the platinum-certified pop album *Speak* in 2004 and followed it up with *A Little More Personal (Raw)* the next year; neither was critically successful. Transitioning to more adult roles in her late teens, she was a member of the ensemble casts of Robert Altman's *A Prairie Home Companion* (2006) and Emilio Estevez's *Bobby* (2006) and played Jude in *Chapter 27* (2007), a dramatization of Mark David Chapman's assassination of John Lennon. These films were generally well received, and Lohan was praised again for her natural acting ability, even by her costar Meryl Streep.[44]

Lohan's persona as a hard-partying, unprofessional, and unreliable performer was already overshadowing her film roles, however. She was arrested for the first and second times in summer 2007, both times for driving under the influence and for possession of cocaine. That first arrest led to several subsequent probation violations, including failing random drug tests, incomplete community service, and failure to appear for court dates. She was also arrested for theft in 2011, for hit-and-run in 2012, and for assault in 2012. Lohan was briefly incarcerated in 2007, 2010, and 2011, serving between eighty-four minutes and two weeks, always released early due to overcrowding in the Los Angeles prison system.[45] She's also been to several drug and alcohol rehabilitation centers and in serious romantic relationships with the singer Aaron Carter, the actor Wilmer Valderrama (with whom she moved to Los Angeles at eighteen) and the DJ Samantha Ronson.[46] Throughout this period, Lohan continued to work, notably in a guest-starring arc in ABC's critically and commercially successful *Ugly Betty* in 2008 and in the box office bombs *I Know Who Killed Me* and *Georgia Rule* (both 2007). Most recently, in addition to *InAPProriate Comedy*, she took a supporting role in the controversial Robert Rodriguez immigration exploitation film *Machete* (2010) and played the titular Taylor in the Lifetime television biopic *Liz and Dick* (2012).

Gossip about celebrity romance, addiction, legal trouble, erratic behavior, on-set unprofessionalism, family strife, and bad driving is not new, of course. As Adrienne L. McLean points out in the introduction to *Headline Hollywood*, "Hollywood has had a long association with scandal—with covering it up, with managing its effects, in some cases with creating and directing it."[47] As my chapter on Jane Russell explains, Hollywood studios had enormous publicity departments, responsible for planting and hiding "news" about everything from star marriages and divorces to new contracts, hobbies, mental illness, and illicit affairs (especially homosexual liaisons) in order to create and market their stars as consumer commodities. Much of this publicity/gossip/news was designed to sate fan appetite for knowledge about the hidden, private lives of stars. At the same

time, most studio-sanctioned publicity supported ideas about the correspondence between performer and role, creating a particular persona, or, in Jeanine
Basinger's words, "the creation of a second self that is believed to be the original
self" combining elements of performers' specific "type" and their own personalities.[48] For the studios, this kind of publicity allowed actors to be especially
believable in certain roles and justified "typecasting" performers as, say, a femme
fatale, swimming champion, tragic mulatto, sexy Latina, or self-parodying celebrity. Not coincidentally, the association between actor and role also established
naturalism as the paradigmatic performance technique and style of film actors.

In important ways, star discourse and naturalist acting pursue similar invest-
ments in the private. According to Carnicke, Lee Strasberg followed Stanislavsky's directive that actors must be "private in public," developing the "private
moment" exercise in order to help actors "who couldn't really let go" through
affective memory.[49] As Richard de Cordova observed about film fans of the 1910s
and 1920s, "The star system . . . depends on an interpretive schema that equates
identity with the private."[50] Contemporary celebrity gossip revels in the private,
and for fans "exhausted by perfect images of stars, nothing entrances more than
the star's own public exposure of the truth," according to Moya Luckett.[51] Rather
than pursuing the private moment as an acting exercise, some performers (like
Lohan and other gossip favorites) present private moments as media spectacle,
available for consumption in a variety of venues. The ubiquity of cell phone
cameras as well as particularly aggressive paparazzi (especially from websites
like TMZ and Radar Online) means that private moments are increasingly captured and even staged for media distribution via television programs, the Internet, and weekly magazines—and often covered by legitimate sources as well.

Julie Wilson, for example, argues that contemporary celebrity gossip outlets,
especially magazines like *Star, Us Weekly,* and *In Touch,* are a "peculiar hybrid of
both fan magazines and tabloid newspapers" that invite their "'younger, hipper'
audiences to relish the glamorous Hollywood lifestyle while engaging in evalua-
tion of those who live it."[52] Gossip is more available and more respectable than it
was at midcentury, suggesting to Joshua Gamson that fans are "simultaneously
voyeurs of and performers in commercial culture" circulated through star bodies.[53]
This younger, hipper audience also embraces online gossip outlets as blogs prolif-
erate on the Internet and seem to especially invite audience participation. One of
the most popular blogs, *Perezhilton.com,* run by Mario Lavandeira, is visited over
ten million times a day, with three million unique visitors per month. Lavandeira scrawls cocaine dust, labia, tongues, and penises on celebrity photographs
and invites readers to comment on his blog (as well as send tips), enabling their
participation in star discourse in particularly immediate ways.[54] Of course, the
interactivity and immediacy of Internet gossip outlets facilitates the existence of
an enormous US (and global) audience for stories, images, films, and quotes
from celebrities. Within moments of a celebrity event (such as Lindsay Lohan

crashing her car), photos, eyewitness accounts, and sometimes even video foot-age can be uploaded to the Internet; as the longtime print gossip columnist Liz Smith complains, "the Internet tells all, and so quickly . . . that gossip colum-nists of my kind couldn't even exist today."[55] Though Smith suggests that gossip has changed since she began writing as "Cholly Knickerbocker" in the 1950s, a focus on privacy, sexuality, and authenticity continues to predominate. But if midcen-tury star discourse followed Strasberg to insist that authenticity and believability were the highest and most difficult kind of acting at the same time that it insisted that stars were identical to the characters they play, current stars suffer from over-exposure. Audiences can know too much about stars' private lives, rendering them unlikable or unbelievable, despite efforts to manage their public images.

Tom Cruise, for example, is arguably one of the biggest action stars of the twentieth and twenty-first centuries and has been vigorously sutured to that persona. Cruise has reportedly rescued nearly a dozen people from injury or even death: five vacationing boaters, a car accident victim, and two young fans in 1996 (all around the time he was promoting the first blockbuster for his *Mission: Impossible* franchise), two other car accident victims in 2006, a woman stranded in a snowbank in 2008, and an injured crew member on the set of *Oblivion* in 2012.[56] At the same time, he has struggled with critical and fan backlash since 2005 because of his courtship of, marriage to, and divorce from Katie Holmes and his reliance on Scientology. In 2005, the *SFGate* columnist Mark Morford warned Cruise that he was "maxing out. Wearing out the welcome. Becoming less the . . . mildly likable megastar and more like an itchy boil on the deranged ferret of popular culture, requiring lancing."[57] Even in 2010, Cruise was still suf-fering from this perception, at least according to the *New York Times* blogger Brooks Barnes: "The couch jumping, the Scientology spouting, the dumping of his power publicist—it has without question hurt his career, perhaps irrepara-bly,"[58] and the failure of the very expensive action film *Knight and Day* (2010) was blamed on his continued unlikability. Further, the "itchy boil" in need of lancing was no longer believable as a romantic lead or action hero. When he and Holmes divorced in 2012, Cruise and Scientology were once again in the news, thanks to a scathing profile in *Vanity Fair.*[59] *Jack Reacher*, a potential Paramount franchise, was in postproduction, and the *Hollywood Reporter* reported that "the studio is left again to hope the media frenzy dies down. But knowing that any reporter who gets near is likely to touch on radioactive topics, a studio executive says that as far as publicity goes, 'You're not going to see him everywhere.'"[60] Cruise was less visible during that film's marketing than usual.

In addition to rumors about his marriage to Holmes and his reliance on Sci-entology, Cruise has also been dogged by speculation about his sexuality: many audience members believe that he is gay but unwilling to damage his blockbuster bankability by publicly coming out. As the openly gay celebrity Rupert Everett notes, "Straight men get every opportunity to play gay parts . . . and then win tons of awards for doing so. . . . But the other way doesn't really work out."[61] When the *Newsweek* columnist Ramin Setoodeh blasted the Broadway production of *Promises, Promises* for casting Sean Hayes, "a guy we all know is gay," as the romantic lead, he ignited an Internet discussion as much about whether his comments were homophobic as about the damage celebrity culture might do to performance.[62] Aaron Sorkin, for example, opined that "the problem has everything to do with the fact that we know too much about each other and we care too much about what we know. . . . The volcanic eruption of tabloids, Internet insanity and . . . reality TV, has de-creepyized voyeurism."[63] For gay actors as well as women, publicity about their sexuality seems to call into question their ability to play particular kinds of roles.

Lohan's career (like Monroe's, Russell's, and Gabor's as well as dozens of other midcentury female stars') has frequently been threatened by her sexuality. As early as 2005, her image overshadowed her film roles. During the filming of *Herbie: Fully Loaded*, Lohan split with Wilmer Valderrama. According to the *New York Times* reporter Sharon Waxman, the broken-hearted eighteen-year-old partied her sorrows away, and Disney executives "debated whether the sexy, party-going tabloid image of its star . . . might discourage parents from letting their children see the film."[64] It did well at the box office, and the *New York Times* film critic Stephen Holden praised Lohan as a "genuine star who combines a tomboyish spunk with a sexy, head-turning strut, executed with minimal self-consciousness."[65] *Herbie: Fully Loaded*, however, was the last time Lohan had a hit film, and the last time a *New York Times* review praised her natural performance without at least referencing her offscreen troubles.

Lindsay Lohan's latest film, *The Canyons*, is a low-budget psycho-sexual thriller written by literary bête noire Bret Easton Ellis, directed by Paul Schrader, who wrote *Taxi Driver* (1976) and directed *American Gigolo* (1980), and costarring James Deen, a porn actor. It was released in August 2013 by IFC Films to nine theaters as well as for on-demand streaming video (VOD). Generally savaged by critics (Manohla Dargis told *New York Times* readers that it was "a dispiriting, unpleasurable work punctuated with flashes of vitalizing vulgarity"), it grossed less than $50,000 at the box office, and its VOD sales are as yet unreported.[66] In "The Misfits" (an obvious nod to Lohan's heroine Marilyn Monroe's final, troubled film), Stephen Rodrick chronicled the film's production in the *New York Times Magazine*; his article uses the naturalist paradigm to explain how and why *The Canyons* might be a successful film, linking Lohan's troubled past and chaotic behavior to her performance.[67] For example, screen test footage demonstrates that "playing Tara [her character] wouldn't be a stretch for her. The large green eyes that read cute a decade ago now conveyed cornered desperation." Lohan dismissed a compliment about her believable performance in a scene of horrifying domestic violence with "I've got a lot of experience with that from my dad." Rodrick was especially impressed with Lohan's performance in "the film's most riveting scene." Lohan, who had arrived late to the set and sniped with her director and costar, briefly left the set in order to prepare. "I was standing by her door," writes Rodrick, "and soon I could hear her crying. It began quietly, almost a whimper, but rose to a guttural howl. It was the sobbing of a child lost in the woods."

Of course, *The Misfits*, which both the article title and article text reference, was marked by its female star's erratic behavior, emotional fragility, and dependence on drugs and alcohol. Though now considered a classic, it was not a commercial success. Its director, John Huston, later commented that Monroe's performance was not acting in the true sense, but that she had merely drawn from her own experiences to show herself rather than a character. "She had no techniques," he recalled. "It was all the truth. It was only Marilyn."[68] Rodrick's eleven-page article, illustrated with seven color photographs from the set, is equally Schrader's story, and follows his struggles to keep Lohan focused on the production despite all the "noise" surrounding her. Rodrick records her many missed days, illnesses, cigarettes, and late arrivals, as well as her frequent drinking and emotional melt-downs, to paint a picture of a young woman who (like the character she plays) is lost in a Hollywood fantasy she can neither control nor understand. His ultimate characterization of her performance as "equal parts vulnerable and dissolute," is made to seem inevitable because of what Rodrick has argued is her psychological connection to the role.

Though certainly much more analytic as well as deleterious than *Life* magazine's chronicle of the making of *Gentlemen Prefer Blondes* (which I discuss below), the objective of Rodrick's article is the same. The behind-the-scenes look at the production process simultaneously records the emotional and physical labor necessary to develop coherent, authentic, and aesthetically appealing performances *and* the resemblance between stars and the characters they play. Lohan's career and the hundreds of column inches devoted to following her films and her private life thus demonstrate how the naturalist paradigm continues to structure film performance and reception.

The roots of contemporary celebrity culture are tied to the star-making processes of Classical Hollywood, especially in terms of the representation of female stars and their presumed influence on their fans. Star histories recover publicity, contractual obligations, and film content in order to explain the current celebrity landscape. Celebrity theory, on the other hand, focuses on the ideological work that stars do and argues for their importance to hegemonic systems. In the work that follows, I attempt to merge these questions through an excavation of the naturalist paradigm, demonstrating how acting itself indicates particular ideologies as well as its imbrication within institutional regimes of film production.

STAR STUDIES, CASE STUDIES, AND SPECTACULAR FEMALE PERFORMANCE

In 1979, Richard Dyer published *Stars*, demonstrating to film and performance scholars that "stars have a privileged position in the definition of social roles and types, and this must have real consequences in terms of how people believe they can and should behave."[69] For Dyer, stars capture tensions over dominant ideologies in particular historical, geographical, and cultural moments. Stars seem to embody these tensions for their audiences as well as for contemporary scholars and historians; the study of stars indicates much about how ideology is negotiated in daily life. For many film, cultural, and performance studies scholars, this negotiation seems to follow the model outlined by Antonio Gramsci, whereby groups of people are "not ruled by force alone, but by ideas."[70] Subordinate peoples agree to their domination because they believe that this order is natural. But for Gramsci and the scholars, such as John Fiske, who follow him, "consent must be constantly won and rewon, for people's material social experience constantly reminds them of the disadvantages of subordination and thus poses a threat to the dominant class."[71] The mass media is one arena wherein this struggle for consent is played out, and stars exemplify how dominant ideology might be made to seem natural and commonsensical.

Case studies are a crucial methodology for investigations of the interplay between stardom and ideology. As Dyer points out, stars are both "culturally and historically specific" but also "read" as indicative of an "eternal universal" and "relate to the social types of a society." Thus, individual stars can illuminate specific ideological crises, but stars *in general* are relatively empty signifiers. Like many others in the field of star studies, I follow Dyer to investigate how particular stars represent "specific instabilities, ambiguities, and contradictions in the culture (which are reproduced in the actual practice of making films and film stars)."[72] In this book, I'm most interested in the instabilities, ambiguities, and contradictions of hegemonic ideologies of femininity, especially as it intersects with race and class; this work therefore adds to important work already developed by feminist film and celebrity scholars. I suggest here that (like other mid-century stars) Jane Russell, Esther Williams, Lena Horne, Carmen Miranda, and Zsa Zsa Gabor as well as Marilyn Monroe make a particularly hypersexualized, spectacular femininity seem natural, authentic, and desirable. Resolutely available to be looked at, the spectacle of their feminine bodies, voices, and actions solidifies notions of appropriate femininity immediately before, during, and after the Second World War. Further, though Dyer suggests that star image is developed through "media texts that can be grouped together as *promotion, publicity, films* and *criticism* and *commentaries*," that is, the making of films and film stars, I emphasize here how star image is also developed through performance.[73] Finally, I explore how these stars exemplify ideologies of femininity (as well as race, ethnicity, and class), that seem to be particularly retrograde but are always already riven with fissures, what Alan Sinfield names "the conflict and contradiction that the social order inevitably produces within itself, even as it attempts to sustain itself" in the Gramscian struggle for hegemonic control.[74] Their performances are often contradictory and ambivalent precisely because they are made to seem natural, understood as both authentic expressions of emotion and personality and also reasonable and logical articulations of femininity.

In the chapters that follow, I investigate how naturalism intersects with various instabilities in representations of femininity and ideologies of the feminine. The first chapter uses Jane Russell to demonstrate how studio publicity invokes the naturalist paradox of acting as labor and as authentic expression of star personality. As this work demonstrates, publicity in the 1940s and 1950s increasingly played on audience knowledge about how stars were manufactured by Hollywood's glamour factory. At the same time, this publicity consistently reinforced assumptions about correspondences between actor and role. This institutional apparatus often trapped stars (especially female stars) within narratives created for them. Russell struggled to write her own narrative in her autobiography, through her gospel music career, and perhaps most especially through the two films she starred in and produced, *Gentlemen Marry Brunettes* and *The Fuzzy Pink Nightgown*. These films specifically critique the publicity system, effectively arguing for a richer understanding of the female performers laboring behind a particular star image.

Esther Williams demonstrates how naturalism can be subversive when the meanings of a "natural" female body contradict the narratives that attempt to contain it. Williams starred in a series of aquamusicals that offered multiple opportunities to view her beautiful, bathing-suit-clad body slipping in and out of the water, often in the arms of her romantic leads. As movie musicals, these films naturalize the idea that the foundation for marriage is romantic love. Williams's characters generally end the films happily married or engaged, but her powerful body and her self-sufficiency in the water undercut the courtship rituals on which these plots are based. Williams also offers an opportunity to query the relationship between physical appearance and character, suggesting that the typecasting endemic to Classical Hollywood is especially enabled by the naturalist paradigm.

Lena Horne's short Hollywood career exposes the tenuous relationship between naturalism and authenticity. As a mixed-race performer typically described as African American, Horne was inserted into a historical paradigm equating light-skinned black women with tragedy, pathos, and sexual license. As I describe below, Horne seemed "authentic" not only because of her performance style but also because she confirmed traditional assumptions about the "tragic mulatto." This chapter also investigates the relationships between, first, the movie musical and the US minstrel show, and, second, the movie musical and naturalist acting. The links between minstrelsy and the musical are well established, but I pay particular attention to their material effects on black performers at midcentury, nearly one hundred years since African Americans first appeared in blackface on US stages (and over one hundred years since white performers began "blacking up"). Links between naturalism and movie musicals are less well established; I argue for a reconsideration of the integrated musical as a response to the naturalist paradigm in nonmusical films and on the legitimate stage. In the same way that monologues and stage business are presumed to indicate the inner emotions of characters, songs in the integrated musical (and, to a lesser extent, in the aggregate musical) are equally indicative of emotional authenticity.

Continuing to explore how spectacular femininity intersects representations of race and ethnicity, I use Mikhail Bakhtin's theorization of carnival to explain the appeal of Carmen Miranda during the Good Neighbor era. In her films, Miranda opens a space for class and ethnic inversion by creating temporary utopic carnival spaces through her dancing body, pattering vocals, and expressive face. Further, as a singularly unnatural performer, Miranda contrasts with the Anglo performers and characters in her films, enabling them to seem "natural" through opposition. Her carnivalesque performance ultimately reinscribes a status quo, both because the romantic and business relationships are ultimately resolved along appropriate class and ethnic lines through her comic interventions and also because it stabilizes the representations of middle-class Anglo femininity through its citation of a Hollywood-manufactured *Latinidad*.

Finally, I use Zsa Zsa Gabor to indicate how playing oneself both extends and subverts the naturalist paradigm. Gabor made about a dozen films but primarily performed on television, either as "herself" on talk shows and variety programs or as "herself" on family sitcoms. First, her performances indicate the flexibility of the naturalist paradigm, as it can be pressed into the service of celebrity persona construction as well as used to create character. In crucial ways, Gabor's performances of self on *Mr. Ed*, *The Joey Bishop Show*, and *December Bride* show how the parodic citation of female norms illuminates the construction of gender within the mass media and in everyday life. Second, I demonstrate how the naturalist paradigm infiltrated television aesthetics, ensuring its continued dominance across medium and through time. Finally, Gabor points toward contemporary celebrity culture, such as the media frenzy surrounding Lindsay Lohan described above, demonstrating that celebrity is as much a product of the naturalist paradigm as gossip and tabloids.

Before developing these case studies, I want to return to Marilyn Monroe, one of midcentury's most spectacular female performers and famous devotees of naturalist acting. After studying with Strasberg, Monroe returned to Hollywood to make *Bus Stop* (1956), a gritty naturalist drama based on William Inge's stage play and directed by Joshua Logan, who had studied at the Moscow Art Theatre in the 1920s.[75] Monroe plays Cherie, the charismatic but untalented nightclub

Figure 3: Marilyn Monroe as Cheri, feeling "That Ol' Black Magic" in *Bus Stop*, 1956, Twentieth Century–Fox.

singer whose rendition of "That Ol' Black Magic" captivates the rodeo cowboy Beau Decker (Don Murray) (see figure 3).

Cherie stumbles through the lyrics, kicking floor switches that activate tawdry lighting effects. The all-male saloon audience ignores the floor show until Beau orders them to pay attention. Buoyed by the admiration of her new hero, Cherie finishes the song more confidently though no more gracefully. Her performance is excruciating but compelling: Cherie is both sublimely beautiful and totally abject. In tatty elbow-length black gloves, torn fishnets, and a black-spangled green leotard, her white skin and blond hair glow. When she sings "Down and down I go/Round and round I go," Cherie closes her eyes, rolls her head, and arches her back. Just as she earlier seemed not to know how bad her performance was, she now seems not to realize how sexual it has become. This sequence is emblematic of naturalist cinema: Cherie's unselfconsciousness signals that she's lost in the moment and overwhelmed by emotion. Because her body responds sexually to the song's lyrics as well as Beau's obvious desire, the moment seems especially "true."

Monroe's performance of "That Ol' Black Magic" illustrates the emphasis on actors' physical bodies as indicative of authentic emotion within naturalist discourses of acting. As this sequence demonstrates, however, the excessively beautiful, sexual, and active as well as specifically raced and classed body destabilizes the naturalist illusion. The body is so compelling that it pulls focus from the narrative and the character, calling attention to itself and underscoring ambivalences within its representation. Monroe's spectacular female performance (that is, the way this sequence calls attention to the aesthetics of that performance as well as the performer's sexuality and femininity, exemplified here by Monroe's beautiful face, soft hair, and hourglass figure) contrasts with its naturalist elements (that is, the way she nearly trips over the switches to indicate her character's self-consciousness but blooms under an appreciative male gaze). This sequence thus clearly indicates the ways in which naturalism and spectacle coincide in Classical Hollywood film, especially in those moments where actresses are "really" performing in musical, dance, or water ballet numbers.

Comparing Monroe's Cherie with her Vicky in *There's No Business like Show Business* is convincing evidence of her talents as a performer. Though both are primarily interesting because of the way her luscious body shimmies in a revealing costume and her breathy voice drips with sexual desire, they also demonstrate her talents as a dancer, her efforts to construct character, and her refusal to be contained by the mawkish narratives of her film. As Vicky, Monroe is simply more engaging than any of the Donahue family, a fact that the narrative itself underscores by juxtaposing their version of "Heat Wave" with hers. The story thus shifts from the efforts of the Donahues to have a successful show business career combined with a happy family life to Vicky's meteoric rise. Though Merman sings her standard, and Gaynor and O'Connor enthusiastically tap-dance and fan-kick, Monroe's performances seem to effortlessly outshine theirs. It's unbelievable that she'd join them in the finale (rather than starring herself) or settle for romance with O'Connell's alcoholic buffoon. In *Bus Stop*, a film with several strong naturalist performances, Monroe's "That Ol' Black Magic" is the "naturally" most compelling. With her vulnerability indicated by her patched costume, gawky movements, and thin voice, Monroe makes Cherie just beautiful and innocent enough to be loved by Beau and just damaged enough to fall in love with the man who virtually kidnapped her. In both films, Monroe appears to be playing herself, despite differences in genre, character, and performance style. As John Huston suggests, her performances were "all the truth. It was only Marilyn." But, he continued, they were "Marilyn plus. She found things about womankind . . . in herself."[76] Like Russell, Williams, Horne, Miranda, and Gabor, Marilyn Monroe seemed simply to play herself, but that performance was both carefully constructed, ideologically contained, and open to multiple and contradictory interpretations. By playing herself, she provides performative models for all audiences compelled to represent and personate femininity.

CHAPTER 1

ENGINEERED FOR STARDOM

PUBLICITY, PERFORMANCE, AND JANE RUSSELL

Jane Russell, Ashton Reid announced in *Collier's* in 1945, is "queen of the motionless pictures."[1] Russell had worked on two films, *The Outlaw* and *Young Widow*, but neither had yet been widely released.[2] Even so, she was better known than many starlets with films in wide release because of the countless pinups, magazine pictorials, billboards, and fan magazine articles generated by the publicist Russell Birdwell for her debut in Howard Hughes's *The Outlaw*. By 1945, photographs of Russell had appeared in almost three dozen different magazines, often more than once;[3] billboards supporting *The Outlaw* were posted in several cities; and gossip about her on-set behavior, her relationship with Howard Hughes, and her marriage to the star quarterback Bob Waterfield were fan magazine staples. According to Reid, Russell had "the best known feminine face in America," she had appeared in more magazines than any other US woman, and "her biography had been published twice as often as that of the next Hollywood star."[4] Russell's celebrity was arguably greater than her acting talents. Her career illuminates the important role of publicity in establishing naturalism as a commonplace understanding of how actors create roles and how celebrity is constructed and maintained, as well as how both may depend on a spectacular female body. Russell is a key case study not only because of the specifics of her career but also because of the ways in which that career followed the general outlines of all actresses' during the Classical Hollywood era.

In 1941, when Russell was filming her debut as Rio McDonald in *The Outlaw*, *Life* magazine ran a three-page feature heralding her as "1941's best new star prospect." In fewer than five hundred words, the magazine communicates several essential points about Russell: she's filming a Western and coincidentally grew up on a ranch; she was an ordinary office worker until Howard Hughes plucked her from obscurity and gave her a $1,000 wardrobe; and she has an astonishingly beautiful face and remarkable figure. Admitting that "whether Jane can act still remains to be seen . . . but . . . with her face and figure she doesn't need to,"[5] the text and photographs suture Russell's biography to the familiar narrative of Hollywood starlets who suddenly discover that their physical attributes and natural personality are all they need to become successful performers. Russell's *Life* photo essay correlates actor and role, lays the foundation for Russell's sex symbol image, and offers readers behind-the-scenes footage of a working film set. As George Kouvaros points out in his important reading of the photographs taken by Magnum Agency photographers on the *Misfits* set, these kinds of publicity campaigns present "a series of meanings both connected to the drama occurring within the film and the historical context of its production."[6] Through their participation in a gendered narrative of stardom that elides women's abilities to influence their film characters as well as their career trajectories, these photographs and text do more than just introduce a rising star. In important ways, they materialize links between actor and role, between persona and self, and between sexuality and performance through the body of Jane Russell/Rio.

Crucially, the photos demonstrate how and why Russell is a "natural" for the big screen. The essay includes eight photographs, the first a half-page shot of Russell in her "Mexican halfbreed" costume as Rio,[7] lolling in the hay with her arms overhead and her beautiful bosom thrust forward. In another, Russell perches on a balcony. She's in her street clothes (a light-colored blouse and skirt, dark flat shoes, and a leather belt with a silver Western buckle) and facing the camera, but the panoramic shot also includes the RKO-constructed Western town—complete with horses, stagecoach, and false-front buildings constructed among real scrub-covered hills and the vast horizon—where *The Outlaw* was shot. Read together, these two photographs place Russell in the film's mise-en-scène: the more candid shot of Russell in the hay includes her costume, while the more formally posed photo features her in street clothes but within *The Outlaw*'s frame of reference.

The photo shoot also includes four close-ups of Russell's face, used to bolster the magazine's claim that she has a promising career. The first asserts that she has an "expressive face"; the second highlights her "excellent smile"; the next two document her "amused distaste" and "annoyance" eating "dried Hopi Indian corn."[8] These photos do not markedly differ from each other; whether she's flashing her excellent smile or picking that annoying corn out of her teeth, she seems pleasant and cheerful. The captions, then, suggest that Russell's face telegraphs a particular emotion and urge readers to interpret her nearly interchangeable expressions in particular ways.

There are two candid shots of Russell with her costars, which link Russell with her character. Walter Huston (Doc Holliday) and Jack Beutel (Billy the Kid) are anchored to the film through their costumes, while Russell is with their characters but dressed as "herself" (albeit in her new $1,000 wardrobe). This arrangement suggests that Russell is Rio, or at least connected to Doc and Billy, even when she's not filming or rehearsing. These images, juxtaposing Russell in and out of costume and character, further collapse distinctions between herself (a self-described rough-riding Californian happiest on her family's ranch) and Rio (the tough, brave, and earthy cowgirl).

As is the case with her character, Russell is either defined by her relationship with the two men or available as spectacle for the audience. Of course, this observation echoes Laura Mulvey's influential assertion that women in Classical Hollywood exist for the viewing pleasure of the audience through identification with male protagonists and "can be said to connote *to-be-looked-at-ness*."[9] In her photo with Walter Huston (Holliday is Rio's first lover), both have their backs to the camera as they stand next to an on-set horse corral. Though Huston is in costume, including his cowboy hat, Russell is in the street clothes she wore in the balcony shot. Her smiling face is turned toward the camera, and she appears to be listening intently to Huston, perhaps as the two discuss their characters or the film (or dinner). The final photo captures Russell with Jack Beutel, the other unknown actor plucked to star in Hughes's film, in front of an adobe house. Beutel is in his Billy the Kid costume, featuring his silver-studded and fringed leather chaps, but Russell is in low-heeled cowboy boots, gabardine pants belted by that same Western belt, and a tight cotton sweater; she appears to be pinning up her hair.

This final shot is especially rich. Though out of costume in this shot, Russell is still marked as a "cowgirl." As Michael Kirby points out in his seminal essay on the acting/not-acting continuum, "costume creates a 'character.'" Coincidentally, he uses the example of a man dressed in Western clothes on a city street, suggesting that at some point "we see either a cowboy or a person dressed as (impersonating) a cowboy. The exact point on the continuum at which this specific identification occurs" differs according to context and audience response.[10] Thus, following from Kirby, Russell is both in and out of costume in all of her photos and may be placed at different points on an acting continuum by *Life*'s readers. Second, Russell's posture (prominent bosom, lowered chin, and hands behind her head with elbows pointing up and out) mirrors the opening photograph of Rio in the hay. Of course, photos of Rio in a haystack/Russell with her arms folded above her head quickly became ubiquitous as well as synonymous with *The Outlaw*, as Birdwell used similar images to suggest the "racy" content of the film. Kouvaros suggests that capturing stars in repeated poses, both in "candid" shots, official portraits, and gestures captured on film, "indicates . . . the disclosure of a biographical detail" and offers a particular intimacy and authenticity. Following from Kirby, while the iconography of the photo suggests a kind of (nonmatrixed) character for Russell, its content suggests a kind of (matrixed) performance. Finally, Kouvaros suggests that postwar actor photography as well as acting itself increasingly prized "absorption," that is, an antitheatrical stance that suggests the performer is unaware of the audience.[11] Defining theatricality as artificiality, Kouvaros demonstrates how representations of film acting increasingly linked actorly absorption on the film set with authentic performances on the cinema screen.

Naturalism functions by suggesting that an invisible "fourth wall" separates actors from the audience: what happens onstage is thus an authentic representation of what really occurs in living rooms, kitchens, diners, offices, hotels, and other spaces of modern life. In naturalist theater, the actors are of course aware of the audience, but they behave as though they are not. Publicity photos like the shots of Russell on the balcony and with Huston or Beutel telegraph this understanding of acting by presenting subjects who, as Kouvaros explains, "are aware of the photographer's presence, yet everything about their bearing suggest an ability to direct their attention elsewhere."[12] Pinning up her hair, Russell indicates both a consciousness of the photographer (she echoes an earlier pose, and most young women—especially those who have worked as models—know that raising their arms over their heads makes their breasts look fuller) and an internal absorption (her hairpin-filled mouth and turned-away head suggest that she's fully engaged in the private act of fixing her hair, something no lady did in public in 1941).

The photo essay, the first in a major national magazine, uses multiple strategies to imply that Jane Russell is a "natural" actress. Presenting her in and out of costume, it reinforces Russell's nascent persona as a brash temptress. The *Life* article further suggests that Russell can act, through the shots of her smiling and eating Indian corn but especially through her absorption and internality. Jeanine Basinger's popular history of the studio system, *The Star Machine*, argues that Classical Hollywood film acting is based on whether or not performers are "believable on screen." Audiences look for authenticity in films as well as publicity images. Stars are created, Basinger argues, by merging character and performer so that roles seem to be "a secret peek into what that actor was really like."[13] Russell, like all the other actresses in this study, was subject to the machinations of the studio system and interpellated by its performance tropes. In this chapter, I use Russell's public image in order to demonstrate publicity campaigns' centrality to public perceptions of acting, performance, and identity. Then I focus on how two of Russell's films, *Gentlemen Marry Brunettes* and *The Fuzzy Pink Nightgown*, directly engage studio-generated links between actor and role, illuminating both how gendered and how commonplace such assumptions were.

BECOMING JANE RUSSELL

Both Russell and many of her biographers agree that there were two Jane Russells (or four, if her breasts were counted separately, which they sometimes were): the glamorous, supremely sexual screen siren and the Pentecostal Christian. Born Ernestine Jane Geraldine Russell (named for her mother and maternal aunt) in 1921 to the daughter of Canadian immigrants living in Bemidji, Minnesota,

Russell moved to California before she was a year old. Elder sister to four brothers, several of whom followed her into film work, she grew up on her family's ranch in Van Nuys.[14] When Russell was seventeen, her father died. According to her autobiography, Russell was a wild teenager, drinking and experimenting with sex. Pregnant at eighteen, she had an abortion, and though her high school football-star boyfriend, Bob Waterfield, believed the child was his, Russell claims she wasn't sure.[15] Waterfield went on to lead the UCLA Bruins to the 1943 Rose Bowl, and he and Russell married in April of that year. After a stint in the US Army Waterfield had a successful career as a pro football player, leading the Los Angeles Rams to three straight NFL championship games (1949–1951). He and Russell adopted three children: Thomas, an Irish toddler, and Tracy and Robert, both born in the United States. They divorced in 1967, after Waterfield began coaching for the Rams. In 1968 Russell married Roger Barrett, an actor she met while appearing in regional theater, but he died of a heart attack just three months after their marriage. In 1974 she married John Peoples, and they were together until his death in 1999. After the 1960s, when her film career declined, she eschewed publicity and public appearances, especially after Peoples's death. She died from complications of a respiratory illness in 2011; she was eighty-nine.

It's important to note that her autobiography, *Jane Russell: My Path and My Detours* (1985), focuses on her struggle to be a good Christian, her challenges as a wife and mother, and her relationship with her extended family and friends much more than on her career as an actress and certainly her reputation as a bombshell. Despite her tremendous religious faith (she claimed to have tried to "save" Marilyn Monroe), Russell struggled with depression and alcoholism, as well as a terrific temper. In her autobiography, she details several instances of physical altercations between her and Waterfield and admits they were unfaithful to each other. She became depressed and alcoholic after the death of her second and third husbands and entered an alcohol recovery center in 2002 at the urging of her children. A political conservative, she claimed in a 2003 interview that she was "a mean-spirited, right-wing, narrow-minded, conservative Christian bigot."[16] Russell's self-presentation, then, represents her as a hardworking, often tested, conservative Christian housewife who happened to sing and make an occasional film rather than as a glamorous, luxury-loving movie star.

Of course, no one would be interested in Russell's path or detours unless she was a movie star, and her autobiography also suggests that she was most happy (and sober) when she was working regularly, especially onstage or singing in nightclubs. After graduating from high school, she took acting classes at Max Reinhardt's studio and with Maria Ouspenskaya at the Actors Lab, where she was trained in Stanislavsky technique. She also modeled for a photographer and worked as a receptionist in a chiropodist's office. In her autobiography, Russell claims not to have pursued an acting career. Instead, Howard Hughes pursued her, casting her as the lead in *The Outlaw* and building its publicity campaign around her scantily clad and provocatively posed body. In 1954, after the success of *Gentlemen Prefer Blondes* (1953), for which she remains best known, Hughes signed her to a twenty-year, $1,000-a-week contract in exchange for six films with his studio, RKO Pictures.[17] She made about a dozen films for RKO and other studios: films noir with Robert Mitchum (*His Kind of Woman*, 1951; *Macao*, 1952); Westerns (*Young Widow*, 1946; *Montana Belle*, 1952; *Waco*, 1966; *Johnny Reno*, 1966); the Bob Hope vehicles *Paleface* (1948) and *Son of Paleface* (1952); and two important dramatic films, *The Tall Men* (1955) and *The Revolt of Mamie Stover* (1956), with director Raoul Walsh. In 1955 she and Waterfield founded a production company, Russ-Field. Later that year Hedda Hopper reported that "professionally," Russell was "divided three ways: Hughes sold three of her six-picture commitments to 20th Century–Fox," and she would "make one annually for Hughes, one for Fox, and one for her independent company."[18] Her plans didn't exactly work out, but Russ-Field produced two of her most interesting and personal films, *Gentlemen Marry Brunettes* (1955) and *The Fuzzy Pink Nightgown* (1957), which I discuss in detail below. She largely retired from filmmaking after her divorce from Waterfield, recognizing that "after the age of 30 . . . there was really very little for a woman to do in Hollywood."[19] Russell continued to work onstage—for example, replacing Elaine Stritch in *Company* on Broadway in 1971—and as a gospel singer until the late 1970s. She also became a spokeswoman for Playtex 18-Hour bras and the "full-figured gals" who wore them, appearing in dozens of television commercials and print advertisements throughout the 1970s and 1980s. From her initial *Life* magazine appearance through her Playtex commercials, Russell's physical assets determined her film roles and her celebrity persona. Though based on her "real" body, this was far from a "natural" or neutral process; Russell became a star through the same publicity apparatuses that structured film careers in the Classical Hollywood era.

The role of studio publicity departments during and in the years immediately following the studio system era has been well documented. As Joshua Gamson points out, studio publicity efforts have long been understood to "focu[s] attention on the worthy and unworthy alike, churning out many admired commodities called celebrities, famous because they have been made to be so";[20] this is an assumption held both by film audiences who purchase these commodities and by film scholars who study audience, text, and performer. As early as 1957, for example, the communication professor Thomas Harris argued that "modern publicity methods decree that the screen star be known to his or her potential audience not only through film roles but also through fan magazines, national magazines, radio, television and the newspapers. . . . This publicity build-up is calculated to make the personality better known to a public which will respond by attending the . . . films."[21] After the breakup of the studio system in 1948, when an antitrust suit against Paramount legally mandated separate film distribution and production corporations, the studios' supposed absolute control over star image is generally understood to have diminished. Further, Leonard J. Leff argues that "around mid-century, neo-realism abroad and 'the method' at home challenged the so-called artificiality of Hollywood."[22] Because Russell's career spans this period, and because she worked with Howard Hughes, an "independent" filmmaker before his purchase of RKO, her case is particularly instructive. While many stars, such as Esther Williams and Lena Horne, underwent extensive studio-mandated makeovers and training, and their publicity was orchestrated within well-entrenched systems of production, Russell's publicity was largely generated on her behalf by a single producer, Hughes. At the same time, Hughes's techniques aped those of the larger studios. Thus, Russell is unique not only for the amount and type of publicity she received but also for its means of production. Further, her history provides a yardstick to measure other midcentury and contemporary performers understood to cultivate an image rather than a career. As her case study confirms, female performers were interpellated into a system that always already nominated them as sexual spectacles and erotic commodities rather than talented and hardworking performers.

Before turning to Russell's specific case study, I want to generally describe the components of publicity campaigns conducted on behalf of most aspiring stars in the 1940s and 1950s, at the height of and immediately following the breakup of the studio system. These were official, carefully plotted campaigns conducted equally through advertising such as billboards and posters, personal appearances, and articles written for fan magazines. Scholars such as Anthony Slide, in *Inside the Hollywood Fan Magazine*, explain that "fan magazines rel[ied] upon the film industry for their survival. . . . At the same time, . . . the fan magazine was a valuable publicity tool." Magazines like *Modern Screen, Movie Life*, and the prestigious *Photoplay* were instrumental in supporting star persona and creating celebrity, and they were familiar to most North Americans, whether in Hollywood or Hoboken. Slide reports that "in the 1940s and 1950s it was not unusual for the best known of the fan magazines to boast sales in excess of one million copies and a readership of three times that number."[23] The primacy of the film celebrity that partially defines Classical Hollywood cinema is dependent upon the manufactured desire to know and consume details about the players' lives, and studio publicity departments were expert at this task.

Richard de Cordova's influential *Picture Personalities: The Emergence of the Star System in America* demonstrates that "the star system leads us toward that which is behind or beyond the image, hidden from sight." Fan magazines but also legitimate newspapers included biographies, personal essays, and gossip that promised to reveal the secrets of the stars' personal lives. In particular, "the star system . . . depends on an interpretive schema that equates identity with the private" and further nominates sexuality as "the most private, and thus the most truthful, locus of identity." The thousands of column inches devoted to star knowledge were therefore explicitly linked to questions of sexuality. "First, fans 'discovered' the secret of the star's real, bodily, existence . . . [then] the star's married life, and . . . [then] the star's sexual affairs and transgressions." Obviously, de Cordova frames his reading of the star system through Foucauldian understandings of confession: "It is in confession that truth and sex are joined through the obligatory and exhaustive expression of an individual secret." These confessions, however, threaten the luminous aura surrounding stars that ensures their status as a commodity. By the 1920s, de Cordova explains, the star scandals that rocked Hollywood (Fatty Arbuckle's rape case or Douglas Fairbanks and Mary Pickford's premarital affair) responded to an escalating but manufactured desire to know personal truths about Hollywood stars. These scandals in turn escalated control over stars' private lives and public images through the detailed and intrusive contracts on which the studio system depended.[24]

The major studios (MGM, Fox, Warner Bros., RKO, Columbia, Paramount, United Artists, and Universal) recognized "that strict, centralised image control" was necessary to ensure that information about stars enhanced and extended their personae.[25] Studios developed large publicity departments that liaised between stars and news outlets. For example, in a 1986 interview with Ronald L. Davis, the publicity agent Walter Seltzer recalled that in the 1940s Howard Strickling ran the MGM department of about sixty people, each of whom was assigned to about a half-dozen stars and the same number of reporters from national, local, and trade papers, managing star personae on both ends.[26] Janet Leigh recalled for Davis in 1984 that actors had two preproduction responsibilities: to go to wardrobe to be fitted for their costumes, and to visit the publicity department so that the studio could make a "'Who?' into a "'Wow!'"[27] Publicity shaped star image in the same way that costumes shaped character.

Publicity workers also buried potential scandal. In *The Fixers*, E. J. Fleming's otherwise lackluster biography of Howard Strickling and MGM's general manager Eddie Mannix, Strickling is convincingly portrayed as a puppet master, the first to be called whenever a star gets in trouble. When Jean Harlow's husband, Paul Bern, was discovered dead on the morning of September 5, 1932, for example, Strickling moved furniture, destroyed evidence, created an alibi for Harlow, and developed a suicide theory. When Irving Thalberg, the head of MGM, finally "called police at 2:30 P.M. Strickling had called the newspapers. Even as police were first racing to [the scene] the *Los Angeles Times* was printing special extra editions . . . of Strickling's suicide version." Protecting Harlow was deemed more important than revealing that Bern was most likely murdered by his common-law first wife, Dorothy Millette.[28] This is not an isolated incident; Walter Seltzer told Ronald Davis that publicity agents "constantly" covered up details from the stars' private lives that might have negatively reflected on them.[29]

In place of negative confessional details, studio publicity departments created acceptable stories and offered suitable news. "Studio-sanctioned disclosure, made available in the form of gossip columns, newsreels, and fan magazines" according to Nick Muntean and Anne Petersen, confessed to stars' romantic desires, family life, and very occasionally their indiscretions.[30] Publicists were assigned to each major picture, and according to Bill Hendricks at Warner Bros., "they turn[ed] in not only just the actual news happenings of the day—some of them imagined—but [they'd] also write features, and [they'd] write all sorts of stories that would go to . . . a column writer who needed that kind of material."[31] Further, at the height of the studio system, says Slide, "virtually all fan magazines were submitting stories for studio approval prior to publication," ensuring that only approved messages about the stars and their lives were distributed to the movie-going public.[32]

The system perpetuated itself. Esmé Chandlee was proud to be the first female "planter" for a major studio, MGM, in the late 1940s. She worked with Hedda Hopper in particular, feeding Hopper items about the studios' rising and established stars and denying scandal when necessary.[33] Based on this key association, Chandlee was the highest-ranking woman in any studio publicity department. Another example of this symbiotic relationship is reported by Walter Seltzer. He recalled that when working at Columbia in the early 1940s, "Lou Smith . . . called our department of fourteen together and said, 'Look, not too much activity going on. If we want to keep the department intact and keep working here, we have to do something spectacular.' And the department collectively went to work on . . . five youngsters, and really developed stars." One of the "youngsters" was Rita Cansino, who later became Rita Hayworth, one of Columbia's biggest stars.[34] Studio publicity agents, who fed gossip to a variety of legitimate newspapers, fan magazines, and trade papers, forged the links between themselves and news outlets for their own career security as well as the stars they represented.

For de Cordova (following Foucault), confession is discursive, generated through written text and oral narratives. In important ways, however, star confession also includes the visual evidence of the body, not only in film, where gesture and stance reveal as much about character as does dialogue, but also in extrafilmic texts. In fact, as Russell's *Life* pictorial analyzed above makes clear, words are secondary to photographic confession. De Cordova focuses his analysis on the emergent star system of the 1910s and 1920s, but by the 1940s star discourse included as much photographic as textual evidence. This shift is especially crucial to understanding how Jane Russell's persona was manufactured. Though her words confessed her deep religious faith and strong marriage, her photographs presented instead a ripe, sensual woman who knew (and longed to share) the secrets of sex.

Because they were so essential to a stars' personality, even candid photographs were carefully managed. Ann Straus, a fashion editor at MGM who oversaw public appearances, recalled that "an MGM actress was never photographed with a drink in her hand. Part of our job, if we went to an opening, a premiere, or a big party with a star, was that we never let them be photographed with a glass in their hand. MGM girls were as pure as the driven snow, and sometimes purer!"[35] Beginning in the 1920s, studios held lavish premieres, inviting movie fans to watch their idols watching a movie, just as they themselves might do—albeit in a more glamorous fashion. According to David Karnes, "these gala openings show-cased the stars, figures who existed both on- and off-screen and who thereby tangibly embodied movie culture's capacity to bridge the two realms." The pre-miere, he continues, was an attraction itself, often more interesting and exciting than the film it celebrated. The audience, made up of movie stars and industry insiders, would arrive at one of the movie palaces on Hollywood Boulevard (such as Grauman's Chinese Theatre) under the avid gaze of "ten to twenty thousand" fans who never saw the film itself.[36] Further, these premieres were often broadcast live via radio, and especially lavish events were filmed for inclusion in newsreels. The film's actors, director, and producer usually attended, but contract players were generally required to attend premieres as part of their training in the art of public relations. Ann Doran "remembered that the studio sent you to the pre-miere. They took you up to the wardrobe department, they put your clothes on, they said, 'you're going with so-and-so because we want to take pictures of the two of you at the premiere,' so you went."[37] Coached by the publicity staff, dressed by studio costumers, and matched with a date by casting directors or drama coaches eager to suggest a romantic partnership before filming began, these bud-ding stars used premiere appearances to further solidify their public personae and extend their fan base.[38]

Photographs of the premieres, including shots of stars as well as fans, were widely circulated in daily newspapers and fan magazines. These photographs testified to the glamour and spectacle of the premiere event but also grounded the stars in an everyday reality, linking their spectatorial practices with those of a mass audience. Further, the juxtaposition of fan with star implies narratives of young men and women plucked from obscurity to become glamorous screen idols; the shining face of an excited starlet in the presence of her screen idols is mirrored by the excited shop clerks and students in the crowd. Premieres thus offered a multilayered and multivalent representation of the audience/performer relationship.

Though the "candid" shots of stars together at industry parties were impor-tant indicators of their personalities and private lives, photographs of stars in their homes were also carefully managed. Simon Dixon explores how the "star's domestic décor is marked by his or her screen role." Photographs of stars in their homes, including John Wayne "surrounded by western art, riding saddles, and Winchesters," participate in the larger project of movie casting, with stars' homes suggesting their past and future roles. In the same way, photographs of Jane Rus-sell on her family's ranch, Esther Williams beside her pool, and Zsa Zsa Gabor with her lapdogs and pink Louis XIV furniture solidify their personae even when, as Dixon points out, these settings are "often to the exclusion of other, more private tastes."[39] Because the star's home and leisure time (like her sex life) are assumed to be especially private, photographic access to these spaces is especially laden with indicators of identity and authenticity.

Press tours and promotional appearances promised access to stars' private identity and further sutured star to role; they too were vigorously policed. According to Ronald L. Davis, major films often occasioned a multicity publicity blitz, with stars "appearing on stage several times a day" performing in skits, singing songs, and answering questions from fans and reporters. Davis continues, "Whenever stars were interviewed, someone from the publicity department usually accompanied them, and newcomers were carefully instructed on what to say."[40] In many cases, stars wore clothing similar to their film costumes, talked about links between their characters and themselves, and presented short live skits. Stars also used promotional appearances to try out new facets of their personae or practice other skills in front of an appreciative audience. Publicity departments and stars worked together to promote both the specific film and the stars themselves.

Jane Russell's experience promoting *The Outlaw* during its 1943 San Francisco premiere (the only theatrical showing of the film until 1946) demonstrates the value of these special appearances. According to Russell, "some idiot" convinced Howard Hughes that she and Jack Beutel should perform an added scene that fit *The Outlaw*'s narrative. They "started rehearsing a playlet on the Goldwyn lot." Hughes had a curtain constructed to look like a forest, then had Beutel, Russell (in a new wardrobe), Russell's cousin and assistant Pat Henry, the publicist Russell Birdwell, and the press "flown up *en masse* at [his] expense and put up in the finest hotels." When Beutel walked onstage to start the scene, the "fabulous, terribly expensive, frigging curtain was stuck." The audience, including the press and the luminaries Hughes had invited, screamed with laughter. They never performed the scene again; Hughes hired a comedian, Frank McHugh, and Russell and Beutel fed him straight lines. For the next nine weeks, as the poorly reviewed film played to packed houses, she, McHugh, and Beutel virtually lived at the theater, performing as many as three shows a day. Clearly, their presence helped sell the picture, and their performance was tweaked to appeal to the audience even though it had little to do with the film. In several cases, Birdwell and Hughes used the tactics of major studios to guarantee big crowds for premieres and extended showings in large cities. According to Russell, Hughes continued to send her on the road in support of her films. In 1946, she toured for *Young Widow*, singing rather than working as straight man for a comic. She was so popular as a singer that Hughes made Lenore Brent in *His Kind of Woman* a lounge singer, which made Russell more willing to do the film, a tired reworking of faded film noir tropes.[41]

Publicity department control went further than planting news items, coordinating promotional tours, and stage-managing photo opportunities, however.

These efforts overlapped with the larger project of actor training and persona development. Davis asserts that publicity agents were charged with creating "an image for each actor and actress. Once the image had been determined, it was important for that would-be star to dress accordingly."[42] Howard Hughes provided Jane Russell not only with the money for a promotional wardrobe but also with an assistant who picked it out. For example, before going on location to film *The Outlaw*, Russell was paired with an ex-model named Slim who made arrangements to fit Russell with "soft cashmere dresses, a camel hair coat, and a tan suit, all simply tailored and stunning."[43] This expensive wardrobe became a key fact in Russell's biography, indicating her humble origins and need for fashion intervention. Emily Torchia worked in MGM's publicity department, styling stars for photo shoots, and remembered that her styling advice extended to personal appearances and stars' private lives as well, and, says Davis, "Della Owens Rice advised starlets at 20th Century Fox on how to dress."[44] Jeanine Basinger's explanation that "audiences responded to actors on film as if they *were* the characters they were playing, and . . . moviegoers saw . . . [an] amalgam of the real person, the character he played, and the interaction between the two" depends on publicity departments working in conjunction with wardrobe supervisors as well as drama coaches and casting agents to reinforce the naturalist paradigm linking star and role.[45] Thus, in multiple ways, publicity determined how stars—and their films—should be interpreted and appreciated.

The publicity campaign for *The Outlaw* is a limit case of the effects of studio publicity. Though that campaign, stretching over seven years, ultimately yielded bigger box office returns than the mediocre film may have deserved, it also delayed the movie's opening, making static images of Russell rather than filmic performance the basis for at least her early career. Because publicity for *The Outlaw* was built around Russell's image more than around the plot of the film or the other actors, it concretized her as a sultry, tempestuous vixen. Not surprisingly, other photographs and stories about Russell built on this image. By the time *The Outlaw* was re-released in 1946 and opened nationally in 1950, Russell was firmly cast as sexy entertainer in both her film roles and the hearts and minds of her fans. Whether as Dorothy Shaw in the musical comedy *Gentlemen Prefer Blondes*, gypsy bride Annie Caldash in *Hot Blood*, cowgirl Nella Turner in *The Tall Men*, or Lenore Brent in *His Kind of Woman*, Russell was a gold-digging bombshell who always got her man by proving she was just as sexy, adventurous, and tough as he was. Even in films like *Hot Blood*, where Russell plays a gypsy rather than her usual entertainer character, she sings, fights, dances, and schemes her way to true love. These roles are all variations on the character implied by Russell's publicity photographs as Rio: the gun in her hand, the half-mocking smile on her lips, and the blouse sliding off her shoulders promise erotic adventure to the men brave enough to tangle with her (see figure 4).

Figure 4: Sultry Jane Russell, ready to tussle, in a publicity still for *The Outlaw*.

Russell Birdwell directed the campaign, working under Howard Hughes's exacting instructions. The *New York Times* reported that Hughes produced as well as directed *The Outlaw* after the initial director, Howard Hawks, "halted production . . . because of a dispute over expenditures"; Hawks believed the film could be produced for much less. Hughes resumed filming December 14, 1940; under his novice direction the shoot continued for another three months and with an additional $1.5 million budgeted for its production (Hawks had wanted to shoot the film for $750,000 total).[46] Hughes, known for his pioneering aviation work (he built planes for the US government and owned three airlines, including TWA) and eccentricities (in the last years of his life he moved from hotel to hotel, seen by only the half-dozen Mormon men who worked as his cooks/secretaries/nurses) as well as his films, had "a flair for publicity" and vigorously promoted his airplanes, his films, his lovers, and even his own mystique, according to his biographers. In 1930, for example, he wrote, produced, and directed *Hell's Angels*, starring Jean Harlow as a promiscuous heartbreaker whose faithlessness almost causes a major British defeat in World War I. Filmed at a cost of nearly $4 million, it is known as the most expensive film of its time, in part because of its aerial sequences and in part because it was converted to sound halfway through production.[47] Despite its budget overruns, *Hell's Angels* was a critical and financial success. Some of that critical success was certainly due to Hughes's promotional efforts, which included, "among other excesses, a three-day cocktail party for the press at the Astor Hotel" and stunt pilots circling over Grauman's Chinese Theatre at the premiere, according to Ronald L. Davis.[48] Clearly, Hughes and Birdwell knew a thing or two about film marketing and promotion.

The Outlaw is notorious for Hughes's battles with the Motion Picture Producers and Distributors Association (MPPDA) and the Legion of Decency over its content as well as its advertising. In 1941, The Outlaw was awarded a provisional MPPDA seal that allowed Twentieth Century–Fox, which had partnered with Hughes for distribution, to exhibit the film at its movie theaters. Hughes was ordered to trim some of Russell's scenes because her costume was "too revelatory" and to change dialogue to make it clear that Billy the Kid and Rio were married when they shared a bed. Though Hughes made the changes, the New York Times reported that "the Hays office [was] said to be anxious to get back the 'preliminary' Production Code seal," and Twentieth Century–Fox pulled out of its distribution agreement.[49] Hughes responded by purchasing theaters in San Francisco and Detroit in order to exhibit the film on his own. According to Peter Dart's history of Hughes's battle with Hollywood censors, Hughes showed the film for four months "by special arrangements and with tremendous publicity . . . before he withdrew the film to develop a new advertising approach." Hughes's new approach called attention to the MPPDA's and Legion of Decency's condemnation of the film, suggesting that it was especially sexually explicit. One poster touted The Outlaw as "the picture that couldn't be stopped" and included a full-color illustration of a reclining Russell, breasts falling out of her blouse, gun pressed to her nearly naked thigh, and hand over head (as in the Life pictorial); another showed Russell kneeling in the hay, blouse slipping from her shoulders, with the caption "How would you like to tussle with Russell?" Putting his aviation interests to work for the film, Hughes had a skywriter "put circles with dots in the middle of them under the title of the picture," which was almost universally condemned for being tasteless.[50]

Hughes planned to re-release the film in 1946 after it had reaped the rewards of the campaign, but the original seal of approval had expired, and it only played in a few theaters. The new MPAA (the name was changed to the Motion Picture Association of America in 1945) refused to recertify it, on the grounds that "all advertising must also be inspected and approved if a picture were to have the code seal."[51] Thus, in its second round, the MPAA censored the publicity for the film rather than its content. With such a concerted effort to sell the film based on Russell's provocative image and the film's presumed racy content, it's not surprising that Russell was a world-famous sex symbol before most audiences had ever seen her films. This image was supported through various publicity efforts that dovetail with naturalist theories of acting to emphasize the correspondence of self and role as well as acting as labor. In important ways, they help illustrate how these naturalist theories are particularly gendered, and potentially detrimental to arguments for and about actresses' agency and labor.

READING RUSSELL'S PUBLICITY KIT

In *The Star Machine*, Jeanine Basinger explains the publicity trajectory most successful 1940s studio starlets followed. First, "candid" shots of aspiring stars at movie premieres, charity functions, war events, and industry dinners were featured in the back pages of a fan magazine. Next, stars moved toward the front of the magazine or into newspaper features about, for example, favorite beauty products. For example, while promoting the films noir *Macao* and *The Las Vegas Story*, Russell told the syndicated columnist Lydia Lane that "if you are going to get the things out of life which are going to make you happy, you have to have a true sense of values." Next, she explained that mascara was the most important cosmetic tool. Her lashes, she said, "are just average lashes. . . . But they look thick because I have made them up well. . . . When you have a dry brush, you will find that by the time you apply a coat to the lashes on one eye, the other eye will be ready for a second coat. Then you can keep going over them until they look long and thick."[52] Next, continues Basinger, stars appeared as "the sole subject of one of the magazine's leading articles."[53] Once established, stars regularly appeared in several fan magazines per month, frequently featured on the cover as well. Finally, stars might get a national magazine cover, as when Betty Grable covered *Time* on August 23, 1948. Though Russell didn't work within the studio system and so did not have an institutionalized publicity department, her career in photographs and magazines follows this rough trajectory.

Russell didn't have a stable of studio-approved stars for her to photographically date, and she eloped with Waterfield in April 1943, before her films were widely released; therefore, few shots exist of Russell in "a rumoured romanced with another star already well known to the public," which Thomas Harris suggests is crucial to developing female star image.[54] Most depict her relationship with John Payne, whom she seriously dated while briefly on the outs with Waterfield. For example, the back pages of the February 1943 *Hollywood* magazine show Payne kneeling to lace up Russell's roller skates. The text uses Payne's pose to suggest that though this isn't the moment, "the question may be popped . . . before John joins the Air Corps."[55] Both are smiling, and Russell's garters are barely visible as she watches Payne fumble with her laces. This photo simultaneously highlights Russell's legs, the innocent activity of skating at a public rink, and Payne's honorable intentions. As with many fan magazine photos, it's sex sanctified as true romance, moderating the photo's erotic content by association with love and marriage.

Though Russell Birdwell's publicity campaign for *The Outlaw* is noted for its salaciousness, he too balanced Russell's sexuality with other signifiers. Birdwell, a

Texan like Hughes, worked as a journalist and director before becoming David O. Selznick's lead publicist in 1935, masterminding the search for the actress to play Scarlett O'Hara.[56] For Hughes, Birdwell hired some photographers and welcomed others to *The Outlaw*'s Arizona location, then made Russell work "overtime to keep up with the bulging publicity schedule to which [he] ... condemned her," as she described the campaign for a 1945 photo essay in *Life* magazine.[57] Russell recalled in a 1943 *Los Angeles Times* interview that because she often had downtime during the location shoot, she posed for thousands of pictures. Representatives from "Life, Look, Click and Catch-as-Catch-Can ... told me to pick up a pail and walk this way and that, and while I was doing it they shot me from in front, on the sides, above and below. It was a photographers' field day—and I was green."[58] Birdwell enlarged photos from the *Outlaw* shoot and mailed them to thousands of servicemen stationed around the world.[59]

According to the *Life* magazine photo essay, Birdwell "concentrate[d] his fire on the service," framing Russell's racy publicity photos as a contribution to World War II efforts.[60] This tactic allowed Russell's sexuality to be viewed as healthy and patriotic. Robert B. Westbrook points out that "the United States government and the film industry cooperated closely during the war in the production and distribution of millions of photographs of Hollywood's leading ladies and rising starlets" in order to sustain "healthy, heterosexual desire and ... [thwart] homosexuality." Substituting Hollywood stars for the wives and sweethearts back home, pinups "functioned as icons of the private interests and obligations for which soldiers were fighting."[61] In order to underscore Russell's importance to US fighting men, Birdwell recalled, he "got a sick looking GI" to pose with Russell's photo—and the sweater he was knitting her—and placed that photograph in the April 13, 1942, issue of *Life* magazine.[62] He also publicized Russell's popularity with servicemen, circulating photographs of Russell being carried by cheering recruits, at the Army Day ceremonies at Camp Roberts on April 4, 1941, being honored as the "mascot of the fourth graduating class of the Army Air Corps advanced flying school" on July 11, 1941 (posing with the plane that bears her photographic image), and as a "Hush-Hush girl" in the navy's campaign to halt "careless talk" about operations.[63] Though her fame as a pinup didn't completely alleviate the negative connotations of Russell's *Outlaw* photos, it did partially excuse her provocative poses as patriotic duty.

Because *The Outlaw* was censored for its advertising campaign as well as its content, Birdwell's attempts to balance Russell's sexy image with morally appropriate motives is especially noteworthy. As Anthony Slide points out, the Production Code's restrictions meant that "it was not enough to present a positive image on screen, it was necessary to continue with that image on the printed page."[64] Birdwell further finessed Russell's pinup popularity by associating it with her own biography: she inspired her own US fighting man as well as countless of anonymous soldiers. After Russell finished promoting *The Outlaw* in San

Francisco in 1943, she traveled to Columbia, Georgia, where she lived as an army wife while Waterfield completed his basic training and waited to be sent overseas. The army itself capitalized on Russell's presence, distributing its own photo of her making coffee in her small kitchen near the barracks (see figure 5).[65]

Birdwell seized on this photograph, using it to illustrate Russell's simple home life. This domestic image is echoed in several fan magazine stories in the 1940s. For example, Westbrook details how "women avidly followed [Betty] Grable's career in the fan magazines where her domestic life . . . was held up as an example to readers," teaching them how to create a happy home despite wartime privations.[66] Thus, Russell was part of a familiar narrative that suggested she was like her fans and modeled appropriately patriotic and heteronormative behavior for them.

Russell's private life was simultaneously framed to align with her star image as a tough and tempestuous temptress in dozens of cheesecake pictorials. The November 11, 1941, issue of *Pic* magazine, for example, features Russell on the cover in a white two-piece bathing suit perched on some rocks overlooking a river. The accompanying story represents Russell's trip with two friends to the

Figure 5: Jane Russell pours coffee during her housekeeping chores at her home in Columbia, Georgia, for Bob Waterfield, stationed at Fort Benning. (AP Photo)

Newhall, California, "drive-in" gold mine: for fifty cents a day, would-be prospectors could keep all the gold they gathered while panning the river. The story
explains that "there were so many things to do that comparatively little time
was devoted to" gold mining. Instead, the three young women (Russell was
accompanied by Lorraine Williams, identified as a dancer, and Patty Durin, a
model) swam, hung their bathing suits out to dry, had a pillow fight, cooked
a campfire dinner ("all . . . are good cooks," the text assures readers), and walked

MISCELLANY

Figure 6: Introspective Jane Russell, drinking coffee on a cold beach. *Life*, January 1945.
(Getty Images)

along the beach. Russell is the sole subject of two photos: in the first she pulls a strapless bathing suit up a bit higher on her chest, the action clearly drawing attention to her bosom, and in the second she steps out of their camping trailer in the same white two-piece she wears in the cover shot, "up at dawn . . . for an early swim."[67]

All of the photos, with the possible exception of the preswim shot, seem to be candid, and none of the women look at the camera, nor seem aware of its presence. At the same time, the photos are undoubtedly carefully posed and no doubt commissioned by Birdwell, who was working through 1941 and 1942 to keep Russell in the spotlight. These photographs balance Russell's sexuality with signifiers of normalcy, innocence, and camaraderie while reinforcing connections between Russell and old-time Western life. The pillow fight, for example, is relatively tame and appears spontaneous—Russell and Durin are wearing chaste cotton nightgowns and are grinning ferociously at each other, rather than, for example, posing for the camera in lingerie and fulfilling male fantasies of what women do when alone together, as they might in a more salacious magazine. Russell here "tussles" with a female friend, but the competitive sparkle in her eye, as well as her flexed muscles, suggests that she's feisty at least (and a wildcat in bed, if the implications of the photo are pushed to their limits). As she sits by the campfire, Russell strums a guitar (an instrument she did not, in fact, know how to play), and the women eat pork and beans, standard cowboy tropes. Finally, Russell wears cowboy boots for her moonlit walk along the beach. This pictorial is representative of those in which Russell appeared while waiting for *The Outlaw* to be released, merging several seemingly random and candid images in order to construct a particular persona.

If this pictorial suggests that Russell is "naturally" outdoorsy, sexy, and feisty, her shots in the January 29, 1945, edition of *Life* magazine suggest that she's also an actress (see figures 6 and 7). The final three pages of that issue offer two photographs of Russell. In the first, she's huddled in a wool blanket, bare feet burrowing into the sand, as she leans against a rock and sips from what the text identifies as "a thermos of hot coffee." The second, a one-third-page shot of her in a flowered two-piece bathing suit, tells readers that a "radiant, wind-blown Russell with a warm, sunny smile is the result of the cold afternoon's work at the beach."[68] The two photographs are nearly polar opposites: the first is introspective, and Russell's heavy-lashed eyes look down at her coffee. She looks cold, tired, and vulnerable. Her body is curled protectively in on itself, and the rumpled blanket, sand dunes, and jagged rock echo each other's roughly textured curves. In the second, Russell stands magnificently tall at the water's edge, leaning on a rock, with her head tilted and her front leg slightly bent. Her torso is twisted away from her hips, and her shoulders are unnaturally raised in order to push her chest forward. She's smiling directly into the camera and looks healthy and vibrant. The juxtaposition of these photos exemplifies George Kouvaros's assertions that star photographs "gave shape to another idea central to postwar

Figure 7: Sexy, smiling Jane Russell showing off her figure on that same beach. *Life*, January 1945. (Getty Images)

culture: acting as work."[69] In his discussion of the Magnum photographs taken on the set of *The Misfits*, Kouvaros determines how the candid shots of Marilyn Monroe, Clark Gable, and Montgomery Clift preparing for their scenes, waiting between takes, and being dressed and made up frame film acting as specific work rather than unmediated depictions of real behavior. In the same way, this *Life* pictorial demonstrates the differences between the photographic image and the labor required to capture it. The contrast between the cold, pensive Russell drinking coffee and the smiling, energetically posed Russell on the beach suggests that Russell had to work to look happy and warm. Further, at a point in her career when Russell was struggling to make serious films and win better roles, the *Life* shots on the beach simultaneously reinforce her sexy image and suggest that there's more to her than great legs, big breasts, and a sunny smile.

In 1953 Jane Russell filmed two blockbuster films, *Gentlemen Prefer Blondes* and *The French Line*.[70] In many ways, *Gentlemen Prefer Blondes* is a better film, with a stronger book and music, as well as more visual spectacle (though *French Line* was filmed in 3D!), but the two films are especially interesting when considered together. Russell essentially plays the same role twice, the films share a setting and are thematically linked, and several of the production numbers mirror each other. Considered as a pair, they help demonstrate the kind of intertextuality that concretizes connections between films and characters that establish star personae. Both garnered tremendous publicity for Russell, but for different reasons and in different ways: as always, her persona is split between the sex symbol and the hardworking good girl. As with most of her films (especially those for Hughes), Russell's publicity for *The French Line* circulated images of her scantily clad curves and focused on the "racy" content of the film, another example of the sexually exploitive publicity that most starlets endured at some point. Publicity for *Gentlemen Prefer Blondes*, on the other hand, focused on the relationship between Russell and her costar Marilyn Monroe. While their sexual appeal was certainly evident, the publicity for *Blondes* foreshadows the kind of "behind the scenes" coverage that George Kouvaros identifies as crucial to emerging narratives of "acting as a social activity" that requires time and labor.[71]

Gentlemen Prefer Blondes, produced by Twentieth Century–Fox, follows two nightclub entertainers, Lorelei Lee (Monroe) and Dorothy Shaw (Russell), across the Atlantic to Paris. A private detective (who eventually marries Dorothy) trails the two women; he's been hired by Lorelei's future father-in-law to catch her cheating on his son. The women sing, dance, and look for romance (and Lorelei finds diamonds) before marrying their respective beaux in a glorious double wedding. Two of its musical numbers, Monroe's "Diamonds Are a Girl's Best Friend" and Russell's "Isn't Anyone Here for Love," are canonical for their campy spectacle. *The French Line*, produced by RKO, has a key musical number as well, Russell's censored rendition of "Looking for Trouble." In the RKO film, Russell plays Mame Carson, a Texas oil heiress who masquerades as a model on a luxury liner headed for Paris in order to find a man who will love her for herself rather than her fortune (in this film, she's pursued by gold diggers, rather than being one herself). She travels with her childhood friend Annie Farrell (Mary McCarty), who has become the successful fashion designer Madame Firelli. Further, because *The French Line* is a Russell star vehicle rather than a partnership (and because her character's sole reason for traveling to France is to find true love), it offers few of the feminist pleasures that critics attribute to *Gentlemen Prefer Blondes.*

Both films take place on a cruise ship, contain a duet between the two female stars that mocks their seeming small-town naiveté,[72] pivot on cases of mistaken identity, and end with the heroines happily married, their fortunes secure, and their reputations intact despite their seemingly scandalous behavior. The similarities were noted by reviewers: Bosley Crowther writing for the *New York Times* called *The French Line* "a fable that looks a faint stencil of 'Gentlemen Prefer Blondes,' touched up with smoking-room humor," and the *Los Angeles Times* critic Philip K. Scheuer complained that it was "uninventively reminiscent of such of its predecessors as 'Gentlemen Prefer Blondes.'"[73] Russell's bodacious curves and singing talent were equally on display in both, proving, in the words of *Variety*'s critic, that Russell could "be a good musical comedy actress . . . when given material and direction" as she was in *Blondes.*[74] Unfortunately, *The French Line* merely exploits Russell's physical charms rather than develops an interesting plot or nuanced characters. From Russell teasingly undressing for a bath in the film's opening sequence to her duet with McCarty, and of course the notorious "Looking for Trouble," *The French Line*'s racy scenes smacked of "rank opportunism," defying Joseph Breen's Production Code Administration (PCA) by presenting little more than a "peep show."[75]

Similarities and differences in plot, sexual exploitation, and characterization aside, the publicity campaigns for both films are equally notable. The May 25, 1953, *Life* magazine put Jane Russell and Marilyn Monroe on the cover, rehearsing their "Two Little Girls" number in matching red sequined dresses and diamond jewelry. Monroe is placed in the foreground and is the focus of the photo essay inside (though Russell was top-billed and paid nearly $80,000 more than Monroe for the film itself).[76] The article explains that Monroe is "the least ingenuous" of the actors to play Lorelei Lee, but she's "full-fleshed and fancy free," singing and dancing "with a surprising technical competence."[77] The photos include three production stills of Monroe and two of Russell in comic situations. In the first, Russell leans against a pommel horse, flanked by two head-standing gymnasts and singing "Isn't Anyone Here for Love"; in the second, she impersonates Lorelei to clear her friend of theft charges. The *Life* article, though certainly a useful and iconic publicity campaign, is a fairly simple and straightforward advertisement for the film and Monroe's specific charms. It's typical of dozens of *Life* stories from the 1940s and 1950s previewing new films, clearly produced in cooperation with studios, which offered access to the set and stills from the film.[78] Importantly, *Life*'s photos of Russell in costume and singing and dancing with her partner are echoed in publicity photos for *The French Line*, which also prominently feature Russell in a sequined costume and with McCarty, her foil in that film.

Though *Life* ran a typical story in support of *Gentlemen Prefer Blondes*, focusing on Monroe's interpretation of Lorelei through both text and images, the photographer Ed Clark took dozens of rehearsal photos that offer different narratives. Shot in black-and-white and available on the Google-hosted *Life* archive as well as scores of fan websites, these photos illuminate the necessary labor involved in making a successful movie musical, as well as the friendship between Russell and Monroe so crucial to the film's success.[79] There are several shots of Russell and Monroe, as well as Monroe alone, rehearsing the song and dance. In most of these, the two women are noticeably out of sync, their bodies turned incongruously toward the camera's lens and their faces focused in opposite directions rather than the perfectly matched pose of the cover image. There are four photographs of Russell watching Monroe rehearse her solo portion of the song: in two of them, Russell looks warmly and encouragingly at Monroe. It appears from the number of photographs of this sequence, all slightly different in terms of Russell's position, lighting, and background composition, that Monroe was rehearsed and shot several times. The affection with which Russell regards Monroe corroborates claims in Russell's autobiography and elsewhere that she took Monroe under her wing during filming, especially by helping her leave her dressing room each morning in order to end the long delays that resulted from Monroe's paralyzing stage fright. In two other photos, Gwen Verdon rehearses the women, demonstrating Jack Cole's choreography. Dressed in a cardigan, loose pants, and character shoes, Verdon looks dowdy compared to the two stars, though she's in the foreground and slightly more in focus. These thirty-odd photographs are an important record of the rehearsal process for Hollywood musicals, and they offer glimpses of the mundane labor women—both stars and technicians—undertook to make these glittering extravaganzas a success. Several critical studies, such as those by the feminists Lucie Arbuthnot and Gail Seneca and the film theorists Florence Jacobowitz, and Richard Lippe, have noted that *Gentlemen Prefer Blondes* represents female friendship outside of normal Hollywood narratives of competition, vanity, and jealousy by creating an especially interesting and nuanced relationship between Lorelei and Dorothy. Despite Howard Hawks's and Jack Cole's supervision of the film and dance sequences, Clark's unpublished *Life* photographs represent the making of *Gentlemen Prefer Blondes* as an equally feminine enterprise.

Two photographs in particular suggest this feminine world of mutual comfort and support; neither was published in *Life*. The pictures appear to have been taken at roughly the same time. In the first, which provides the cover for this book, Monroe drinks a bottle of Coca-Cola while Russell touches up her makeup. The two women are sitting on the steps of the film set's nightclub, where they've just rehearsed. Monroe is caught in profile, one leg bent and crossed over the other, which is angled beneath her. Though it seems like a candid shot, Monroe also seems supremely aware of the lines of her body, and her legs—revealed up to her waist by the dress's slit—are flexed, her elbows, hips, shoulders, and knees offering photographically interesting angles. As Jacobowitz and Lippe point out, Monroe's photos "are never simply candid and spontaneous; there is always present an underlying sense of a real person who is also an actor, aware of a performance."[80] Russell seems less studied, with her legs crossed at the ankles and thrust in front of her, but the slit in her skirt exposes her legs as well. Though the two women aren't paying attention to each other, they are sitting so close that their hips touch. Further, their comfort in performing such intimate actions as swigging a bottle of Coke and reapplying lipstick suggest an easy familiarity. In the second shot, Monroe has put down the now nearly empty bottle, and Russell has kicked off her shoes. She's moved up a step and sits behind Monroe, leaning into her friend's shoulder; Monroe rests her back on Russell's thigh. Both women are looking off to the right and smiling; Russell looks as though she's been caught in midsentence. This seems like a completely unguarded and candid moment for both stars, and their body language suggests they are close friends. Though certainly the two may still be performing for the camera (as many assert Monroe always was), the performance here is about female friendship, camaraderie, and intimacy, which is quite different from the official *Life* images, which highlight the comic moments of the film and focus on Monroe.

Though these rehearsal photos are remarkably rich images, it's unsurprising that *Life* chose not to run them. In the first case, they are evidence of actors actually working: as Danae Clark points out, in Classical Hollywood film, "the labor of performance becomes less the provenance of actors and more the property or product of the studio."[81] That is, the finished film was generally understood to have been created by an anonymous group of editing, lighting, makeup, costume, scenographic, sound, and other technicians led by a visionary director rather than discrete performances developed and delivered by actors working alone and with each other to craft character and further narrative. The inclusion of Verdon in particular suggests that the dances performed by Monroe and Russell are not their own, and thus threaten the narrative fiction that Lorelei and Dorothy are successful cabaret performers (while simultaneously underlining that they are hardworking performers). As I argue throughout this book, the erasure of the labor required to develop musical comedy in general, and the spectacular female performances it engenders in particular, is an explicit devaluing of female performers' agency and subjectivity as well as evidence of the naturalist theories of acting that insist performance is merely recorded "natural" behavior. Rehearsal photographs trouble both these assumptions.

Second, the kind of intimacy and casualness on display in these photos, especially the closeness of the two stars' bodies, Russell's bare feet, and Monroe's indulgence in Coca-Cola, is an unacceptable image of glamorous Hollywood stardom. The incongruity between Russell's chipped pedicure and her diamond necklace, or Monroe's mussed hair and her perfectly tailored costume, undercuts the myth of glamour that studios strove to construct around their process and products. Unlike the "candid" shots of stars at movie premieres meant to demonstrate similarities between them and their audiences, or pictorials of, for example, Esther Williams swimming with her children (which are always staged and choreographed events in their own right), Clark's *Life* outtakes do too much to demystify the magic of moviemaking.

Nearly sixty years after they were made, it's equally unsurprising that they have been commercially reproduced (the first photograph is available in a variety of sizes and frames for purchase on Allposters.com and hangs on my office wall) and uploaded to many fansites (of Monroe, Russell, even Coca-Cola). Audiences are still interested in the "real" star behind the image, especially in the case of Marilyn Monroe, and film scholars are committed to deconstructing official narratives of Hollywood history. At the same time, these kinds of rehearsal images and relaxed moments are de rigueur in contemporary entertainment magazines. Stars mugging for an automatic photo booth in *Entertainment Weekly* have replaced Edward Steichen's striking portrait of Gloria Swanson peering from behind black lace, published in the February 1928 issue of *Vanity Fair*.[82] Unlike the formal studio portraits of the 1920s–1940s or the studio-approved production stills once used to "publicise films and the stars who help sell films,"[83] publicity images no longer follow strict aesthetic or commercial codes. Instead, they are generally less consistent, more ambiguous shots, as are the *Life* outtakes.[84]

Howard Hughes followed his own specific publicity codes when selling Russell and her films to a mass audience. Repeating the formula that had proved successful for *The Outlaw*, Hughes built the publicity campaign for *The French Line* around Jane Russell's physique and the threat of censorship. Posters for the film showed Russell in costume for "Lookin' for Trouble" with the tag line "J.R. in 3-D. It'll knock both your eyes out." According to a report in *Time* magazine, Hughes once again "reaped the free publicity of scandal when the film, like *The Outlaw*, was rated Condemned by the Catholic Legion of Decency."[85] As Leonard J. Leff and Jerold Simmons point out in *The Dame in the Kimono: Hollywood, Censorship, and the Production Code*, *The French Line* was one of several significant challenges to the PCA in the mid-1950s, though most understood Hughes as stirring up controversy in order to stir up interest in the film. Older and wiser than she was when she made *The Outlaw* (and a mother and more committed Christian), Russell contributed to the controversy by denouncing the film. *Life* magazine quoted Jane Russell "earnestly" complaining that she "fought and beefed and argued over scenes in the picture."[86] Several fan magazines also reported on the debate between Hughes and the PCA, always including pictures of Russell in her infamous bikini.[87]

Both *Movie Life* in April 1954 and the first issue of *Exposed* (1955) featured Russell on the cover as well as a story about *The French Line* and the need to revamp the Production Code. "Howard Hughes, the zillionaire owner of RKO," exhibited *The French Line* without the PCA seal of approval and showed "Jane Russell throwing around and about all the ladylike muscle, backside and bosom" in a dance designed to drive men mad, said Charles Samuels in *Exposed*. Samuels's article asserts that the outdated code will be gone soon and compiles a list of films and court cases that had recently tested its value. *Exposed* uses Russell's image in the sequin-blazoned and cutout suit both on the cover and to introduce the article but also includes Russell's condemnation of the film. "Jane Russell," writes Samuels, "has vociferously agreed with the blue noses that her dance scenes should be cut or toned down. She said she never wanted to do the sexy dance in the first place but that the studio had insisted."[88] Thus, *Exposed* used Russell's racy image but effectively divorced it from her "real" biography, severing links between character and role.

Like *Exposed*, the April 1954 issue of *Movie Life* used *The French Line* to both comment on the outdated PCA and demonstrate that Russell was (at least as far as overt sexuality was concerned) different from the characters she played. On the cover, Russell wears a low-cut red sequined dress; in the article "Hot Stuff!" she appears in her *French Line* costume to support allegations that her "screen-scorching dance . . . added fuel to the burning issue" of censorship. Although Russell's images highlight her curves, the caption under the *French Line* photo reminds readers that "Jane Russell sided with censors who demanded" that the dance scene by reshot and edited.[89] Similarly, the January 1955 *Movie Play* ran the article "Russell Uncensored" to demonstrate that although Russell speaks "just plain sex" simply by "walking across the camera," she's a committed Christian with "a soft tender heart" hidden by her "boisterous sometimes coarse attitude."[90] These articles all suggest that Russell's films and image may be censorable, but when she speaks and acts for herself, she's above censure. Further, by separating her private person from her screen persona, they suggest that acting is labor, even when it seems natural. Russell's body may naturally and authentically "speak sex," but her heart speaks to Jesus.

Though *Movie Life* suggests on page 21 that Russell is markedly different from her film characters, the article "Designing Women," twenty-five pages later, reinforces links between Mame, her *French Line* character, and her own biography. Accompanied by six photographs, the article discusses Russell's friendship with Della Russell (no relation), a fashion designer who makes some of her favorite clothes.[91] In *The French Line*, Mary McCarty plays Mame's old friend Annie Farrell, who's left Texas to become the New York designer Madame Firelli. When Mame visits her shop, she chats, chooses handbags and hats, and models dresses, just as Russell does in the photos of her and Della in the designer's Beverly Hills boutique. If photos of Katharine Hepburn reading novels in her WASP-y living room were meant to remind fans of her role as Jo in *Little Women*,[92] certainly Russell's visit to her friend's shop consciously echoes a pivotal plot point of *The French Line*.

Though the content and theme of the *Life*, *Exposed*, *Movie Play*, and *Movie Life* articles and photo essays are quite different and even contradictory, all "reach beyond" the films to "examine and reveal the 'real' personality" of the star, as Anthony Slide suggests all film publicity must do.[93] Whether they demonstrate the labor involved in moviemaking or elide the star with a role (or divorce her from it), the fan magazine stories and photos promise an authentic experience of Jane Russell. Promising that Russell's new career as a gospel singer is "no joke" while reminding viewers that she usually "spouted sex," *Movie Play* uses the seeming incongruity to demonstrate how its readers can access the real Jane Russell.[94] Further, simultaneously highlighting differences and similarities between performer and performance, as well as documenting the labor that goes into making a number like "Two Little Girls" seem effortless and fun, fan magazines underscore naturalism's key paradox: it is a conduit for authentic emotion but also a technique that can be learned and honed to perfection. Jonathan Rosenbaum's description of Classical Hollywood film as "the notion of documentary imposed over fiction" is made visible by the *Life* images of Russell and Monroe drinking a soda on a rehearsal break, as well as the delight that Dorothy and Lorelei share in each other's company, and points toward the audience's desire to read the constructed image of the star/character but also to believe they've accessed its reality.[95] This emphasis on authenticity, then, links Jane Russell's publicity photos, fan magazine stories, and movie roles with naturalist acting, which promises an authentic performance by examining and revealing the real personality of the star.

STAR AND SELF IN *GENTLEMEN MARRY BRUNETTES* AND *THE FUZZY PINK NIGHTGOWN*

In 1955, after the success of *Gentlemen Prefer Blondes* and with her contract with Howard Hughes guaranteeing her $1,000 per week for twenty years,[96] Russell was in a position to create her own production company. The resulting Russ-Field, founded with her husband, Bob Waterfield, released two films starring Russell, *Gentlemen Marry Brunettes* (1955) and *The Fuzzy Pink Nightgown* (1957).[97] In addition, Russ-Field produced another two films without the star: the Western *The King and Four Queens* (1956), starring Clark Gable and Eleanor Parker; and the adventure romance *Run for the Sun* (1956), starring Richard Widmark. The Russell vehicles illustrate her familiarity with the publicity machine that created her, real and imagined connections between self and role, and public (mis)understandings about the nature of film acting. This section interprets the two films as metacommentary on naturalist acting, publicity, and stardom in postwar Hollywood.

After the 1948 Paramount antitrust decision effectively ended the studio system and diminished the power of individual studios to guarantee distribution, studios could no longer afford to produce as many films as they had in the 1930s and early 1940s. With demand exceeding supply, independent production companies, "often established by former studio personnel [became] the central suppliers of movies in the postwar period."[98] Though independent producers, such as David O. Selznick (*Gone with the Wind*, 1939) and of course Howard Hughes, had long worked in partnership with but outside of the major studios, Denise Mann points out that in the postwar period "greater autonomy for actors, writers, directors, and other members of the creative community was attained."[99] As was the case with Jane Russell, these independent production companies were often headed by stars who developed films for themselves as well as projects that extended their star image. Thus, Russ-Field produced musical comedies, Westerns, and films noir, the three genres in which Russell worked.

Although Russ-Field was financially and critically unsuccessful, *Gentlemen Marry Brunettes* and *The Fuzzy Pink Nightgown* successfully concretize Russell's persona and its links with institutionalized systems of publicity and marketing. Further, though I'm not suggesting Russell is an *auteur* in the traditional, *Cahiers du Cinéma* sense, these films' preoccupation with promotion and publicity, as well as distinctions between star image and talent, are valuably interpreted as personal expressions of Russell's experience in the 1940s. In his obituary for Russell in the *Guardian*, Mark Cousins argues that as a producer she "read scripts, worked hard," and produced "intelligent" films. As for *The Fuzzy Pink Nightgown*, Cousins suggests "those in the know could see how personal it was, and how sardonic its comments were on Hollywood."[100]

Gentlemen Marry Brunettes is an equally sardonic representation of the importance of publicity, and the way that promotional tactics capitalize on performers' sexuality rather than their actual talent. The film's source material is Anita Loos's 1927 novel *But Gentlemen Marry Brunettes*, a sequel to her *Gentlemen Prefer Blondes*. In Loos's version, Dorothy Shaw breaks hearts as she breaks into show business, marrying a succession of men who fail to fulfill her dreams. The 1955 film, however, constructs an entirely new narrative, written by Loos's niece, Mary Loos Sale, who was married to Richard Sale, the film's director. Columbia Pictures originally planned to make the film with Jeanne Crain and Debbie Reynolds but passed on its option; instead, United Artists partnered with Russ-Field to produce the film and star Russell.[101] The film follows the sister act of Bonnie (Russell) and Connie (Crain) Jones from New York to France and back again. The two arrive in Paris and find out that their mother (Mimi, also played by Russell) and aunt (Mitzi, also played by Crain) were the toast of 1920s cabaret society. Rudy Vallee plays a character named Rudy Vallee, but he's a rich Parisian impresario who loved Mitzi and Mimi rather than an American big band singer. The future *Mr. Ed* star Alan Young plays the hapless but extremely wealthy Charles Biddle, who wants to break into show business and loves Connie (he also plays his mother, his father, and a hapless but extremely wealthy admirer of Mitzi and Mimi); the B-movie regular Scott Brady plays David Action, the theatrical agent who entices the Jones sisters to Paris and falls for Bonnie. Gwen Verdon, who trained Russell and Monroe for *Gentlemen Prefer Blondes*, was featured in the final "tribal" dance sequence, though the *New York Times* reported that her section was cut by US and UK censors because her "dance and abbreviated costume" were "objectionable."[102] As with *Gentlemen Prefer Blondes*, Jack Cole choreographed and Travilla designed the costumes; Earle Hagen orchestrated both films.

Like *Gentlemen Prefer Blondes*, *Brunettes* opens with Russell and her costar dressed in tight, glamorous gowns and singing in front of a curtain, complaining that love has left them alone and misunderstood. The similarities between the films mostly end with the opening number, however. Connie and Bonnie's song wasn't written for the film; rather, Guy Lombardo, Billie Holiday, and Frank Sinatra all had already released "You're Driving Me Crazy" before Russ-Field licensed it. Most of the music (including "Ain't Misbehavin'" and "My Funny Valentine") is Crain and Russell reinterpreting jazz standards, which Russell had been doing for more than a decade in live shows and on record albums.[103]

Where *Blondes* is noted by feminist critics for the self-consciousness of its sexual spectacle, as well as Hawks's knowing reversal of the gendered relationships and sexual structures of his other, homosocial films,[104] *Brunettes* is self-conscious about the institutions of entertainment. In one of the film's most knowing and genuinely funny moments, for example, Connie and Bonnie are presented with sparkling butterfly "costumes" that would only cover their nipples and pubis. The sisters refuse to wear them, and Russell sardonically comments that "they'll never get past the Breen office." Further, *Brunettes* lacks the strong central female relationship that allows feminist critics to recuperate *Blondes*. Connie and Bonnie are sisters, but they are less protective of and affectionate toward each other than Lorelei and Dorothy. Instead, Bonnie abandons Connie to hapless Charlie in order to romance debonair David; Mimi and Mitzi come to blows over Rudy Vallee in one of many flashbacks; and Connie and Bonnie suspect each other of sexual immorality and deceit, privileging their relationships with Charlie and David over their sisterly bonds.

Finally, instead of being a smart and sharp-tongued businesswoman—that role went to Crain—Russell's Bonnie is shallow and naive. In fact, Russell seems to be channeling Monroe's dumb blonde persona (or at least Dorothy's courtroom impression of Lorelei) for her characterization. Bonnie has a soft, breathy voice, frequently utters malapropisms, and can't say no to a man, even when she knows she should. Perhaps Russell wanted to escape her tough-talking persona and felt able to do so in a film she was producing with a relatively unaccomplished director, but the effect of her performance is fairly jarring. Russell slips in and out of her breathy diction and her naive characterization to occasionally deliver sardonic quips. Rather than seeming to self-consciously highlight femininity as a performance, as in Hawks's film, these moments make Russell look like an acutely untalented and inauthentic performer.

Critics largely agreed, noting that the sparkle was missing from this production, especially in terms of its dialogue, music, and individual performances. *Variety* called it "a rather inept musical comedy"; the *Los Angeles Times* noted that "the girls have been saddled with dull and listless dialogue"; and A. H. Weiler reported in the *New York Times* that the "aimless, uninspired charade" was "saved from being a complete dud by a clutch of sturdy standard tunes and a quick . . . tour of Paris and the Riviera." Further, most agreed with Weiler that at least the costumes of "the spectacularly dressed Misses Crain and Russell," as well as the location shooting, were excellent.[105] Indeed, the film highlights several Paris landmarks, lavish showgirl costumes, and Christian Dior's 1954 haute couture in the sequence when Connie and Bonnie receive gifts from unknown admirers. In short, it's visually pleasing throughout.

The production numbers, despite *Variety*'s accusation that they were "either droned or breathlessly raced through for comedy that never comes off," are genuinely spectacular. Travilla designed gorgeous, glittering showgirl costumes for the 1920s flashbacks and outfitted Russell and Crain as leopards-cum-birds-of-paradise for the finale, the "African" "tribal"-themed rendition of "Ain't Misbehavin'" that included Young in a gorilla suit, a grass-cloaked "witch doctor," and a chorus of scantily clad, black-faced tribesmen. Of course, this number is appalling to contemporary audiences, as it trots out tired tropes of African savages and helpless white women (I can't help but wonder what Verdon's excised dance sequence included in terms of costume, makeup, and movement) and it's frankly musically uninteresting as well. Despite the failings of the finale and the "seemingly interminable" rendition of "My Funny Valentine" as "dragged out" by Crain and Young in the Musée Rodin,[106] the production numbers are a welcome respite from the obvious plot machinations, wooden performances, and clichéd dialogue. It's not a very good film.

Even so, the film's attentiveness to the importance of publicity to show business careers documents a keen understanding of the interplay between image and talent in postwar Hollywood. For example, when Connie and Bonnie arrive in Paris, they are greeted by the disappointed Charlie, Rudy, and David. At first assuming that two bejeweled and fur-coated women are the Jones sisters, the men are shocked by Connie and Bonnie's dull traveling clothes. They rush the girls to their hotel, explaining that they've arranged a press cocktail party in their honor, but they must look much more glamorous in order to capitalize on the fame of their mother and aunt. All three men frantically make over Connie and Bonnie, cinching them into tight corsets; transforming their leopard-print show costumes into short, chic cocktail dresses; restyling their hair and applying fresh, dramatic makeup; and adding feathered headdresses and opera gloves. This scene, of course, echoes fan magazine narratives about the manufacture of Hollywood glamour. When the Misses Jones, introduced through "Have You Met Miss Jones," are a tremendous hit with the press, Charlie, David, and Rudy take credit. David further explains that this cocktail party was a necessary step in their careers: only after they've become famous as the American daughters of Mitzi and Mimi can they secure nightclub bookings.

The sisters soon discover that their mothers were the toast of cabaret society, even though "all they could do was hold feathers in the right places, and sometimes they didn't do that very well," Rudy says, waxing nostalgic. Through a series of flashbacks, the audience (and Connie and Bonnie) learns that though the press loved Mitzi and Mimi, they were utterly talentless; an extended version of "I Want to Be Loved by You" features both Crain and Russell tunelessly singing, lifelessly dancing, and unable to find their marks. Rudy Vallee sings well and manipulates them across the stage. As Rudy frequently explains, it didn't matter that their mothers weren't very good performers: they had *je ne sais quoi*, which seems to translate to a willingness to commodify their sexuality, both onstage and off.

Connie and Bonnie, on the other hand, are presented as hardworking and captivating performers (though reviewers complained about their lackluster performances, the film narrative asserts that they are strong singers and graceful dancers) who refuse to pander to the prurient desires of Parisian audiences. They audition for several prominent clubs, but when they find that their costumes will be nothing but silk stockings and heels, or fur mitts, or jeweled butterflies, they walk out. Finally, they agree to perform at Le Cocteau wearing nothing but large ostrich fans, tights, and heels. David and Charlie are shocked; Rudy and his fellow roué and Mitzi/Mimi's ex-lover the Earl of Wickenware (Guy Middleton) are delighted. Connie and Bonnie perform a song behind the fans and also behind large silk screens, suggesting that they are in fact naked. But when the audience demands an encore, the two drop their fans, revealing that they're fully and plainly dressed in shorts and sweaters pulled off their shoulders. The crowd loudly boos, and David tells them they'll never work in Europe again. Even so, the film audience understands that the girls have kept their American values and senses of humor intact.

Before Connie and Bonnie can return home in defeat, they receive a roomful of Christian Dior haute couture, chocolate, jewelry, champagne, perfume, and matching poodles. The press, which reviled them the day before, again takes interest. Connie and Bonnie are concerned about what they will have to do in return for the gifts, but they are rescued from having to find out by a booking in Monte Carlo. It is clear that all of Paris, as well as the disgruntled Charlie, David, Rudy, and Wickenware, is once again fascinated. Newspapers print daily photographs of the well-dressed girls and speculate about the identity of their wealthy admirers. Thus, despite the failure of their nightclub act, the publicity about their imagined sex lives ensures that they remain in demand as performers.

After the final production number in Monte Carlo, "Ain't Misbehavin'," the plot speedily and predictably resolves. Charlie is actually a millionaire and bank-rolled the gifts, paid for the Monte Carlo booking, and planted the press notices. Mimi arrives to rush her girls home, but Charlie, David, Wickenware, and Rudy charter a plane and stop them before Connie, Bonnie, and Mimi can sail to the United States. The young couples pair off as Mimi has a drink with her old beaux. Again, the film as a whole is unremarkable, but its preoccupation with publicity makes it an interesting document of stars' relationship to their public personae. The Jones sisters are the toast of France not because of their talent and charm but because of speculation over their private lives. Just like their mother and aunt, they are sexually interesting rather than talented—a point that also references Russell's early fame.

The Fuzzy Pink Nightgown, which Russell called her favorite film, is based on Sylvia Tate's novel about a Hollywood actress who is kidnapped for ransom and falls in love with her kidnapper. Russell believed the film suffered from its incon-sistent tone: she wanted to make a suspenseful noir, like her successful films with Robert Mitchum, but the director, Norman Taurog, wanted to make a comedy.[107] Neither fully prevailed. The *New York Times* reported that the title nightgown was a "flimsy excuse" for a "long, long movie"; the critic for the *Boston Globe* complained that "Miss Russell, never my favorite cinema star, is mildly effec-tive. . . . Ralph Meeker is always effective but this time he has to be good without the aid of a believable plot"; John L. Scott, in the movie's most favorable review, promised audiences that "some individual scenes provide amusement but con-sistency is the jewel that's missing."[108] The plot is, in fact, relatively unbelievable; the love story is unconvincing; and though only eighty-eight minutes long, the film drags interminably. Not particularly successful as a film noir, screwball com-edy, or romance, *The Fuzzy Pink Nightgown* is best understood as a sustained exe-gesis on postwar celebrity. Though it's certainly not a feminist film (Laurel agrees in the final moments that Mike is her "boss" and gives up the career she struggled to build and then control), its critique of Hollywood's "star machine" does offer a female perspective, one that acknowledges the difficult choices actresses in Clas-sical Hollywood must make.

In the film, Russell's character, Laurel Stevens, is kidnapped on her way to the premiere of her film *The Kidnapped Bride*. Everyone—including Laurel, her fans, the police, and the press—except the studio head (Adolphe Menjou), who knows it's not planned, is convinced it's a trite publicity stunt. Benay Venuta, playing a gossip columnist with a very cozy relationship with the studio, spearheads the campaign to discredit Laurel. She uses her columns to promise Laurel that if the kidnapping is the stunt she believes it to be, Laurel's fans will turn against her: thus Laurel must either give up her career or send her kidnappers to prison. It's a tough choice. Over the course of two days, Laurel falls in love with Mike (Ralph Meeker), a convict on parole after being framed for murder, and befriends his accomplice, Dandy (Keenan Wynn). McBride (Fred Clark), the sympathetic police officer who blames himself for putting Mike away the first time, is on their trail. When the two lovers are caught trying to escape, they reveal that the suitcase holding the cash is full of copies of *Variety* and claim the whole adventure was a publicity stunt. Though the *New York Times* critic complained there is "no quick unraveling to the happy ending,"[109] when the film does finally wrap up, Laurel is understood to be grateful that her career is over. At last, she can forgo the persona building, playacting, and hypocrisy that characterize Hollywood stardom in order to experience ordinary but true love.

The film opens with Laurel watching the trailer for *The Kidnapped Bride* with her agent, Barney Baylies (Robert Harris), and the studio head, Arthur Martin (Menjou). She is angry that a scene with her "looking sexy" in a bathtub has been cut from the film because "it won't make it past the censors." She insists that she'll pull her financing from the film and skip that night's premiere unless it goes back in. Later, talking to her assistant, Bertha, Laurel complains that Barney and Arthur are unhappy that they can't boss her around now that she's producing her own films. They call her "tough and temperamental" for making the same choices they once made for her. Laurel explains that she sells a "funny, phony little commodity called sex, and if the customers are hungry enough to buy it, I run my own factory in my own way." The parallels between Russell's public image as a screen temptress, her desire to control her career by producing her own films, and her reputation as "temperamental" are clear from the outset of the film, inviting audiences to read Laurel Stevens as a stand-in for Jane Russell. This setup, then, gives especial credence to the critique of Hollywood celebrity and hypocrisy—both explicitly tied to the discourse of naturalist acting—that follows.

Late in her first night with the kidnappers, Laurel pretends to cry in order to get Dandy on her side. She stands beside her locked bedroom door and sobs expressively. Sure that she's got his attention, she hurries to the bed, carefully arranges herself in a tableau of vulnerable but sexy sorrow, and boo-hoos loudly. When Dandy doesn't immediately appear, she cries more hysterically, facing the door and projecting her sobs in that direction. When she hears Dandy approach, Laurel buries her face in her arms and continues to sob and whimper. When Dandy rushes sympathetically to her side, Laurel lifts her tear-streaked face to his and begs him to let her go. She continues to wipe wet tears from her cheeks as Dandy tells her that Mike is a convicted murderer recently released from prison. What's most interesting about the scene is how it shifts between pretense and authenticity. The audience knows that Laurel is faking her sobs and recognizes her careful arrangement of her body on the bed as a clever actress's impersonation of seductive sorrow. At the same time, Laurel is really crying: we see tears fill her eyes and spill down her face, and they continue after Dandy has entered and rejected her plea for rescue. This shift from pretending to cry to really crying illuminates a key tenet of naturalist acting. Though the signs of emotion may be faked, they can also become real. Though of course Russell may have used eye drops or some Stanislavsky-derived technique to conjure her tears (and the audience will never know from whence they actually came), Laurel is "really" crying. Further, when her tears fail to move Dandy, she switches emotions and tactics. Wiping her wet face one last time, Laurel tries to seduce Dandy, promising that she'll be a true "friend" if he just takes her home. At that moment, Mike bursts in and orders Dandy out, excoriating Laurel as a phony.

Throughout the film, Laurel and Mike argue about the "phoniness" of actors. In their first exchange, Laurel tells Mike that he doesn't play the part of the kidnapper very well, smoking a pipe instead of chewing a cigar, and wearing a soft sweater instead of a bold suit; she knows because she's been in movies about gangsters. Later, Mike tells Laurel that he doesn't like her because she's a phony, pretending to be "a big man expert, phony act, phony everything." She points to her nightgown-clad body and responds that "this just happens to be the legitimate article. People pay good money to look at it." In this exchange, Laurel defends her profession and persona by referencing the sexually alluring body on which she's built her career. She may be an actress, but her beauty and sex appeal are real. In fact, throughout the film Laurel insists that though actors may, in the words of the theorist Michael Kirby, "feign . . . simulate . . . represent [and] . . . impersonate," she is sincere in her relationships with her friends and in her emotions.[110]

Mike and Laurel's debate neatly captures the antitheatrical prejudice that has long equated performance with hypocrisy, as well as naturalism's presumed counter to this charge. In *Fangs of Malice*, Matthew H. Wikander points out that the "malicious charge" that all actors are hypocrites "finds expression in innumerable tracts railing against the theater." "Western civilization" places a high value "on sincerity, authenticity to one's own true self," Wikander continues, and thus actors are necessarily suspect. At the same time, actors insist that they are themselves sincere, and that "the lies actors play" are only temporal and contingent on the theatrical frame.[111] Of course, as David Krasner points out, naturalist acting is "an acting technique that stresses truthful behavior in imaginary circumstances."[112] According to the Hollywood character actor and Group Theatre member Morris Carnovsky, naturalist actors believe in the authenticity of their actions and emotions and present them as "truthful" and "beautiful":[113] they are the opposite of phony. While washing dishes (the kind of quotidian behavior naturalist representation seems to prize), Laurel explains how to reconcile inner truth and outer appearance. She tells Mike that he needs to use "the Stanislavsky method" in order to be a more convincing kidnapper. She informs him that in this "theory of acting, you say to yourself over and over and over 'I'm a heel, I'm a heel, I'm a heel' and pretty soon you get to be one." "Then what?" Mike asks, and Laurel replies, "You get to be a success." He responds "Just like you?" and she ruefully acknowledges, "Just like me." This is a remarkable exchange, not only because it introduces by name a version of Stanislavsky technique to a mass audience and refers to the kind of training that Russell herself, and presumably Laurel, underwent before becoming a star, but also because it acknowledges the potential pitfalls of successful acting. Not only might an actor begin to believe her character, she might become successful impersonating something she's not, and thus become trapped in an uncomfortable persona. Later in the film, after Laurel and Mike have fallen in love, Mike worries that she's had lots of love affairs. She urges him not to "get me mixed up with that girl in the movies." Unable to separate the Laurel he adored onscreen from the woman walking with him on the beach (despite the fact that she's taken off her platinum wig and is wearing his dungarees and dress shirt), Mike replies, "She's you, isn't she?" Her eyes soft and her voice quavering, Laurel assures Mike that "she's make-believe, and so are the guys." For Russell, who struggled to reconcile Christian values with her temptress image, this is an especially trenchant observation. Ultimately, though *The Fuzzy Pink Nightgown* isn't much of a movie (and Russell told the *Washington Times* reporter Vernon Scott that its failure meant she "may never appear in pictures again"),[114] it is an acute critique of Hollywood celebrity and public misunderstandings about acting.

Though Jane Russell never received critical acclaim for her acting, her performances in several major movie marketing campaigns say much about how acting was understood in Classical Hollywood and illuminate how film was framed for postwar American audiences. For Russell and her contemporaries, photographs and articles about actors solidified correspondences between actor and role and demonstrated how acting is also labor. Further, though her film performances do not reveal an overlooked talent, Russell was trained in naturalist techniques. More importantly, she was closely associated with the femmes fatales of film noir and the man-hungry Dorothy Shaw of *Gentlemen Prefer Blondes*, despite her devotion to Pentecostal Christianity. Her case study, then, is a useful demonstration of how personality, persona, and publicity coincide, always already dependent on a naturalist paradigm that fuses self and role, and even in contradiction to the "facts" of a performer's biography.

CHAPTER 2

MORE THAN A MERMAID

ESTHER WILLIAMS, PERFORMANCE, AND THE BODY

In 1948, wounded by critics who excoriated her acting ability and frustrated with MGM's resident acting coach Lillian Burns, Esther Williams approached George Schtanoff, a Russian drama coach who trained starlets off the studio lots. He refused to help her: "Anybody can do Portia, but I don't know anyone except you who can sing and swim at the same time. I'm afraid I should not tamper with your successful career."[1] His response reveals assumptions about film acting during the Classical Hollywood era as well as about Williams's special talents as a performer. First, acting, even Shakespeare, could be learned by anyone. Second, Williams was unique: the specifics of her athletic but feminine body could not be taught to other actresses. Clearly, this assumption expresses naturalism's crucial paradox. On one hand, it is a specific technique that can be learned and even perfected, but on the other, it is always rooted in the inner self of the performer. In this chapter, I tease out the connections between naturalist acting and the "natural" female body in Classical Hollywood film. As Williams's case study demonstrates, physical appearance and the body, undertheorized elements of film acting, can facilitate feminist interpretations of character and narrative. Esther Williams enables a nuanced understanding of the relationship between performance, embodiment, and agency.

MGM created "aquamusicals" for Williams, many choreographed by the master of spectacle, Busby Berkeley, and shot in the enormous tank constructed for her films. Those films were unique in the postwar musical comedy boom, adding water and bathing suits to the standard song-dance-and-romance plot.[2] Williams started in film, it is generally understood, to provide MGM with a novelty actress like Twentieth Century–Fox's ice-skating Sonja Henie.[3] Her status as a champion swimmer gave MGM various opportunities to display her partially clothed body while adhering to the strict Production Code. Unlike Henie, who performed in fur and velvet jackets and short skirts, Williams performed in bathing suits, form-fitting leotards, or lingerie. She swam through tropical waters and moonlit pools, slipping sensually through the water and twisting her body through hoops, around underwater poles, and inside fantasy grottoes. As Catherine Williamson points out, "the languorous swimming scenes offered an excellent opportunity to display the female body in various stages of undress while the wholesomeness of the narrative deflected any possible reprisals from the Breen office." Williamson goes on to argue that Williams's success was based on "the brilliant way she merged 'femininity' and athleticism into an aesthetically pleasing yet politically innocuous form."[4] Because her body was coded as beautiful as well as strong, wholesome as well as sexy, her feminist address may have escaped censure by critics, fans, and the industry. Further, unlike Henie, Williams was an all-American girl, born in Kansas, raised in the California sunshine, and with a history of representing the United States in competition. Williams's star persona combined patriotism, motherhood, and athleticism with the standard star attributes of glamour and beauty. Her case study provides an important example of how cinematic bodies may carry ambivalent meanings even when conventionally framed and contained.

Schtanoff was right that Williams was a unique performer. Though her films are often criticized for recycling their plots, and Williams played basically the same (swimming) character in each—a criticism leveled at all the performers I consider here—she was a versatile performer. As a swimming star, she created three distinct modes of water performance: elegantly graceful (as in the water ballets in *The Ziegfeld Follies* [1945], *Duchess of Idaho* [1950], and *Jupiter's Darling* [1955]); charmingly funny (for example, parts of her animated swim with Tom and Jerry in *Dangerous When Wet* [1953], and her clowning with Red Skelton in *Texas Carnival* [1951] and with a Seabee doll in *Skirts Ahoy!* [1952]); or powerfully thrilling (any of her collaborations with Busby Berkeley, such as *Million Dollar Mermaid* [1952]). These modes differ in tone and aesthetics, but Williams's body is always long, lean, and languorous. Wearing a variety of mostly one-piece bathing suits that show off her extremely muscular back and shoulders as well as her powerful legs, Williams is a charismatic performer as well as a supremely accomplished athlete.

All three performance modes are visible in *Easy to Love* (1953),[5] her final collaboration with Berkeley and her frequent costar Van Johnson. As the *Variety* review asserts, "the sock entertainment values in the presentation are the musical water numbers,"[6] and they more than make up for the trite plot. Julie Hallerton, a model, secretary, and aquatics star (Williams), is pursued by two hunky, successful, rich men (John Bromfield and Tony Martin) while pining for her oblivious boss, Ray Lloyd (Johnson), who of course realizes in the final act that he has always loved her after all. Because Julie is so busy, so is Williams, and this film has more swimming scenes than any of her others (only her 1960 television special includes more numbers, and none as elaborate as those directed by

Berkeley). She swims two graceful ballets, one in the pool at Cypress Gardens, Florida, where most of the film was shot, and the other with the ubiquitous water tank on the MGM set standing in for a New York City theater. In the Gardens children's show, Williams is funny. Dressed as a clown, complete with red curly wig and full face paint, she falls out of a handstand on a chair being propelled through the water, plays catch with a trained seal, evades a papier-mâché crocodile, bounces on a trampoline made of "dynamite," and cannonballs into the water. In the finale, she is incredibly athletic, and the number still amazes with Berkeley's technical and Williams's physical prowess. In a seven-and-a-half minute extravaganza of waterskiing, Williams swerves in and out of sixty-eight professional water-skiers, the Cypress Gardens Aqua Maids, dozens of ramps, and jets of shooting water before being lifted by helicopter to a trapeze. She finishes by diving eighty feet into the midst of the skiers and their boats and then ski-jumps straight toward the camera and over the live orchestra from a twenty-foot ramp. These three modes present contradictory images of the female body. The water ballets, which highlight her curving legs and her generous buttocks and breasts, conform to what Aagje Swinnen and John Stotesbury identify as typical representations of the female body that mark it as erotic spectacle.[7] The clown routine and waterskiing finale, on the other hand, are athletic tours de force. As such, they demonstrate the limits of the "natural" female body as well as the limits of its representation in the Classical Hollywood era.

Williams made *Easy to Love* while pregnant with her third child, Susie, and that pregnancy illuminates some of the pressures put on spectacular female stars who depended on their physical appearance for cinematic intelligibility. In her autobiography, Williams recalls that *Easy to Love*'s producer, Joe Pasternak, "would not be happy" about the pregnancy. She was right: he first asked what was wrong with her and then asked, "What are *you* going to do?" Since it was her baby, it was her problem, and Williams "had to get everybody on the film rallied to finish the work before [she] started showing."[8] Fortunately, she was able to do so, since the de rigueur bathing suits made it impossible for her to hide a pregnancy under baggy clothes or behind strategically placed pillows, lamps, or handbags.[9] Clearly, though female celebrities were often popularly represented as natural wives and mothers, their pregnancies weren't necessarily blessed events and could derail their careers. For musical comedy stars, who nearly always fell in love in the first act, met complications in the second, and ended about to live happily ever after, visible pregnancy usually meant they were removed from their current picture and even released from their contracts.

Williams's pregnancy also threatened Busby Berkeley's planned water spectacles. The waterskiing finale would have been challenging anyway, since Williams didn't know how to water-ski and "was probably the only person associated with this picture who understood that waterskiing really has nothing to do with swimming and demands an entirely different set of muscles and skills," but she quickly learned. After she demonstrated her proficiency at skiing (she looks like a professional rather than the beginner she claimed to be), Berkeley began adding more stunts, describing the final number: "You're skiing along and we drop you the swing from the helicopter: You kick off your skis, and the chopper pulls you out of the water. You climb up onto this trapeze swing, and we fly you over eight speedboats that're pulling the skiers in V-formation. Then you dive into the lake and hit right in the center of the V." Williams expressed concern about wind drift forcing her off center so that she'd land on a skier rather than open water; Berkeley expressed concern that the skier would sue and they'd "have a lawsuit that would kill us." In the end, she insisted that Berkeley hire Helen Crelinkovich, a platform diver, to perform the actual dive because Williams feared a miscarriage if she dove eighty feet into Lake Eloise. In her autobiography, she recalls that she told Berkeley, "I'll do everything else you ask of me, Buzz—I'll even do the ski-jump over the orchestra at the end—but not the dive. I want to hang on to this baby."[10] Indeed, Crelinkovich dove three times (Berkeley was a perfectionist), and Williams apparently did the rest of the helicopter stunt, as there are unbroken close-ups and close shots of her grabbing the bar, skiing up a ramp, and dropping her skis while being towed through the sky.

She did not, however, do all the other stunts in *Easy to Love*. Her concern about filming *Easy to Love* as well as the earlier *Pagan Love Song* during her pregnancies reflected the fact that "there was no swimmer on the lot to replace" her,[11] but also that some of her sequences were difficult and dangerous to do. Though she doesn't admit it in her autobiography, Williams appears to have been doubled in both the clown number and when jumping over the orchestra at the beginning and end of the water-skiing finale. It's notable that though she discusses Crelinkovich's participation at great length, painting herself as a concerned future mother as well as a savvy negotiator for her fellow swimmer, she doesn't mention any other stunt doubling in any of her films. As the only woman in Hollywood—perhaps the world—who could combine such extreme athleticism with such charm and screen presence, she was a unique talent. Her autobiographical elision of her other stunt doubles (none of whom appear in the credits of her films) clearly serves her narrative of sine qua non performance, but also of femininity.

A male swimmer almost undoubtedly doubles some of *Easy to Love*'s stunts. In the clown number, Williams is pushed into the water by her chimpanzee costar, evidenced by the large splash that's only partially obscured by a red cloud of smoke and the massive box of "dynamite" that doubles as a trampoline. Though the splash proves that Williams lands in the water, her clown character immediately begins a series of flips, somersaults, and belly flops before diving out of the box. Next, the clown is pulled into a sideways cartwheel by a nearly invisible towline onto a chair and then dragged around the pool. The film cuts and Williams crouches on the chair, waving and smiling as she rushes toward the camera and a final close-up. Both the editing of the sequence (the unbroken trampolining as well as the break before the final close-up) and the shot distance signal the use of the stunt double, of course. But in this short sequence, the clown's legs and shoulders are heavier, the face is broader, and the center of gravity is lower. Simply put, a heavier, stockier, more traditionally masculine body does this series of stunts.

Similar strategies are apparent in the ski jumps over the orchestra in the finale. The camera cuts to a close-up of Williams after each jump, but the skiing body (dressed in a shiny, flowered pink bathing suit) that clears the ramp and lands on the other side is not hers and is markedly more masculine. It's doubtful that many audience members would have noticed the doubling—the other performer only appears in about eighteen seconds of the three-minute clown segment, and eight seconds of the finale. Further, few audience members scrutinize Esther Williams's body with such scholarly attention. It's nonetheless notable that Williams hides the fact that she's apparently doubled in these sequences by a *man*. First, her "natural" female body, which is always larger and stronger than all the other onscreen women and most of the men, can do things that other available women can't do. Second, a male body can stand in for hers without causing comment from most audience members.

SWIMMING TOWARD STARDOM

Esther Williams was in this unique and irreplaceable position on the MGM lot because of her past as a champion swimmer as well as her own efforts to become a pleasing singer, lovely dancer, and believable actress. Born in 1921 to an aspirant middle-class family, Williams began swimming after her brother Stanton, a successful child star and financial support of the family, died at sixteen; her enterprising mother thought Williams's athleticism might one day turn a profit. Only eight years old, she handed out towels in exchange for swimming lessons at the Los Angeles City Pool, and three years later won the city-wide children's fifty-meter freestyle race. In 1939, Williams won gold medals for the hundred-meter freestyle, freestyle relay, and hundred-meter breaststroke at the US National Championships. Though Williams was expected to be a strong contender in the 1940 Olympics, those games were canceled because of World War II. Williams continued to reference her competitive history throughout her career, suggesting that acting and water ballets were her second choice to competitive swimming. Denied the opportunity to race, Williams alternated clerking at I. Magnin in Los Angeles and starring in Billy Rose's San Francisco Aquacade with Johnny Weissmuller. Returning to Los Angeles and only seventeen years old, she married Leonard Kovner, a medical student, and planned to give up swimming and focus on a career as an assistant buyer at I. Magnin. Though MGM pursued her, Williams had decided that "show business was no business for me."[12] But in 1941, with Kovner struggling to pay his medical school bills, she reconsidered.

Kovner, however, was adamant that she stay out of show business. Of course, she signed with MGM and divorced her first husband. Recognizing that she was terrific when she was wet but not particularly interesting out of the pool, Williams insisted on nine months of singing, dancing, diction, and acting lessons.

Williams starred in her film debut, *Andy Hardy's Double Life*, in 1942. This film was a blueprint for all others: Williams sang, danced, swam, and romanced the leading man. Determined to capitalize on Williams's unique body and athletic ability, MGM built a twenty-five-foot-deep, ninety-foot-square water tank for 1944's *Bathing Beauty*, and she made blockbuster musicals for the next decade. Williams married Ben Gage in 1945 and had three children: Benjamin (1949), Kimball (1950), and Susan (1953). While raising her family and starring in lavish musical productions featuring multiple water ballets, she was held up as an exemplar of Hollywood's working mothers in spreads for many fan magazines (see figure 8).[13]

In 1954 she explained to Hedda Hopper that she felt fulfilled as a mother: "First I loved Ben . . . and didn't need anybody else. Then I had my first child and I couldn't have been happier. Then Kim came to keep his brother company. . . . Now Susan completes the circle."[14] Of course, Williams's marriage to Gage was always rocky because of his alcoholism and laziness (and her extramarital affairs, with costars Victor Mature and Jeff Chandler, among others). According to her autobiography, they would probably have divorced sooner if she hadn't gotten pregnant with Susan during a reconciliatory trip to Washington, DC, in 1953.[15]

In 1955 MGM dropped her contract, presumably because at age thirty-three she was nearly past her bathing beauty prime.[16] She continued to appear in B-movies filmed outside Hollywood and without the support of the major studios, such as *The Unguarded Moment* (1956) and *Raw Wind in Eden* (1958). These films recycled the Girl + Water + Boy formula of her earlier pictures, but without the spectacular swimming sequences, extravagant costumes, or lush orchestrations. In *Raw Wind in Eden*, for example, Esther Williams/Laura's small plane crashes on a Mediterranean island. The secluded coves and rocky beaches give her many opportunities to swim alone and with her love interest, Jeff Chandler/Moore. But the film was a drama rather than a musical. Further, its small cast and location shoot meant that the swimming sequences were simple and comparatively lackluster. The film received terrible reviews. Bosley Crowther for the *New York Times* complained that "it looks as if halfway through shooting . . . the producers lost the script and went right on shooting without it. . . . For it is hard to believe that any story could otherwise go as haywire and obscure as does this drama from Universal."[17] Though the film wasn't successful, away from Gage, Williams enjoyed romances with both Jeff Chandler and an Italian she identifies in her autobiography only as Giorgio.[18]

Williams and Gage divorced in 1958, and Williams gave him $75,000, paid off several of his debts, and took full custody of the children.[19] In 1960, she made her

Figure 8: Esther Williams and her daughter Susie at their pool for *Modern Screen*, September 1956.

final musical extravaganza, *Esther Williams at Cypress Gardens*, an NBC television special promoting that Florida location, sponsored by the United Brewers Association and costarring her lover Fernando Lamas. Williams retired in 1961 to keep house for Lamas, and the two married in 1969. After Lamas's death in 1982, Williams produced and starred in *Swim, Baby, Swim* (1984), using techniques she'd developed with her own children to teach youngsters to enjoy the water and practice water safety. Hailed as the inventor of synchronized swimming, she provided color commentary for the 1984 Olympics synchronized swimming coverage. In the late 1980s, married to her fourth husband, Edward Bell, Williams returned to swimsuit design, producing a successful retro collection based on her film suits.[20] She published her autobiography, *The Million Dollar Mermaid*, in 1999; it spent several weeks atop the *New York Times* best-seller list. Esther

Williams suits, based on her iconic bathing costumes, are available for sale on the Internet and in department stores, but Williams largely disappeared from public view and died in 2013.

In all her films, Esther Williams was certainly glamorous and beautiful, but she was also physically strong. Though these are physical attributes, they also imply character.[21] Thus, I interpret her spectacular female body in order to reframe naturalism as intervening within as well as supporting Classical Hollywood narratives of femininity and domesticity. Williams's muscular, sexy appearance is incorporated as spectacle but also supports narratives of strong, independent women. In this chapter, I recover the history of actor training at the major Hollywood studios, especially MGM, during the 1930s and 1940s in order to demonstrate how and why naturalism became the dominant acting technique as well as the popularly understood definition of successful performance. Then I evaluate Williams's performance in aquamusicals as both cinematic performance and the performance of gender through a sustained discussion of feminist and performance studies theories of agency and embodiment. Finally, drawing on this theoretical and historical background, I read three of Williams's most popular films, *Million Dollar Mermaid* (1952), *Skirts Ahoy!* (1952), and *Dangerous When Wet* (1953), paying particular attention to the meanings carried by her spectacular body.[22]

THE NATURAL BODY AND THE NATURALIST PARADIGM

Esther Williams claims that the "nine-month [training] clause" in her contract "was the funniest thing [the studio had] ever heard,"[23] but her demand merely formalized the process that the major studios, especially MGM, usually offered its newly contracted stars. Though popular histories like Ronald L. Davis's *The Glamour Factory* and Jeanine Basinger's *The Star Machine* make clear that Hollywood studios in the 1930s–1950s ran a highly regimented organization that turned out the commodities known as movie stars, there has been little concentrated work on those studios' official procedures for actor training. While a definitive history of studio actor training is not the focus of this project, I want to gather archival and anecdotal evidence in order to demonstrate how naturalism achieved its paradigmatic status, as well as how discourses of naturalist acting impacted the performances and careers of all the actresses I consider here.

For the most part, studios in the 1930s used on-site acting teachers, generally called either drama coaches or dialogue directors, to train newly contracted players as well as work with established performers. According to Cynthia Baron, "by 1939 all of the major studios had actor training programmes."[24] The instructors were generally women who had worked in New York City and regional theaters before coming to Hollywood, sometimes with their husbands. The veteran stage producer and director Lillian Albertson started as a dialogue coach for Paramount in 1933, and Phyllis Loughton, married to the screenwriter and director George Seaton, headed that studio's talent department before moving to MGM to become a dialogue director. MGM also had Lillian Burns, who had appeared with the Belasco Company and the Dallas Little Theatre and was married to the director George Sidney. Sophie Rosenstein, who had started acting onstage as a child and who had taught drama at the University of Washington, worked at Warner Bros., and when she retired Estelle Harman took her place before becoming head of Universal's talent department.[25]

Studio drama coaches disagreed on whether film acting could be taught, echoing the naturalist paradox. Lillian Burns insisted, "I don't believe you can teach acting. Anybody who tells me that is a charlatan," preferring to describe herself to Jamie Lee Curtis, daughter of her longtime pupil and friend Janet Leigh, as "a developer of people."[26] Estelle Harman, on the other hand, believed that "it is possible to teach the craft and art of acting, especially of film acting."[27] But whether or not these women taught acting or helped develop a film persona, young men and women were regularly sent to them for training, and they worked privately with major stars like Lana Turner (Burns) and Rock Hudson (Rosenstein). Further, according to Baron, studio and off-set drama teachers "played a significant role in articulating and formalizing the periods of acting" by publishing dozens of manuals for drama students and teachers. For example, Paramount's resident acting coach Lillian Albertson published her method in *Motion Picture Acting*, a textbook that included endorsements from Paramount and RKO stars, directors, and producers.[28]

Like nearly everything in the studio system, actor training generally followed specific steps. Al Trescony, an MGM casting director and onetime head of its talent department, described the initial process: first, he interviewed likely prospects, and if they seemed promising, his staff prepared a screen test. Candidates rehearsed with contract players, and then a director filmed them on an existing film set, "using one of our cameramen under contract, such as Joe Ruttenberg, George Folsey. . . . To be able to have someone like a Joe Ruttenberg test a beginner was like having Picasso paint their portrait."[29] Phyllis Loughton remembered that actors with successful screen tests usually joined her Paramount Studios school.[30] At other studios different drama coaches took over. Then actors worked singly or in groups with drama coaches. Sophie Rosenstein was well known for the showcase performances she produced for Universal executives as well as producers and directors from the other studios. Hugh O'Brian remembered doing "scenes with other people there on the lot who were under contract," including Rock Hudson, Tony Curtis, and Piper Laurie.[31] When Estelle Harman took over for Rosenstein at Universal, she "had classwork for general training and the private for when they were doing special roles."[32] Burns never worked her actors on a stage: "I had a very large room set up like a living room. . . . It even had a grand piano in it and a fake fireplace, a fake mantel," so that her charges would become relaxed and natural working in a film-set environment rather than framed by a proscenium.[33]

These dialogue directors and drama coaches had considerable influence over contracts and casting as well as film performances. Trescony recalled that new contract players were given script pages to study and then read with Lillian Burns, who "would find a ... scene which would enhance the ability of the actor being tested." If she was impressed, the two would recommend a screen test. Trescony asserted that Burns "was a very important and tremendous power at MGM."[34] Phyllis Loughton was proud that she was able to "find places for my kids who were ready to do it" by reading optioned scripts and making suggestions to directors and producers.[35] The actress Joan Leslie remembered going to Sophie Rosenstein's "house at night and she would work with me on the scene, one-to-one dramatic coach."[36] In her interview with Ronald L. Davis, Loughton bitterly recalled that although she "should have been directing ... they're never going to let a woman direct." Instead, she "did all the putting together of the scene, and then [the director] took it over. But if I didn't like the shot I would say so—whisper of course—because there is nothing more invisible than a dialogue director if he's smart."[37] Thus, not only did drama coaches and dialogue directors help actors craft performances, they also influenced film production.

Of course, Burns, Albertson, Loughton, Rosenstein, and others primarily taught classes and coached actors. Based on their recollections, as well as those of their students, they stressed naturalism, authenticity, and believability; according to Baron, they used strategies from "their understanding of Moscow Art Theatre productions and Stanislavsky's System."[38] This understanding is specifically tied to the techniques and aesthetics of the Group Theatre, which had a profound personal as well as conceptual influence on film acting. Not only because their mode of acting, which Morris Carnovsky, a founding member, described as "real, living drama" rather than "the old romantic theater,"[39] models the kinds of performance prized by studio directors and producers, but also because Group members trained many film performers. The actor, director, and producer (and Group Theatre member) Norman Lloyd, for example, told Ronald L. Davis that the Group Theatre made the greatest impact on US film and theater, "mostly from the point of view of acting."[40]

Founded in 1931 by Harold Clurman, Cheryl Crawford, and Lee Strasberg, the Group Theatre developed techniques for acting based on members' understanding of Stanislavsky as taught and promoted by Richard Boleslavsky and Maria Ouspenskaya. The founding three as well as several other Group members had studied with Boleslavsky and Ouspenskaya at the American Laboratory Theatre in New York City in the 1920s. Many members worked as actors and teachers in Hollywood while also performing Group productions in New York.[41] In 1937, for example, Carnovsky took supporting roles in Clifford Odets's *Golden Boy* on Broadway as well as in the Academy Award–winning *Life of Emile Zola*.[42] When the Group Theatre disbanded in 1941, its members continued to develop their Hollywood connections, as both actors and teachers. Ouspenskaya (not a Group actress, but a major influence) opened the School of Dramatic Art and played character roles in the Wolf Man and Tarzan series as well as other supporting parts. Carnovsky, Phoebe Brand, and Roman Bohnen worked in film (Carnovsky and Bohnen each appeared in several dozen films before being blacklisted) and founded the Actors Lab.[43] Of course, Lee Strasberg and Stella Adler offered competing versions of Stanislavsky technique to American film and theater actors from their base in New York City. By disseminating their ideas in acting schools, on the set to their fellow actors, and through studio connections, the members effectively made the techniques and goals of the Group Theatre the principal influences on cinematic performance in the 1940s and 1950s.

Not surprisingly, these Group-influenced and stage-trained acting coaches used techniques comparable to the core principles of Stanislavsky's system. They believed that all actors needed vocal training in order to speak clearly and evocatively, physical training to develop a flexible instrument, and practice with "emotional recall . . . and observation and concentration" in order to create believable characters, according to Baron.[44] Studio teachers urged focus and concentration on what Stanislavsky termed "the given circumstances" of the text. Focusing on the script, they urged actors to imaginatively re-create their characters' emotions and then live them out onscreen.[45] Janet Leigh, who worked extensively with Lillian Burns throughout her career, recalled that Burns had her students bring characters to life "by establishing a complete person, a complete life," and urged them to think about "what would she do in this circumstance because of her relationship with her mother and her father and her sister and her brother, or her friends, or whatever."[46] Joan Leslie was a successful dramatic actress and a favorite of the director Raoul Walsh, with major roles in *High Sierra* (1941) and *The Revolt of Mamie Stover* (1956). In 1981, when she was regularly guest-starring on television, she recalled that she still used Rosenstein's teaching: "You make a character for yourself. You think what perhaps she did before this show started, and what perhaps she's going to do after this story ends. . . . Of course, we automatically use everything that we've ever known in our lives to make that character as real as possible."[47] Estelle Harman explained to Ronald L. Davis that she helped her charges "peg the character": working together, they developed a list of adjectives that described the character and then divided those into three columns. The first column held traits the actor and character had in common; the second was for those that described the character and "the actor feels, 'I had that once,' or 'I have a little of that"; and the third was "very foreign to him."[48] Again, actors used parts of their own biography in order to seem authentic onscreen. By finding correspondence between actor and role, performers developed believable characters.

These techniques, of course, support James Naremore's assertion that "the typical dramatic film regards acting as an artful imitation of unmediated behavior in the real world":[49] film actors seem natural. Naturalist acting was the goal of supporting players as well as major stars. For example, the comic actress Jean Porter, who played minor roles in several Esther Williams vehicles, explained that "you just absolutely become the character. You don't act. . . . It's living the part, completely living the part."[50] Esther Williams agreed. In her autobiography she recalled her second screen test for MGM, after she'd been working with Burns. "The truth was [myself] was all I could be. I was not a graduate of the New York stage; I knew nothing about Stanislavsky or Stella Adler. I had no pretensions that I was an actress."[51] Despite Williams's insistence that she wasn't an actress, her assessment of her screen test clearly articulates the primary discourse on acting available to film actors during the studio system. After being trained in naturalist techniques, they played exactly themselves in order to embody a cinematic character. This discourse emphasizes the presentation of an authentic "self"—to the exclusion of other factors such as rehearsals, specific training, and the director—as the hallmark of successful film acting.

Film acting makes specific technical demands as well, both in terms of hitting marks and playing to the camera. As a "truth machine," the camera demands that actors project "from the eyes instead of just the voice," according to MGM's Burns, "because you cannot say 'dog' and think 'cat' because 'meow' will come out if you do."[52] Further, film acting demands significant individual preparation in lieu of formal rehearsals. Burns taught her students to create background histories for their characters in order to determine how those characters would react in particular circumstances.[53] These strategies crossed studio lines. In her textbook, *Modern Acting: A Manual* (published while she was teaching at the University of Washington), Warner Bros.' Sophie Rosenstein included lessons on making up internal dialogue in order to motivate action and then used these techniques to compensate for films' lack of rehearsal and nonchronological shooting sequence.[54] Clearly, both Burns's and Rosenstein's methods are influenced by Stanislavsky's "magic if" and the belief that an actor is natural, realistic, and believable in a part if he or she lives the character.

The studio apparatus further supported the naturalist paradigm. In particular, the production of extratextual knowledge about actors emphasized the ease with which they were able to create their characters: publicity consistently stressed that acting is fun, and it's easy to play yourself. In general, mainstream discussions of stardom in Classical Hollywood ignored the labor undertaken by actors, in terms of both their long on-set hours and sometimes dangerous or distasteful working conditions, but more importantly regarding their development of performance technique and cultivation of talent and skill. Syndicated gossip columns, fan magazines, and newsreels downplayed the effort required to be a movie star, much less an actor. The gossip columnist Hedda Hopper's trademark "I just got off the phone with . . ." not only indicates her intimacy with Hollywood stars but also suggests that actors call to chat with the press about their new projects, rather than that these conversations are a crucial and time-consuming publicity chore. Further, Hopper's breezy columns made moviemaking seem like a game. In 1954, for example, she reported that Williams's "next picture at M-G-M, 'Jupiter's Darling,' is laughable. . . . Mermaid Esther makes her debut in the picture rising out of the Bay of Naples, and she probably will have a sunken swimming pool as big as the Atlantic Ocean. . . . It will be more Cinemascope, Technicolor, and M-G-M than history, but it sounds like fun."[55] Hopper's columns were syndicated throughout the United States during the Classical Hollywood era; she had a radio show for much of the period as well. Hopper was an important source for information about Hollywood actors' private lives, film production, and the links between the two. For the most part, she presented film sets as playgrounds and actors as happy performers who rarely realized they were working.

This erasure of labor in order to emphasize the correspondence between self and role is evident in filmed interviews as well. In February 1955, Williams appeared on *Person to Person*, the famed newsman Edward R. Murrow's interview program.[56] Murrow visits Williams and her husband, Ben Gage, and children, Benji, Kim, and Susie. The carefully produced segment purports to show Williams at home with her family, enjoying domestic life. The adults eat dinner with two-year-old Susie before the nanny puts her to bed; they look through a scrapbook; Williams shows off her laundry room; they check out the beautiful backyard pool, where the whole family swims daily. On one hand, this segment reinforces the idea that Williams is a warm, maternal, domestic woman, especially when she explains to Murrow that she'd rather have a laundry room than a diamond necklace. She's also athletic: she and Gage swim at least twenty laps in their competition-sized pool every day, even if she plans to swim at the studio later. But the segment also demonstrates (whether intentionally or not) that Williams is in charge. Early in the interview, Gage interrupts Williams to tell Murrow that she doesn't like to be interrupted. With an icy stare, Williams replies peevishly, "That's *not* true." Later, when Susie bangs her cup on the dinner table, Williams turns to her daughter and says calmly but quite firmly, "Mother's talking." One of the most illuminating moments comes when Williams gets up to show off the laundry room. The hem of her crinoline skirt is flipped up in back, and Gage hustles after her, obsequiously smoothing it down. She gives him a disdainful look and swishes through the door. This carefully choreographed glimpse at the "real" Esther Williams is as ambivalent a representation as any of her film roles. It's notable that even the presumably unintentional moments of Esther Williams ruling her family support the idea that she's in charge. Thus, Williams seems to be an authentic leader, a characterization of her movie roles, as I discuss below.

At the end of her career, Williams appeared on television again, in 1960's *Esther Williams at Cypress Gardens*.[57] She plays herself rehearsing for a television special when she meets Fernando Lamas's Arabian prince, Ahmed. The two swim, sing, and fall in love. The production numbers, then, are explicitly framed as performances for television cameras. Further, because Williams introduces the story, the location, the host (Hugh Downs), and the supporting players to the audience before the narrative unfolds, she underscores the reality of their situation. Several features of the narrative further enhance the correspondence between the television special and real life. Williams's biography as a competitive swimmer and movie star is referenced several times. Prince Ahmed has a harem, an obvious nod to Lamas's reputation as a ladies' man. Of course, he gives them up for a chance to marry Esther. Finally, because many audience members likely knew that Williams and Lamas were romantically involved, their interactions indicate "real" rather than narrative love.[58]

Though studio schools mandated training in specific naturalist techniques, starlets were also offered extensive makeovers designed to uncover their beauty and heighten their personal charm. From Rita Hayworth's hairline-raising electrolysis to Judy Garland's studio-provided diet pills, the story of actresses being "improved" by experts in order to become more beautiful is a familiar one. As Sharon Marie Carnicke and Cynthia Baron point out, the studios promoted the view that starlets were "inert matter, bodies without minds" who emerged as screen goddesses after the ministrations of hair and makeup personnel, advice from wardrobe supervisors, and fitness classes held at the studios. As they demonstrate, studio publicity suppressed information about acting training, suggesting instead that "actresses were produced by Hollywood's expert makeup and publicity men."[59] In this account, actresses have little inherent talent, need no technique, and lack the agency to exercise either.

Williams's description of her acting training confirms the studio's emphasis on technical training and focus on physical appearance but also suggests actresses' agency. In her autobiography, she discusses her acting training at length, presenting a narrative of a hardworking actress striving to do better than the "A's for Anatomy and barely D for Dramatics" with which critics graded her performances.[60] Despite Cynthia Baron's assessment of Burns as a naturalist teacher bringing Stanislavsky-influenced training to Hollywood stars, Williams complained that all the MGM starlets "learned the same mannered technique."[61] In fact, Lana Turner, one of Burns's most successful protégés, was criticized for merely imitating Burns, which Burns agreed, "in a way, was the truth."[62]

Williams understood herself to be limited as an actress: "I can't act, I can't sing, I can't dance," she famously complained.[63] Even so, she was an engaging and appealing performer who used her body to signal plot, character, and theme. Though Williams seems to have rejected Burns's version of naturalism, she did develop her own "natural" style. She watched films of MGM's great stars in order to learn how they connected with their characters. She also worked on her diction, singing, and dancing.[64] And she trained every day at the Beverly Hills Hotel pool—an unlimited guest pass was the second clause she had written into her initial MGM contract—which did at least as much to develop her specific performance style (see figure 9).

Williams's account of her early screen tests suggests that she understood her body as her primary tool for communicating with audiences. Less than a month after signing her MGM contract, Williams was tested without dialogue in four

Figure 9: Publicity photo of Esther Williams at the Beverly Hills Hotel, 1941.

outfits: evening gown, business suit, cocktail dress, and, of course, a two-piece bathing suit. The director, George Sidney, edited the footage so that as Williams spun around, her costume changed; the test succeeded in showing "an Esther whose personality would take her wherever she wanted to go."[65] Her second test, for a Clark Gable vehicle, was more substantive. Williams was sent to rehearse the scene with Dan Dailey, a member of MGM's stable. Terrified that she'd make a fool of herself, she begged Dailey for extra support, assuming that he would do the scene with her because Gable was too important to test with an unknown. Dailey urged her to "just be yourself." Gable did the test—and tossed out the script, kissed Williams three times in front of his wife and the crew, and left with a wink and laugh. After the star left, Williams "was a basket case. Real life emotion had taken over where on-screen drama had left off. My lip was quivering and my eyes had started welling with all-too-genuine-tears." Sidney rolled camera, cued Williams's lines from the scene, shot a close-up, and then edited the shots together in order to make a solid test.[66] In both cases, according to Williams, MGM executives were thrilled by her natural potential.

These two screen tests, of course, recall the notorious Kuleshov experiment: the Russian silent film director intercut an expressionless actor with shots of soup, a young girl, and a child's coffin; audiences read the actor as hungry, loving, and grieving.[67] As in narratives of the experiment, Williams's performances were made intelligible by editing. Though this seems to confirm the Russian formalists' emphasis on montage as meaning, I want to offer another interpretation: Williams's *body* suggested narrative. Of course, I'm relying on Williams's account, and she uses the events to construct a specific star persona. It is notable, however, that she highlights her natural body and its unmediated response to physical stimuli. If nothing else, Williams establishes a link between her body and her performance style at its originary moment. Her story suggests that while the lessons, the screenings, and even Burns's suggestions may have helped her manipulate that body, her physical appearance alone was enough to represent a confident, fresh young woman who was ready for business and love, which is how she describes herself in her autobiography.

Further, Williams framed her conflicts with Lillian Burns and the importance of developing her own authentic style as mandated by her body. Comparing the usefulness of Burns's advice to a starlet like Debbie Reynolds and to her own career, Williams "knew instinctively that a five-foot-eight-inch girl could not behave like a feisty, indignant little poodle with quick, jerky movements."[68] Her "five-foot-eight-inch" body, though voluptuous and conventionally beautiful, did place specific demands on her directors and costars. For example, her first major aquamusical, *Bathing Beauty*, paired her with Red Skelton, a comedian who usually exploited his small frame, with its connotations of quick wit and wiry strength, to get the girl. As Steven Cohan points out, Williams, of course, has "a more imposing physique than any of the men" in the film and physically

dominates Skelton.[69] Though the narrative resolves with the two happily married, in their next feature together, *Neptune's Daughter* (1949), Skelton played
comic sidekick to Ricardo Montalban's romantic lead. In her autobiography,
Williams reports that Gene Kelly, her costar in *Take Me Out to the Ball Game*
(1949), resented her height, which was at least six inches greater than his own.
After he complained that she "sat tall," Williams snapped. "I have perfect propor-
tions in a swimsuit, and that's why I'm here making movies at MGM. . . . I can't
make myself five-two, and I can't make you six-three, either. For this scene, it
would help a lot if you'd just sit up straight. If that's not enough, try tucking one
foot under your ass."[70]

As she became more successful at the box office, Williams began to look for
costars, like Montalban, Chandler, and Lamas, who could match her physical appearance and swim well enough that she didn't have to support them in
the pool. Thus, in order to be a believable romantic heroine, Williams had to
be paired with a specific type of athletic, muscular leading man. Her body
demanded that its power be matched with an (almost) equally powerful partner.
In this way, Williams's characters modeled a partnership between equals rather
than a comic pairing of a domineering woman or the more typical coupling of a
vulnerable woman and protective man.

Williams's performances are also structured by the technical demands of her
underwater ballets. Few other actresses had such constraints on their breathing and movement: few other actresses had to act while swimming. Williams's
performance style therefore incorporated her physical body more directly than
most. MGM's water tank, though designed specifically for Williams's water ballets and intended to allow maximum flexibility, still imposed significant limits. Tight framing, James Naremore points out, "requires [all actors] to cultivate
unusual stillness or restraint." As anyone who swims knows, it's especially difficult to remain still when underwater. Following from Naremore, Williams had
to "modulate behavior to fit a variety of situations," adjusting her actions to "a
medium that might view [her] at any distance, height, or angle," but she had
to do it in the pool as well as on land.[71] She developed much of her own choreography and worked with directors like Busby Berkeley to incorporate underwater shots of her swimming alone as well as group scenes featuring dozens of
swimmers in tightly framed, technically precise sequences.

As a swimming champion, veteran of an outdoor water show, and the "inventor" of synchronized swimming, Williams was particularly skilled at water choreography. But to focus on her "naturalness" in the water may discount her abilities
as a performer. David Thomson remarks, "It is often preferable to have a movie
actor who moves well than one who 'understands' the part" because movement
focuses the audience on a character's actions and suggests the actor's motivations, a reminder particularly applicable in Williams's case.[72] In her first feature,
Andy Hardy's Double Life (1942), Williams was filmed through a window in the

side of a tank and had to remain in a particular spot at a particular depth to stay in frame. When filming began, Williams "did something that nobody had told [her] to do": she rolled "languidly" in the water, "convey[ing] the sensation that being in there was absolutely delicious."[73] In this early sequence, she "moved well," using her body to signify unexpected meanings within technical constraints. This anecdote is central to my analysis of Williams. From the very beginning, she signaled her delight in the water, her comfort with her body, and her relaxation while swimming. Though usually directed at the camera and clearly available as erotic spectacle, Williams's swimming body is always also satisfying to her. Williams's "natural" body is active and controlled by its owner as well as a visual spectacle; the pleasure is both her own and her audience's.

This intersection of pleasure, spectacle, and agency is usefully complicated by performance studies' discussions of embodiment. Marvin Carlson suggests that performers "[draw] upon their own bodies . . . made performative by their consciousness of them and the process of displaying them for audiences." The body is not merely something to be molded by outside experts nor an accident of genetics but also a process of subjectivity. Williams's bodily experiences as a dutiful daughter, swimming champion, and water showgirl offered her a specific repertoire of presentation and movement on which she drew as a film actor. Further, concentrating on physical appearance offers the opportunity to interrogate what Carlson terms "the expressive qualities of the body, especially in opposition to logical and discursive thought and speech."[74] These communicative systems might be at odds with each other, opening texts to multiple interpretations and audiences. This is certainly the case for Williams's films, as I demonstrate below.

Though these early examples demonstrate how Williams is not the sole author of her film performances (a caveat true of all film actors), they also indicate how her process to create characters seems to have included an especial understanding of the limits and potentials of her body. As Sharon Marie Carnicke suggests, "viewing the actor's body and voice as productive of performance offers . . . a methodology that transcends the limitations of identifying styles with specific acting techniques."[75] Williams used her body's size, shape, and strength to signal her characters' internal motivations as well as relationships between characters. Though traditional accounts of the links between beauty and stardom seem to suggest otherwise, the material body offers opportunities for the exercise of performer agency.

Terrific/Dangerous When Wet: Feminist Readings of the Spectacular Star Body

In *Million Dollar Mermaid*, James Sullivan (Victor Mature) espouses a particularly patriarchal view of Annette Kellerman's (Williams) value in and out of the pool: "Baby, you're a swimmer. You belong in the water. Wet, you're terrific. Dry, you're just a nice girl who ought to settle down and get married." A close read-ing of several of her films demonstrates, however, that Esther Williams is equally powerful and interesting on land as she is in the water. Williams made over thirty films in the 1940s and 1950s; in 1953 the Hollywood Foreign Press Association named her the number-one movie star in the world.[76] Her films are best remem-bered for their ingenuity in getting Williams into a bathing suit at least once per picture, but they're equally notable for their recognizably feminist narratives. Almost without exception, Williams's heroines pursue personal and professional goals, rejecting romance in order to swim the English Channel, join the navy, or manage their own careers as circus performer, swimsuit designer, fashion model, theme park manager, water ballet star, or bullfighter. Her films are remarkable not only for their glorious swimming sequences but also for their insistence on female independence secured by physical and emotional strength. Of course, as a World War II–era star, Williams undoubtedly reaped the benefits of the "Rosie the Riveter" campaigns, but as Catherine Williamson points out, "as the war drew to a close, tolerance for 'strong women' (onscreen and off) dropped off dramatically."[77] It's worth noting that Williams continued to portray indepen-dent women well into the 1950s, after Hollywood films stopped suggesting that wartime shortages justified women doing the same jobs as men. In the analysis of *Million Dollar Mermaid, Dangerous When Wet,* and *Skirts Ahoy!* that follows, I insert Williams's body into the cinematic apparatus, developing a more nuanced understanding of naturalism and its subversive potentials.

Steven Cohan notes that although a casual viewer might assume that Esther Williams's "swimming numbers were all the same," she developed as a performer, and her "numbers increasingly became more spectacular and technically com-plex," requiring her to develop her body's musculature, flexibility, and stamina.[78] I take Cohan's point further, suggesting that by the 1950s Williams had devel-oped a performance style that negotiated Classical Hollywood's demand that star, body, and character align against her own body's increasing size, strength, and almost freakish beauty. While the plots of most of her films suggest that Williams's character is torn between romantic love and athletic competition, her body and performance style make clear that she will embrace her body's com-petitive power as well as find love on her own terms.

Williams's heroines generally begin by explicitly rejecting marriage or romance, then continue to pursue their own goals throughout, a significant departure from most movie musicals. Rick Altman demonstrates that musicals are organized on "radically different principles" than most Classical Hollywood films. Rather than following one protagonist's trajectory, creating momentum through the sequence of scenes as well as editing, framing, and sound, the musi-cal develops according to "dual focus": two (male and female) protagonists trade scenes and songs, usually paralleling each other in terms of theme and emotional development. Altman argues that through such generic convention, audiences learn how to "read" a film and accept its conclusions. Movie musicals "[set] up a series of male/female oppositions, eventually resolving them to harmonious unity through the device of marriage."[79] Scenes of the heroine and hero's journey toward each other and a happy ending structure the musical, and the couple who once seemed impossible becomes inevitable. Supported by discourses of naturalist acting, these love stories seem authentic and rooted in real behavior; thus, following from Altman, the dual-focus structure of most movie musicals underscores the certainty of marriage and the immutability of sex and gender characteristics.

Williams's films do not employ dual-focus organization. First, she's not part of a famous couple, like Fred Astaire and Ginger Rogers. Though she made multiple films with Montalban, Chandler, Lamas, and Johnson, she wasn't popularly associated with a particular actor. More importantly, she is the sole protagonist of most of her films. She generally has many more songs and production numbers than her love interest, and their scenes do not echo or parallel each other. In an Esther Williams vehicle, men are supporting players. Of course, Williams's characters generally accept marriage proposals in the final scene, but her powerful physical presence and status as single protagonist undercut the romantic finale.

In *Million Dollar Mermaid*, Williams plays the real-life Australian swimming champion and US Hippodrome star Annette Kellerman (1886–1975). The film begins with Kellerman as a young girl, swimming in secret in order to strengthen her crippled legs enough to take dance lessons. After she wins several swimming races, she and her beloved father leave for London and eventually New York; Mr. Kellerman (Walter Pidgeon) dreams of opening his own music conservatory. En route, they meet the promoter James "Jimmy" Sullivan (Victor Mature) and his assistant, Doc Cronnol (Jesse White). Annette and Jimmy fall in love, and he promises to make her a star. First he gets her arrested for indecent exposure on a beach in Boston: Annette was planning to swim twenty miles in a one-piece men's racing suit. Using that publicity to draw an audience, Doc, Jimmy, and Annette set up a water carnival whose only draw is Annette's demonstration of swimming strokes in brightly colored "indecent" swimsuits. Jimmy and Annette clash over her career, and they part. Annette begins swimming at the Hippodrome, her father dies while conducting its orchestra, and she agrees to marry the theater manager, Alfred Harper (David Brian). Of course, she still loves Jimmy, and when she's injured filming a scene for a silent movie, he rushes to her hospital bedside, flush with his success promoting the movie (dog) star Rin Tin Tin. Alfred graciously concedes defeat, and Jimmy and Annette embrace as he promises her she'll be able to swim again.

Williams spends much of the movie in the water: she races in Australia, swims the Thames as a publicity stunt, performs in the water carnival, stars in one of her most elaborate and iconic Busby Berkeley–directed film extravaganzas, and "films" a silent movie (represented solely by scenes of Williams in a water tank). Out of the water, she falls in love, cares for her father, takes a stand for women's rights, and negotiates her Hippodrome and movie contracts. In all of her scenes, she is pleasant, charming, and energetic; in the Hippodrome sequences, she is nearly delirious with joy. Her acting, then, creates a "believable" character who takes such enormous pleasure in swimming that it carries over to all other situations. In many ways, this exceptional happiness mutes Annette's independence, business acumen, and feminist allegiances. Nothing moves her so much as being in the water, and her character comes across as a nice woman rather than a show business pioneer and early sports celebrity.

This impersonation of pleasantness seems to be just what the director ordered. Williams was excited to work with the acclaimed Mervyn LeRoy and assumed that he'd bring "insight and sensitivity" to the film, especially the complicated (for an Esther Williams picture) romance. She was disappointed; according to her autobiography, the only direction she ever received—whether in a swimming scene, a love scene, or a fight—was "Let's have a nice little scene."[80] Williams suggests that LeRoy resented being assigned to an Esther Williams vehicle and could barely be bothered to advance an opinion on anything. Left on her own, Williams struggled with the role, her costars, and the demanding water choreography.

Sharon Marie Carnicke suggests that "screen actors accommodate different directorial visions by adjusting their performances to suit the aesthetic and narrative styles of the films in which they appear."[81] In *Million Dollar Mermaid*, Williams used her body to present this "niceness." For example, when she prepares to swim in Boston, she walks through the scandalized beachgoers, whimpering that she feels ashamed and afraid and begging to go home. The camera frames her lower body, focusing on her "offensive" legs. Her muscles flex and tense as she walks. At the edge of the beach, Jimmy removes her robe and she stands up on her toes with her left leg held at an angle away from her body, creating a pretty triangle. Her legs are gorgeous, and her upper body is muscular, strong, and voluptuous (see figure 10). Though she says she's embarrassed and angry, her body suggests that she's poised and proud. This isn't a scene of humiliation but a nice scene of a gorgeous woman in a bathing suit. Annette's complicated emotions are resolved by this spectacular pose. In important ways that are repeated throughout her film career, Williams's body contradicts the cinematic narrative presented. Though her words and the plot suggest one thing, her body proclaims another.

The water ballets in *Million Dollar Mermaid* are spectacular, and familiar to many from their inclusion in *That's Entertainment II*; Williams's body in these numbers communicates joy, energy, and strength. She performs one to music from *The Nutcracker Suite* in a fantasy grotto with a giant oyster bed. First, she holds on to a pole and "dances" en pointe, articulating the ballet positions, and presenting several graceful arabesques. With the pole as a partner, she twirls

Figure 10: Williams's gorgeous legs certainly make this a "nice little scene" for *The Million Dollar Mermaid*, 1952, MGM.

slowly around and around with her knees to her chest, her fluffy pink tutu incongruously revealing her muscular buttocks and thighs. After nearly three minutes without a cut for breath, she propels herself bulletlike toward a large oyster. Once there, her skirt mysteriously missing, and presumably after breathing, she does a duet with the shell, mirroring its shape with her body, stretching herself out and curling herself close before she plucks the pearl, climbs inside, and closes the shell around her. Throughout the sequence (which takes place as her father is suffering a heart attack in the orchestra pit below!), Williams smiles and poses. Though the music and costume are almost stereotypically feminine, Williams's upper body, torso, and thighs are extremely muscular, and her graceful backbends, arabesques, and bullet-shaped propulsion emphasize their musculature.

The final Hippodrome show is elaborate and exciting, indicative of the MGM "house style" that Steven Cohan associates with camp, "present in the form of the studio's musicals as well as their distinctive look, and made most evident when the aggregate energies of numbers, viewed individually and collectively, visually and contextually, pull against aesthetic conventions centered on an expectation of integration."[82] The sequence begins with colored jets of water spurting twenty feet in the air; the camera swings behind these jets to reveal a V-shaped ramp. Beautiful girls in yellow sequined suits slide face first between the legs of muscular men wearing red loincloths and holding streaming red banners overhead. When all the girls have entered the water, the men "ski" on their bare feet down the ramp. Finally Williams, dressed in a red sequined bathing dress with a crown of flames on her head and posed on her tiptoes, appears atop the ramp. Hands overhead in the victory gesture, she "skis" like the men and is pulled through the water between the men's and women's swinging legs. She speeds directly for the camera, smiling as though it's Christmas, her birthday, and her honeymoon rolled into one, and then plunges backward into the water, presenting her breasts, stomach, pelvis, and finally long legs to the camera (see figure 11).

The ballet continues with groups of men and women swinging through clouds of yellow and red smoke until they dive in tandem into the water. Williams swings through the smoke and somersaults into the water, where she grabs a suspended ring and is pulled fifty feet above the pool; the camera shoots from over her head to show the swimmers in undulating rings below her. She drops straight down only to instantly resurface poised on a platform and framed by smiling

Figure 11: The joy of swimming in *The Million Dollar Mermaid*, 1952, MGM.

girls and a sparkling arch. She holds this pose—arms curved away from her body, triangle legs, head lifted and turned in a three-quarter profile—smiling and even laughing a little until the platform begins to sink again into the water. That Williams is laughing in this scene suggests that she relishes the spectacle that's been created to highlight her unique talents as a performer. She's delighted to use her body in dangerous and complicated stunts, and delighted that her body responds to the camera and choreography in such a pleasing, "nice" way. This sequence, indicative of MGM's spectacular, camp house style, is equally indicative of the pleasure an athlete takes in her trained and toned body.

Despite Williams's seeming joy in this scene, she might well have been nervous or even terrified about its outcome. Though LeRoy directed *Million Dollar Mermaid*, Busby Berkeley staged the two extravagant water ballets, at Williams's request; she knew "he'd bring a real sense of showmanship to the film." Williams appreciated his vision, but she also knew that "Busby didn't give much thought to my safety. He just expected me to do whatever he dreamed up for me....As a result, I risked my life every time he said 'Roll 'em.'" Her complaint isn't hyperbolic. When shooting the film's first Berkeley ballet, Williams broke three vertebrae in her neck and upper back, spending six months in a cast "from the back of [her] neck all the way to [her] knees." She continued to suffer from headaches because of the accident.[83]

In her autobiography, Williams blames herself for the accident. Her costume included a metal crown that was "a lot stronger and less flexible than my neck." Because she was the only trained swimmer and diver on the MGM set, Williams believed that it was her responsibility to consider all the elements of her stunts, costumes, weather conditions, and on-set distractions: "I didn't think it out in advance, and shame on me, because I was the only one who would understand something like that."[84] Here, Williams seems to internalize what Danae Clark understands as the actor's presumed position during the studio era. Audiences, studios, and critics fetishized stars as objects.[85] Rather than subjects entitled to labor protections, for example, stars were products of their studios. By taking responsibility for her accident (which was in fact compounded because the cast and crew left Williams in the pool and took their lunch break), Williams participates in the construction of the actor as an artist who expresses something truthful and beautiful rather than a worker who produces a commodity. For Clark, understanding the "actor as worker ... permits actors' voices to be heard" and establishes them as social subjects rather than objects in a representational frame.[86] Though Clark develops a Marxian analysis of Hollywood labor, her insistence on actor subjectivity parallels my own feminist recovery of performance labor.

Finally, Williams's broken neck illuminates how movie musicals mask the effort that goes into their production. Though most of the water ballets in *Million Dollar Mermaid* are staged for audiences, we never see Williams rehearsing,

trying on costumes, or working with the orchestra at the Hippodrome or Hollywood film technicians. Instead, we see the final, spectacular product. In her autobiography, Williams suggests that the swimmers, camera operators, technicians,
costumers, makeup artists, and other film crew personnel worked very hard to
make her films a success, and she certainly presents herself as a dedicated studio employee who logged long hours in and out of the pool. But *Million Dollar
Mermaid*, which ends with Annette in the hospital because an underwater stunt
in her Hollywood debut has gone awry, erases all the labor and all the danger
inherent in making movies. As film theorists like Steven Cohan point out, movie
musicals were appealing as "escapism from wartime hardships and consumer
shortages." This appeal especially rested on the spectacular sequences of "lavish, outlandish imagery and gratuitous motivations" that denied the performer
hardships and consumer concerns without which these sequences could not have
been made.[87]

In *Dangerous When Wet* Williams plays Katie Higgins, a swimming champ and
Arkansas farm girl sponsored by Liqui-Pep to swim the English Channel. Training in England, Katie meets the dashing French champagne maker André Lanet
(Fernando Lamas). André tempts her (with champagne, a lingerie-inspired bathing suit, and a secluded private pool) to drop out of the race and enjoy life with
him. Though it's never explicitly stated, the scenario implies that he's a glamorous Frenchman interested in a sexual fling, while Katie is a good American girl
looking for true love and marriage. Katie refuses; her wholesome family is too
important to her, and they'll lose their farm and she'll lose their respect unless
she wins the race. Battling fog, cold, rough seas, and André's entreaties to quit,
Katie struggles. In a sudden reversal, André joins her in the final stretch, swimming with and encouraging her. With André's support, she reaches France and
wins by default because the other female competitors have dropped out. The next
morning, André opens her hotel door to her shocked family, but Katie flashes her
new wedding ring. He joins in with the family anthem ("I Woke Up Today on the
Right Side"), and the two follow her family down the stairs and back to Arkansas.

Though a purely textual reading might tease out the feminist and nonfeminist
implications of the narrative, I focus on Williams's body, arguing that she choreographs gender in both conventional and challenging ways. In the nonswimming
scenes, Williams uses her body to signal femininity and fragility. Though she's a
large woman, she makes herself small, especially in her scenes with Lamas (see
figure 12). For example, after he meets her during a training session and takes
her to his yacht, she perches on a bench with her legs tucked under her, her head
tilted down, and her arms crossed in front of her body. She's compact and curvy
(though of course still muscular). She seems contained and vulnerable, quickly
covering herself in a blanket. Lamas is relaxed and elegant, spread across the
screen with one leg perched on Williams's bench and the other solidly anchored
on the deck. He reaches one hand over her head to grasp the mast. Where she

Figure 12: Self-contained Esther Williams with Fernando Lamas in a publicity photo from *Dangerous When Wet*, 1953, MGM.

curls into a corner of the frame, he ranges across its expanse. In all their dry scenes together, her body is curved, closed in on itself, and small in comparison to his. Though Lamas is slightly taller than Williams, she consistently contracts her body to further signal femininity with its size and shape: she eats dinner with her elbows tucked into her sides, she walks with short steps that cross over each other, and she sits with her ankles tucked under her or her arms wrapped around her pulled-up knees.

In the water, Williams is long, rangy, and expansive. When she and Lamas swim together in their water ballet, she uses her superior speed and strength to avoid his physical advances.[88] Williams is clearly really swimming in open water during the training sequences, which underscores the authenticity of her performance. Here, I borrow Adrienne McLean's analysis of Rita Hayworth as a model for evaluating Williams's swimming sequences. McLean suggests that dance in Hayworth's musicals subverts the narrative closure that Classical Hollywood films are understood to require. "Dancing . . . betray[s] the essential duality, the distance between, narrative and spectacle. Dance cannot be a fictional treatment of itself in performance. To dance, one has to be able to do it, not merely suggest it. . . . In film, then, dancing can make plain . . . the distance between the real-life authority and complexity of a film's performers and the narratively defined and bounded fictional characters they play."[89] For McLean, Rita Hayworth's dancing body undercuts film narratives that establish her characters as passive, vulnerable, or unsympathetic. Williams's swimming body is a similarly subversive instrument for challenging the conservative conventions of the Hollywood musical, offering ambiguities within her films' narratives by reinforcing her body as active at the same time that it functions as spectacle. Because Williams is really swimming in the ocean, and really battling waves and cold temperatures, her articulation of strength and courage seems more authentic than her landlocked vulnerability.

Importantly, she's equally powerful in segments of the film's centerpiece water ballet. A dream sequence featuring Tom and Jerry, the ballet dramatizes Katie's conflict between swimming for glory and settling for romance. Against an animated background, Williams sets off across the Channel with the cartoon characters; Lamas voices an octopus who sings and offers champagne to distract Williams from her goal. Though the ballet opens with some underwater somersaults and poses, the majority of the number contrasts tight, twisted movements while she's with Lamas with languid but purposeful swimming. For example, when she sits down at a bistro table with the octopus, she curves her body in on itself. When Jerry is able to remind her of the race, she immediately swims powerfully and expansively toward France and victory. But Lamas's octopus follows her through an exotic underwater landscape, and the dream sequence ends with Tom and Jerry struggling with Williams to free her from his multiarmed embrace.

Though Williams is not on record as a feminist, and her autobiography suggests she made conservative professional and personal choices, her body itself offers feminist meanings. Susan Knobloch suggests a model of "resistance through artistry," arguing that even if feminist ideals aren't self-consciously engaged or endorsed by either actress or narrative, the "imaged body" may introduce them, allowing audiences and critics "to explore how screen acting can be read for its political significance precisely because it in and of itself does signify, adding and even changing meaning."[90] I suggest here that though Williams may not have consciously developed a *feminist* performance style, her body enables audiences to develop feminist analyses. Importantly, this style seems "natural" because it's predicated on her embodied experience. As a former swimming champion, Williams knew that her strength and stamina made her successful. As a box office star, she recognized the importance of her charm and beauty. Further, Williams undoubtedly recognized that her viability as a star depended on her believability in musical romances as well as water ballets. Her choreography of gender echoes Judith Butler's claim that only felicitous performances of gender and sex render all men and women "culturally intelligible."[91] Thus, she offers a combination of familiar, conventionally feminine movements and displays of incredible strength and power. She's clearly a woman, but she's a woman who sometimes usurps masculine prerogatives; her performance of gender suggests new ways of harnessing female physical and emotional strength while remaining femininely attractive.

Dangerous When Wet marks Esther Williams as a choreographer of gender. The dance scholar Susan Leigh Foster expands Judith Butler's emphasis on speech as performative, calling for an assessment of "the articulateness of bodies' motions as well as speech." Her description of the choreographer of gender provides the frame through which I read Williams's water ballets: "The choreographer constructs relationships of body to momentum, stasis, impulse, and flow and articulates the relationships of the body's parts one to another. She engages the body's semiotic field . . . and situates the body within the symbolic features of the performance space. . . . In so doing, she fashions a repertoire of bodily actions that may confirm and elaborate on conventional expectations for gendered behavior, or she may contrive a repertoire that dramatically contravenes such expectations."[92] In the water ballets as well as the narrative scenes, Williams choreographs gender in order to create a coherent character. She develops a specific repertoire of movement, one that suggests that women are strong and independent when they trust their bodies to perform physically. She presents herself as stereotypically feminine on land in order to directly contrast her swimming scenes. The pattern of small, vulnerable, and contained when on land or with men juxtaposes her long, powerful, and expansive body when alone or in the water. This, then, is Williams's "natural" performance style, incorporating Classical Hollywood expectations of feminine behavior, her lived experience of gender, and the unique capacities of her body. She uses this contrast in many of her films, especially at the height of her career in the late 1940s–mid-1950s. This performance style offers audiences several representations of femininity, but especially the assurance that success and happiness can be achieved independent of a male partner.

Skirts Ahoy!, less spectacular than Million Dollar Mermaid or Dangerous When Wet, further demonstrates how Williams's "natural" body enables feminist narratives. As the debutante Whitney Young, Williams leaves her groom at the altar and joins the US Navy WAVES. She bunks with two other young women, Mary Kate Yarbrough (Joan Evans) and Una Yancy (Vivian Blaine), also escaping the perils of romance. The three work and play together, graduate at the top of their class, and receive plum assignments in Washington, DC. Of course, they also settle their romantic difficulties, but importantly, the film ends with the women setting off together and leaving their romantic partners behind. *Skirts Ahoy!* presents an overtly feminist theme covertly facilitated by Williams's "natural" body.[93]

Skirts Ahoy! makes several truth claims about the authenticity of the characters and plot, demonstrating how naturalist discourses and film publicity worked together to present seamless representations of "real life." According to her autobiography, Williams collaborated on the film treatment with screenwriter Isobel Lennart, who talked to Williams about loyalty, love, and responsibility to other women, weaving those ideas into her script. Williams portrayed a woman with values, conflicts, and desires modeled on her own: "I liked the fact that the story lines of their loyalty to one other, and the way they adapt to life in the navy, took precedence over romance." This anecdote demonstrates how Williams perpetuated links between her "natural" personality and the characters she impersonated. Second, because *Skirts Ahoy!* was made in cooperation with the WAVES, the film "had to go by the book about official navy attire. There would be no adding extra sparkle or substituting high heels for sensible oxfords."[94] The demands of verisimilitude kept Williams and her costars in the "sensible" but not particularly feminine or sexual WAVES uniform, and these costumes project competence, authority, and virtue. Finally, Williams's "natural" body further signaled strength and honor: she's physically larger and stronger than all the other women in the film and is their leader. The film poster, for example, shows Williams flanked by Evans and Blaine; though their arms are linked, suggesting equality, Williams towers over the other two. This stance is repeated throughout the film, and Williams often leans over one or both of her friends, her arm around their shoulders, indicating her superior strength and wisdom.

Though Williams is positioned as the leader (not only is she taller and stronger, but she's also from a wealthy family with military connections), the film suggests that the women equally sustain each other. This friendship among near equals, Lucie Arbuthnot and Gail Seneca propose, "invites the female viewer to join them, through identification, in valuing other women and [them]selves"; thus, audiences can "discover feminist pleasures within films of the dominant culture." As with *Gentlemen Prefer Blondes*, the "narrative of romantic adventure is continually disrupted and undermined by other narrative and non-narrative elements in the film. This disruption is so severe and continual that we have come to regard the romantic narrative as mere pre-text, a story which co-exists with, contradicts, and disguises another, more central text."[95] Arbuthnot and Seneca focus on Marilyn Monroe and Jane Russell's relationship by examining several elements of the film (use of space, costuming, lighting, generic convention, and the like) to demonstrate how the film avoids the objectification of women as well as focuses on their connections with each other. Not surprisingly, they pay particular attention to the film's musical numbers, pointing out that Monroe and Russell only duet with each other rather than with their putative love interests. The same is true of *Skirts Ahoy!* Williams, Evans, and Blaine sing and dance in a coffee shop, put on a talent show, and sing while teaching others to swim. Their romantic partners are shown only briefly, and only as connected with the women. The musical numbers create a female-centered world where women can enjoy their bodies, voices, and friendships because the songs and dances are directed to each other, unobserved by male eyes. Again, as Steven Cohan points out, musical numbers suggest authenticity because audiences witness the performer rather than the character in displays of virtuosic singing and dancing. The film thus suggests that women can build strong communities, such as the Navy WAVES, and thrive within them. Clearly, the content as well as the structure of the production numbers in *Skirts Ahoy!* further enables a feminist narrative.

Williams's body does much to develop her character as well as establish her relationships with Evans, Blaine, and Barry Sullivan, who plays her love interest, Dr. Paul Elcott. Sullivan seems much weaker than Williams. Not only is his character never developed—in his single scene without Williams, he's talking about her, and she immediately enters—but he's never represented as her physical match. They do not swim together, the usual hallmark of a Williams love affair. She is at least his height (thank goodness the WAVES kept her in "sensible" shoes!), and she's presented as more athletic and physically capable than he. When they go for dinner, some WACs attempt to flirt with Elcott. Whitney stands up and marches over to their table, towering over the other women. When the restaurant erupts into a WACs/WAVES brawl, Elcott is clearly dismayed by Whitney's defense of his and the navy's honor. When she is brought up on disciplinary charges, he refuses to defend her. His masculinity threatened, he urges her to be more feminine, to sit down and sit still, and to wait for him to take the lead in their relationship.

The water ballets in *Skirts Ahoy!* stress Whitney's independence and further the theme that there's more to life than romance. After the disciplinary hearing, she goes to the base pool to cool off and encounters two small children (Kathy and Bubba Tongay). They are without parental supervision, and Williams settles a dispute between the two by promising to swim with them. The three frolic in the water, and Williams seems maternal: these two swimming prodigies could be her children. She executes fairly standard Williams choreography (twisting her body languidly, rolling sensually, pointing her toes and thrusting her bosom), but her movements are mimicked by the children, rendering her swimming playful rather than erotic. Though the choreography is nearly identical to what she performs in *Million Dollar Mermaid*'s *Nutcracker* fantasy, the context is very different. The *Skirts Ahoy!* ballet, then, suggests that Williams is moving in the water the way she (and children) naturally might, rather than performing for an audience interested in the erotic potential of her swimming body. The ballet ends with a race between the three—she gives the Tongays a head start and engineers a tie—and all do the butterfly, a stroke mostly associated with male competitive swimmers. This race is unlike any other in Williams's oeuvre.[96] Shot first head-on and then from the side, Williams lifts her powerful upper body far out of the water before crashing into the pool; unlike her other water ballets, this is a display of brute strength rather than grace or elegance. Further, she's dressed in an athletic swimming suit and wears a baseball cap on her head, signaling that she's swimming for exercise and enjoying the children, the water, and her athleticism. Her history as a competitive swimmer as well as her current physique supports this analysis; in other words, this is Williams swimming as she "naturally" swims.

The second water ballet is motivated by Whitney's anger over Elcott's admonishments to be more ladylike. Demonstrating that she's strong but feminine, she strips to a pink, lacy bra and tap pants to relax with a moonlight swim. Though we see her remove her blouse and skirt, the bra and tap pants are only briefly visible as she dives into the water; her costuming in this film is generally less revealing than in most of her vehicles. In this sequence, she swims with a floating "Seabee" doll, cradling him in a waltz, tangoing aggressively, then waltzing again before kissing him passionately. The music changes as her movements change, and she is definitely "leading" the dance, just as Sullivan has accused her of trying to take the lead in their relationship. Finally, she squeezes the doll so tightly that he explodes. After the Seabee's deflation, Williams sets him aside and begins swimming lazy laps across the pool. She has worked out her tensions through a comic interlude, and she's ready to enjoy physical exercise, alone and on her terms.

These two water ballets are different in tone and meaning from most swimming sequences in her films. Williams swims to release her frustration, and her swimming is understood as a physicalization of her mental state. The correspondence between physical action and mental state especially signals naturalist authenticity, as Williams is gripped by overwhelming emotions and spontaneously acts them out. Unlike the ballets in *Dangerous When Wet* and *Million Dollar Mermaid*, these are not performances for an appreciative audience nor a dream sequence. Instead, Williams uses her body and the pleasure she takes in that body for emotional escape. She's actively swimming because she wants and needs to swim, not because someone else wants her to. Further, because there isn't an imagined spectator, the camera frames Williams differently: there are fewer underwater shots or shots of her entire body lolling in the water. Instead, most shots are close-ups of her head and shoulders, or medium shots of her entire body cutting through the water. Unlike in most of her water ballets, the camera doesn't segment her body into component parts, and there's little emphasis on her spectacular legs. Williams's real, natural body enables *Skirts Ahoy!* to include a woman enjoying her body's strength and power instead of primarily presenting it as an object of sexual desire.

Esther Williams illuminates how physical appearance and the beautiful feminine body may provide subversive performances of gender. Her aquamusicals, and the water ballets that are their raison d'être, demonstrate how her body demands narratives of strong, independent, even aggressive women. Of course, Esther Williams is not the sole author of her performances, nor is it necessarily her intent to offer feminist meaning. Even so, as Paul McDonald argues, performance analysis "need not be caught up with questions of intentionality. . . . It does not matter how the details got there, only that they are there and seem significant."[97] Reassessing her water ballets as choreographies of gender offers a reconsideration of the spectacular female body and indicates the subversive potentials of naturalist acting. Her especially powerful and articulate musculature and bone structure (and the cultural meanings they carry) offer multivalent representations of women. Though Williams's athletic body may be an extreme example of how subversive meanings inhere in feminine bodies, other spectacular bodies might be read for significance in excess of or contrast to narrative. Representing the body as active *at the same time* as spectacular, Esther Williams demonstrates how the material body crafts cinematic performance, suggesting feminist possibilities within conservative texts.

CHAPTER 3

LIGHT EGYPTIAN

LENA HORNE AND THE
REPRESENTATION OF BLACK FEMININITY

In 1942, Lena Horne was offered an MGM contract; like Esther Williams and countless other aspiring stars, she underwent the standard makeup, wardrobe, and lighting tests for MGM executives and producers. But where Williams remembers this as a necessary if sometimes frustrating experience, Horne's experience indicates the failings of the studio system regarding performers of color. In her bitter account, performed in interviews, memoirs, cabaret shows, and her 1981 autobiographical tour de force *Lena: The Lady and Her Music*, Horne explained that her "copper-colored" skin didn't effectively signal blackness on film. Max Factor, MGM's chief makeup artist, developed the pancake base "Light Egyptian" to darken Horne's skin so that she could pass as African American. Ten years later, MGM used Light Egyptian again, this time to darken Ava Gardner, the daughter of North Carolina white sharecroppers,[1] so that she could play the biracial Julie in *Show Boat*, a role for which Horne was rejected. Horne had played this classic tragic mulatto role for a segment in the Jerome Kern biopic *Till the Clouds Roll By* (1946). When MGM produced the full-length film version of *Show Boat* in 1951, Horne's biographer James Gavin explains, "an obviously black actress could not play an octoroon who had survived in turn-of-the-century Mississippi by passing for white . . . and until 1952, the Hollywood Production Code barred miscegenation on-screen—not in scripts but in casting." Whether or not Horne's acting ability was up to the demands of the role (doubts shared by Gavin as well as MGM decision makers like George Sidney),[2] she could not be cast in what she described as her dream role because of institutionally racist policies. Instead, a white performer "blacked up" in order to play the role of a black character, as had been done on US stages and screens since the early nineteenth century.

Light Egyptian, then, is the makeup used to make a white or light-skinned black woman look mulatto. Its invention and use demonstrates the ways in which Horne was compelled to negotiate an authentic black femininity in 1940s Hollywood rooted in the conventions of the nineteenth- and early-twentieth-century minstrel stage. In short, black performers must be a particular color and play particular parts in order to be culturally intelligible. Like Thomas D. Rice in 1836 and Bert Williams in 1910, Horne blacked up for the sake of her career. The casting of *Show Boat* illuminates one of the cruel ironies of this tradition. On one hand, Horne was too light to be "naturally" black; on the other, she was too "naturally" black to play a mixed-race character.

Horne's case study illuminates how embodied and visible signs of race (as well as sex, class, and gender) with a particular history and set of codes produce cinematic authenticity. Authenticity is performative and citational, building onstage, onscreen, and in everyday life performances to, in Butler's felicitous phrase, "produce the effects that it names."[3] As such, it is intimately bound to the discourses and practices of naturalist acting, as this chapter makes clear. In important ways, singing, whether in front of a live cabaret audience or in a movie musical, demonstrates a distinctive authenticity founded on (and produced by) the discourses and the techniques of naturalist performance, most especially the correlation of performers' bodies and voices with their roles as well as the gendered and racial histories of the genres in which they sing.

This chapter places Lena Horne within the history of the movie musical, exploring some of its roots in the minstrel tradition as well as its links to theatrical and cinematic naturalism. After a biographical sketch of Horne's personal life and career that demonstrates how her shifting persona was always already marked as her authentic self and a symbol of black femininity, I sketch those broader histories. Finally, I read some of Horne's film performances: as Georgia Brown in *Cabin in the Sky* (1943), as Julie in *Till the Clouds Roll By* (1946), and her "pillar songs" (none actually sung in front of a pillar) from *Till the Clouds Roll By* and *The Duchess of Idaho* (1950), an Esther Williams vehicle. Horne performed for over six decades, and though these performances cover only her very early career and persona, they effectively demonstrate how Horne manipulated—and was manipulated by—the discourses and techniques of naturalism in order to appear intelligible in Classical Hollywood film.

Lena Horne's Biographical Performances

Lena Horne was born in 1917 to Edna Scottron Horne and Edwin Horne Jr., both scions of prominent black Brooklyn families. Though Horne's family was and is understood as representative of the black bourgeoisie and Horne described herself as black, she had a multiracial genealogy. According to James Gavin's biography, *Stormy Weather*, her mother was "the fair-skinned, green-eyed daughter of a Native American mother and a successful Portuguese Negro inventor." Her paternal grandfather, Edwin Horne, "wasn't even a Negro, but the son of a white

Englishman and Native American mother" who passed as black during Recon-
struction. His wife, Cora, who largely raised Horne, was three-quarters white: her
father, Moses, was a "mulatto . . . house slave" who became a prominent business-
man and "married a white woman" after the Civil War.[4] Horne's parents separated
when she was two years old, and she lived with her paternal grandparents until
1921, when Edna reclaimed her daughter and took her to Philadelphia, where
she was starring with a black theater troupe, the Lafayette Players. For the next
eight years, Horne shifted between her paternal grandparents' Brooklyn home,
boardinghouses, and family friends or relatives (some of whom reportedly physically and sexually abused her) in Florida, Ohio, and Alabama while her mother
pursued her acting career; she spent a brief period with her father, who joined
her when she lived with an aunt and uncle in Fort Valley, Georgia. In 1929, she
returned to her paternal grandparents in Brooklyn, staying with them until her
mother, now married to a white Cuban named Miguel Rodriguez, reclaimed
her in 1932. A year later, living in poverty in Harlem with her mother and stepfa-
ther, Horne started in the chorus at the Cotton Club.

In the 1920s and 1930s, Harlem's segregated Cotton Club was famous for its
white "slumming" audience, black jazz headliners, and beautiful, light-skinned
chorus girls. Jayna Brown's excellent recovery of black chorines in the late
nineteenth and early twentieth centuries, *Babylon Girls*, notes that female chorus members were the lowest-paid and the hardest-working employees of the
Harlem nightclubs, dancing and singing in up to six shows a day and rehearsing afterward. Many of these clubs were unofficially segregated, allowing black
celebrities to join the audience but keeping all other blacks out.[5] Still, as Jazzy
Jasmine Adelaide Hall, a Cotton Club dance captain, explained, "It was the case
of having the chance of being first and foremost. . . . You met the best artists."[6]
This was certainly true for Horne, who quickly became a featured performer,
singing with Cab Calloway, Avon Long, and the Nicholas Brothers. According
to Gavin, Horne hated working at the Cotton Club, which she said was run by
gangsters and thugs. She was insecure about her singing and dancing, and even
doubted that her beauty (which she credited with her early success) was enough
to support a long-term career. She branched out, appearing on Broadway in a
supporting role in the voodoo melodrama *Dance with Your Gods* (1934); in 1935
she began touring as well as recording with the Noble Sissle Orchestra. Though
her career seemed promising, she took a break to visit her beloved father, who
was living in Pittsburgh. There she met Louis Jones, a college-educated aspiring
politician and Baptist minister's son. The two married in 1937, and after a rocky
few months, Lena became pregnant with their daughter, Gail. After her birth, the
couple continued to struggle financially as well as emotionally, and just over a
year after their marriage, Horne left Gail with Jones to make *The Duke Is Tops*, an
independent all-black film. She returned to Broadway in *Lew Leslie's Blackbirds
of 1939: A Harlem Rhapsody*, bore the couple's second child, Teddy, and left Louis

for good (though they didn't officially divorce for several years) in August 1940 to pursue her show business career.

In 1941, Horne signed a multiyear, multipicture contract with MGM (see figure 13). Walter White, a family friend and executive secretary of the NAACP, had been applying pressure to all the Hollywood studios to sign a black performer and offer her the same treatment available to white starlets. Horne's contract specified that she would not play stereotypical parts such as mammies, domestics, or "native" dancers. Unfortunately, this limited her casting, as these were the only parts generally deemed acceptable for black actresses.[7] Except for her supporting roles in the all-black musicals *Cabin in the Sky* and *Stormy Weather*, both released in 1943 and designed, says Arthur Knight, "to *make* the first black movie star," Horne never played a character within the narrative.[8] In fact, according to her *New York Times* obituary, Horne bitterly remembered that "the only time I ever said a word to another actor who was white was Kathryn Grayson" in the *Show Boat* segment from the Jerome Kern biopic *Till the Clouds Roll By.*[9] She did play character roles in *Death of a Gunfighter* opposite Richard Widmark (1969) and as Glinda in *The Wiz* (1978), but in the rest of her twelve studio films, made

Figure 13: Lena Horne, looking very much the "bronze swan" in an MGM publicity photo, 1941.

between 1942 and 1956, she sang specialty numbers, some of which were reportedly cut for southern distribution. Though still under contract to MGM, Horne
appeared in nightclub acts throughout the United States, both above and below
the Mason-Dixon line. She also carried on affairs with Joe Louis, Orson Welles,
and Artie Shaw, as well as Leonard Hayton, a married composer and conductor
with MGM's celebrated Freed Unit. Divorced from Louis Jones in 1943 (she got
custody of Gail, but he kept Teddy), she and the now-widowed Hayton married in Paris in 1947, since interracial marriage was illegal in much of the United
States (Hayton was white and Jewish). That marriage, though not without its
challenges, lasted until Hayton's death in 1971.

When MGM did not renew her contract, Horne returned to cabaret performances. Horne had always been frustrated in Hollywood. In 1946, right before
MGM dropped her, she told *Ebony* magazine that "it's easier for a colored person
to be a singer than an actress" in Hollywood films.[10] A lifelong advocate for civil
rights (Gavin's biography includes the photograph her grandmother Cora had
taken to commemorate Lena's 1919 induction into the NAACP), Horne became
an increasingly vocal proponent in the 1950s and 1960s. In June 1950, her name
appeared in the pamphlet *Red Channels,* a publication that demanded the boycott
of Horne and 150 other entertainers who were suspected of being communist/
fascist sympathizers "taking over the broadcast and film industries." She attended
a rally in Jackson, Mississippi, at the request of Medgar Evers in 1963, marched
with Dr. Martin Luther King Jr. later that year, and "identified passionately" with
Malcolm X. She remained active in black advocacy until the end of her life: her
last public appearance was at a 1999 benefit gala for the Lena Horne Youth Lead-
ership Scholarship Awards, which offered training in community organization
for urban black youth.[11]

A frequent guest from the 1950s through the 1990s on television programs like
The Tonight Show (from Steve Allen's version in 1955 to Johnny Carson's in 1966)
and *The Muppets* (1976), as well as the specials *Monsanto Night Presents Lena
Horne* (1969) and *Harry and Lena,* with Harry Belafonte (1969), Horne wanted
her own musical variety/talk show. Though she taped three episodes of *The Lena
Horne Show* for British television in 1958, she was not able to secure a US network
contract, which she blamed on US prejudices. She told a reporter in 1957 that "it's
pretty clear why I've never had my own show. So I won't go into it."[12] She performed her signature "Stormy Weather" for the last time on *The Rosie O'Donnell
Show* in 1998.[13] Though she was unable to launch her own series, her television
appearances over five decades ensured that she remained a popular and familiar
performer and activist.

Whatever the hazards of her television and film careers, Horne was always
a successful nightclub performer and important recording artist. She head-
lined shows in Las Vegas, Miami, Los Angeles, Chicago, London, Paris, and
her home base of New York City. Though not all were critical or commercial

hits, she released more than thirty albums between 1942 and 2006.[14] In 1981, she reached her largest and most integrated audience with *The Lady and Her Music*. Held over at Broadway's Nederlander Theatre for 333 performances and then toured throughout the United States and in London until 1985, her solo autobiographical performance generated a Grammy Award, as well as an Emmy nomination for the Showtime network's televised version.

After *The Lady and Her Music*'s phenomenal success, Horne's popularity as a recording artist and television guest star revitalized. She also hosted a segment of the third installment of *That's Entertainment* in 1994. Horne continued to sing in nightclubs, guest on television, and record until the late 1990s. These later performances tended to draw attention to her status as a black legend as well as her still captivating voice, nuanced interpretations, and charismatic presence. Living just blocks from her daughter, Gail, and mostly homebound in her last decade, Horne died May 9, 2010.

For most performers, Horne's success was remarkable. For a black female performer, she was sui generis. Her résumé is studded with firsts and near-firsts: one of the first black female singers to front a white band (Charlie Barnet's swing orchestra in 1940); the first black performer to play the Copacabana, in 1944; the first Broadway kiss between African American and Latino performers (with Ricardo Montalban in *Jamaica* in 1957); the first black woman to have a sold-out solo show on Broadway (1981's *Lena: The Lady and Her Music*).[15] (The claim that made her most notable, that she was the first female black performer to sign a long-term contract with a major Hollywood studio, was refuted in her *New York Times* obituary.[16]) Clearly, Horne's career is remarkable for her artistic achievements as well as her dismantling of many show business color barriers. As a Grammy and Tony winner, inductee at the Kennedy Center, recipient of two stars on the Hollywood Walk of Fame, and holder of honorary doctorates from Howard and Yale universities, Horne is one of the twentieth century's most celebrated entertainers.[17] Not surprisingly, she was successful at least in part because of her willingness to serve as a symbol of her race, crafting a flexible persona that exploited stereotypes of black femininity, whether in the integrationist 1940s and 1950s or the more militant 1960s and 1970s.

It is important to note that although her film, recording, television, and cabaret persona was generally understood as an authentic expression of a "real" Lena Horne, it was not static. Indeed, Horne shifted from the embodiment of a well-bred, demure, but aloof ideal 1940s "Negro" to an angry, sexy, and wise black diva. This shift, as well as its flexible authenticity, is perhaps best demonstrated by her performances of "Stormy Weather." Though Horne sang several numbers that crossed over from film appearances to recordings to live shows, spanning several decades of performance ("Can't Help Lovin' Dat Man" from *Show Boat* is just one example), "Stormy Weather" is her standard. Defined by Shane Vogel as the "song that a singer is always prepared to perform and that an audience is always prepared to recognize" as well as the "banner by which one announces her advance," the standard encapsulates a performer's persona.[18] The lyrics, music, and performance patterns inscribe a particular narrative for the singer, and its repetition throughout different media and across time help concretize particular notions of the performer. Though Ethel Waters is also associated with "Stormy Weather," and in fact debuted the number in *The Cotton Club Parade of 1933*,[19] the link between Horne and Harold Arlen and Ted Koehler's Tin Pan Alley classic is stronger than that between many female singers and songs. Thus, her multiple versions of the song offer a richly complex model of how cabaret singing might indicate personality and how singers might exploit discourses of naturalism.

The film *Stormy Weather* follows Bill Williamson (Bill "Bojangles" Robinson), a World War I army musician and naturally virtuosic dancer, as he works his way to show biz success and woos Selina Rogers, the pretty, singing sister of his dead buddy Clem.[20] Told mainly in flashback and, according to the *Variety* review, "chockful of cream-of-the-crop colored talent" like Ada Brown, Cab Calloway, Katherine Dunham, Harold and Fayard Nicholas, and Fats Waller, along with dozens of black musicians and chorus girls, *Stormy Weather* ends with an extravaganza celebrating twenty-five years of black entertainment staged as a benefit for black World War II troops.[21] Bill, who split with Selina several years earlier when he accepted a Hollywood contract and she pursued a career in Paris nightclubs, has been living in the gracious California home he designed for the two of them. Still in love with Selina and still dancing, Bill accepts an invitation from his old friend Cab Calloway to attend the benefit. Bill arrives in time to see Selina sing "Stormy Weather" and (of course) to join the show himself. When Selina spies him in the audience, she sheds a single tear and meets him backstage to tell him that she's finally ready to accept his proposal. The two close the show, backed by Calloway, the full band, dozens of dancers, and uniformed audience members with their well-heeled dates. Directed by Andrew Stone and released by Twentieth Century–Fox, the film was a critical success, because its "cavalcade of Negro entertainment" made it "just the kind of spirited divertissement that will make you forget all about your own . . . troubles," at least according to its *New York Times* review.[22]

When Bill arrives at the benefit, he watches Calloway from backstage and then goes out front to watch a special act that Calloway "is sure [he'll] like." Bill picks up the title card on his table, reads that Selina Rogers and Katherine Dunham will be performing, and takes his seat at the edge of the stage. The nightclub curtains rise, Calloway cues the band, and Horne stands with her back to the audience, looking out a curtained window onto a windy, rainy street. She turns and begins singing, and her face is pleasant but nearly immobile throughout. Dressed in a sheer-sleeved, sequined gown with diamonds in her ears, a perfectly matched manicure, and smooth hair worn half up, Horne keeps her feet relatively still, her elbows close to her sides, and gently sways back and forth. As she sings the second verse, she starts down a short staircase to the area in front of the band. Her movements are still contained: for example, when she laments that "since you went away/the blues walked in and met me," she raises her hands about chest high and opens her arms only about three-quarters wide before curving them back toward her body, soon dropping them to her sides on "old rocking chair will get me." On the line "since my man and I ain't together," she spies Bill at this table and almost pauses. She remains in this spot at the front of the orchestra to deliver the rest of the song, alternating glances between Bill and the rest of the audience. Selina's voice trills pleasantly that she "can't go on/ everything I had is gone," that she's "heavy-hearted and sad," and that it "keeps raining all the time." Her voice and body finally reach (what passes for) a crescendo at "this pittering, pattering, beating, and spattering drives me mad," delivered directly to Bill. A single tear visible in the corner of her right eye, Selina pulls herself together to deliver the final chorus. Her closing "can't go on/everything I had is gone" is relatively quiet, signaling resignation to her loneliness. When the thunder crashes outside and the orchestra speeds up its tempo to match, Horne is almost animated. She moves her arms from side to side (though they are still curved and about waist high), turns, and hurries up the stairs to shut the window. The song segues into "Katherine Dunham and her troupe doing a short, blistering jungle dance." Though the reviewer for the *New York Times* also notes that "Miss Horne digs deep into the depths of romantic despair," her voice is light, delicate, and controlled throughout. Horne herself admitted that she gave a naive performance because, as a member of the black bourgeoisie, "I'd always been taught not to show my feelings."[23] (See figure 14.)

This performance of "Stormy Weather" is especially interesting in light of Lena Horne's MGM roles and persona. Though she's playing a character, Selina has virtually the same movement vocabulary and vocal repertoire of her non-character performances in *Till the Clouds Roll By, Words and Music, Two Girls and a Sailor,* or *The Duchess of Idaho,* some of which I discuss below. It is likely that many audience members who saw these films had also seen *Stormy Weather,* especially Horne's black fans, many of whom reportedly made significant efforts to see all her pictures.[24] Thus, her character performances as well as specialty numbers solidified Horne's aloof, contained, reserved performance style, which both Horne and her audiences associated with her "authentic" self. As Shari Roberts points out, black audiences read her "stylized, distant, inaccessible performance . . . as masquerade . . . and parody of the racist expectations" of white audiences. At the same time, Roberts continues, her performance seemed "blank," allowing white audiences to read her as neither white nor black.[25] Further, publicity in both the black press and Hollywood fan magazines stressed Horne's biography as an exemplary (and mixed-race) black woman, suggesting that she embodied the bourgeois ideals middle-class African Americans shared

Figure 14: Reserved and refined Lena Horne, singing the title song in *Stormy Weather*, 1943, MGM.

with whites.[26] In the 1940s, the glamorous, self-possessed young woman who merely hints at desire and despair is the authentic Lena Horne.

Horne's performance in *The Lady and Her Music* recasts her standard,[27] making it newly authentic through the "act of repetition and revision" that characterizes cabaret performances of singers' repertoire. Standards, continues Shane Vogel, "accumulate multiple meanings as they are performed, reinterpreted, and improvised . . . meanings that exceed the textual record. . . . In their instantiation, songs may inscribe their historical moments with echoes of past performances. They are simultaneously reinscribed by these subsequent and successive enactments."[28] In this way, Horne reworks "Stormy Weather" to produce a different but no less authentically performed persona. As Frank Rich, reviewing the show for the *New York Times*, remarks, "she transforms each song, however familiar, into an intensely personal story that we've never quite heard before. . . . She's singing with an abandon, range, and feeling" that she's not previously offered audiences.[29] This performance, despite its differences from previous versions of her standard, is also understood as authentic.

For *The Lady and Her Music*, Horne is dressed in a floor-length couture Giorgio Sant'Angelo red jersey dress with a gold brocade jacket. Her close-cropped hair is curly, and she wears enormous gold "tribal" earrings. Accompanied only by piano, the song begins with a mellow, almost spoken version of the third verse of "Stormy Weather." Horne then admits that "I know he's gone" but asserts "I don't let it stop me" to transition (with a key change and a drawn-out *ah*) to the familiar "don't know why" lyric. As she begins, the audience breaks into applause. Backed by a full jazz orchestra that relies heavily on saxophone, she mostly sings with her eyes closed, microphone clutched in her left hand, rocking back and forth and bobbing up and down. She opens her beautiful red lips as wide as she can, peeling them back from her strong white teeth. She fills the spaces between words with grunts, ahs, oh-yeahs, and mm-hmms.[30] If her film body language suggested a curving inward, in this performance she reaches forward, grasping at the air and clutching it back to herself. Her elbows remain close to her sides, but she is much more dynamic, pulsing up and down to the beat of the music. In the second chorus, as she sings "can't go on," she pushes her fully extended right arm out to the side as she rocks up and down and back and forth, tossing the microphone from hand to hand, punctuating her frustration and grief. She crouches ferally on the stage and finishes the song covered in sweat, drawing out a final "raining all the time" for almost one-eighth of the entire song time. The song seemingly pours out of her, and Horne appears powerless to control her emotional response to the music.

She is controlling it, of course, just as she controlled her presentation of self in the 1940s. The discourse suggesting that singers "lose themselves" in the emotion of their songs mirrors the naturalist paradigm that actors present their own intensely felt emotions when in character. Further, the naturalist paradox that there are specific, nearly scientific techniques available to actors parallels the practice, rehearsal, and performance that Horne undertook to become the performer of *The Lady and Her Music*. Her film performances, mediated by MGM's training and dictates and structured by the demands of naturalist acting, revealed Horne as a dignified and even aloof black woman. Her persona offered a sharp contrast to stereotypes that suggested primitivism, excessive sexuality, and comic overemotionalism. In *The Lady and Her Music*, on the other hand, she offers herself as a sexy, strong, embattled (but still fighting) diva. In 1981, Horne had been performing in cabarets for five decades, modifying her performance to incorporate new musical styles, changing notions of black femininity, and her own biography. Though neither presentation is necessarily "true," they are both "natural," supported by discourses of naturalism linking performance with persona for singers as well as actors.

NATURALISM, AUTHENTICITY, AND THE MOVIE MUSICAL

"The musical," asserts Scott McMillin, "is arguably the major form of drama produced so far in America," a claim borne out by the large number of US theater history and dramatic literature syllabi devoted to the subject.[31] What

makes the musical uniquely American is arguably its development, from minstrelsy, nineteenth-century burlesque, and twentieth-century vaudeville through
the complex book musicals of Rodgers and Hammerstein and their descendants to concept musicals like *A Chorus Line* and *Dreamgirls*. According to Raymond Knapp, the musical's origins in earlier forms of popular entertainment
offered "the American musical . . . a jump start in acquiring the specific capacity
and implicit charge of projecting a mainstream sense of 'America'—of what
America was, what it was not, and what it might become." Further, musicals
accounted for many of the songs on the *Billboard* Top Forty, at least until the
1960s, making their audiences a "community with songs to be shared, providing
at least some basis for achieving a sense of unity" among geographically, ethni-
cally, economically, and culturally diverse groups.[32]

Knapp discusses community in theatrical musicals; Jane Feuer takes up the
question of community in movie musicals by focusing on the genre's rhetorical
and cinematic conventions. She argues that the movie musical, more than any
other genre, "perceives the gap" between performer and audience because of its
specifically theatrical and popular culture antecedents. The sense of community
that comes from tapping toes in the audience along with Al Jolson on the vaudeville stage, as well as the frisson of liveness such performances engender, cannot
be replicated in the movie theater. Instead, movie musicals in the Classic Hollywood era offer "'community' as an ideal concept. In basing its value system on
community, the musical . . . creat[es] humanistic folk relations in the films; these
folk relations in turn act to cancel out the economic values and relations associated with mass art."[33] This community, argues Richard Dyer, represents a utopic
America where happiness bursts from its citizens and is expressed in exuberant
song and dance. Of course, as Dyer points out, this community is largely limited to whites, and the movie musical "disturbingly constructs a vision of race"
by excluding blacks from the "physical and cultural spaces of other peoples."[34]
Horne's roles in all-black productions like *The Duke Is Tops, Cabin in the Sky*,
and *Stormy Weather* as well as her "pillar songs" in other musicals make Dyer's
point abundantly clear.

Many film historians, including Dyer, understand Lena Horne's Hollywood
career as an inevitable result of white racism: MGM needed a beautiful black
woman to appear in its spectacular movie musicals but also needed to be able
to cut those appearances for southern distributors refusing to show films with
black performers. Though institutional racism undoubtedly contributed to
Horne's Hollywood "failure," the conventions of the movie musical, shaped by
both minstrel performance and the dictates of the naturalist paradigm, limited
Horne's roles to the familiar and presumably natural "high yaller gal" or tragic
mulatto. Her film roles, as the readings of "Stormy Weather" suggest, were largely
understood as performances of an authentic self (a claim I make on behalf of
all the actresses in this study). In Horne's case, historical tradition as well as the

apparatuses of the studio system supported a particularly racialized interpretation of character and performer.

Raymond Knapp condemns the minstrel tradition, asserting that "blackface minstrelsy . . . has stained the history of musical theater in American with the seemingly indelible imprint of burned cork, grotesquely painted smiles, and whitely protruding eyes."[35] Certainly this stain is shameful, but the structure of the minstrel show, borrowed by female burlesque troupes like Lydia Thompson and the British Blondes as well as early-twentieth-century vaudeville shows,[36] presented audiences with different musical styles, dramatic reenactments, and comic moments loosely organized around a common theme. Structurally, US stage and film musicals are direct descendants of minstrel shows. Further, as Knapp points out, "minstrelsy established and maintained an important generative link between the theatrical stage and music that was genuinely popular."[37] Eager audience members purchased minstrel sheet music, often featuring engravings of key performance moments, and enjoyed the songs in their homes, just as later audiences purchased soundtrack albums and listened to movie musical songs on their radios while reading fan magazines.[38] Burlesque, on the other hand, used topical humor and local references (as well as the spectacle of scantily clad women) for its appeal, making it less easily consumable outside of the theater or by a mass audience. Second, says Knapp, minstrel "music was presented first and foremost in coordination with either narrative aims or choreographed movement (or both)."[39] The specialty acts of the vaudeville stage were ordered for maximum performance impact—a sentimental ballad followed a flea circus and was followed in turn by a raucous dance and then a fire-eater—rather than narrative, and dancers were not always singers, or vice versa. Linking narrative and song, minstrel shows thus suggested the format for early musicals as well as populist theatrical entertainments.

At the same time, "the minstrel show was very much in the aggregate vein," explains Martin Rubin, "a conglomeration of diverse parts in which each act was presented as a self-contained unit designed to stop the show."[40] In important ways, Horne's appearance in aggregate musicals that allowed her songs to be cut for southern distribution followed the tradition of nineteenth-century minstrel shows. Northerners, the main white audience for both Horne's films and blackface minstrelsy, might well have made connections between Horne's "pillar songs" and the high yaller gal of minstrel tradition on the basis of form as well as content.

In terms of narrative, antebellum minstrel shows presented an idealized version of plantation life, marked by comedy based on demeaning racial stereotypes as well as nostalgia for simpler, happier times. Theater historians generally use the Irish American Thomas D. Rice's 1830 debut of his blackface "Jim Crow" dance at New York City's Bowery Theatre as the origin of US minstrelsy. In 1843, Dan Emmett's Virginia Minstrels mounted a full-length production of the kinds of blackface specialty acts that had been crowding northern, urban stages for the last decade.[41] Like Rice, Emmett's troupe spawned imitations, and by the late 1840s minstrelsy was the most popular form of theatrical entertainment in the northern United States. These minstrel shows, explains Eric Lott, featured white male performers "made up with facial blacking of greasepaint or burnt cork, and adorned in outrageously oversized and/or ragged 'Negro' costumes."[42] According to Robert Toll, the minstrel show generally followed a tripartite structure: a "walkaround," or exchange between the interlocutor and the other members of the troupe focused on jokes and comic patter; an olio of novelty acts, including wench songs, stump speeches, dances, and acrobatics; and a one-act skit, usually depicting plantation life but sometimes burlesquing familiar plays or topics of local interest. Standard characters included the grotesque and sexually voracious "funny old gal"; the dandy and his foil, a simple-minded "Jim Crow" character; elderly, gentle "Uncle Tom" figures; and the wench, or high yaller gal.[43]

Nineteenth-century audiences understood these minstrel characters and minstrel songs as authentic depictions of black life. As Jennifer Fuller points out, "blackface performance was regarded as 'realistic' in many ways, no matter how ridiculous it may look and sound to us now. Blackface performers were praised for approximating the audience's notion of 'real' blackness."[44] Rice's blackface character was based, he claimed, on a real black stableman's song and dance; he further secured the performance's authenticity by his costume. Cuff, a porter at his hotel, loaned Rice his own clothes, hat, and shoes for the performance, at least according to Rice.[45] Following Rice's template, minstrel groups authenticated their performances by claiming inspiration for the songs, skits, and characters from "real" blacks they'd seen on northern streets or trips down south. Naming themselves "Virginia Minstrels," "Plantation Singers," or "Georgia Serenaders" even if they'd never been below the Mason-Dixon line fortified their southern bona fides. So complete was this illusion, claims Lott, that many audience members, including Mark Twain's mother, believed they were seeing authentic, biologically black performers on New York stages.[46]

Of course, wench characters seem to especially test the bounds of authentic performance. Played by men, wenches were nonetheless read by audiences as beautiful women: the nineteenth-century actress and feminist Olive Logan described the performers as "marvelously well fitted by nature for it, having well-defined soprano voices, plump shoulders, beardless faces, and tiny hands and feet."[47] Further, extant photographs and engravings of wench performers do not always represent them as blacked up, suggesting that their light skin was explicitly contrasted with their funny old gal and male counterparts.[48] At the same time, as Peter Stanfield points out, the wench characters "continued [minstrelsy's] common project of feminizing blackness."[49] In antebellum minstrel shows in particular, signs of masculinity (such as large shoes and even pants visible beneath the wench's skirts) coexisted with the femininity portrayed in song, hair, and makeup of the performer, casting doubt on the possibility of legitimate black masculinity.

In antebellum minstrel shows, wench songs were most often sung *about* mulatto women rather than by them. Annemarie Bean suggests that minstrelsy "combined both the erotic and the commodification of the sexual being of the characters, usually involving a mulatta wench and two darker skinned men rivaling for her attention."[50] The wench had no voice of her own and was presented as an object for the audience as well as within the narrative and dramaturgical structure. This love triangle was rarely resolved in minstrel shows; just as the tragic mulatto of legitimate drama and Hollywood film is unable to find love with white men because of her taint of blackness nor with black men because they are inferior to her white blood,[51] the wench remains untouched and unloved by the other minstrel players, despite their de rigueur presence. According to the historian William J. Mahar, for example, the Virginia Minstrels' first show included the "Lucy Long Walk Around," performed with a silent, cross-dressed performer as Long. The singer narrates his courtship and marriage to "Miss Lucy," and describes her as attractive and a good dancer.[52] As Bean points out, the effect of the lyrics about the beauty of silent but visible black bodies "assured their value as sexual objects" and gave audiences license to project their own desires onto male minstrels impersonating beautiful black women.[53] In general, wench songs described black women (often portrayed onstage in light or no makeup and elaborately costumed) "as objects of male desire, . . . as defenseless victims of abduction or early death, and as ideal subjects for sentimental veneration."[54] Several of these songs were about interrupted courtships or violently ended marriages. "Lucy Neal," an extremely popular song that existed in several versions, told the story of a mixed-race woman loved by a black man, from his perspective. Their romance is interrupted by "a nigger with a wooly lip" claiming he is betrothed to Lucy. This gentleman "pull'd out a cane of steel/An' run himself right into it." His convenient suicide allows the two to marry, but when Lucy bears a child with telltale resemblances to the "wooly lipped" gentleman, the singer leaves her, broken-hearted.[55] William Mahar credits the popularity of lost-love songs to an acknowledgment of the actual breakup of slave families coexistent with experiences of "similar disruptions, broken promises, or breaches of contract among audience members."[56] These stories, then, allowed audience members to sentimentalize both their own romantic misadventures and the material consequences of slavery for black families, especially when voiced by white men in blackface, an established and obvious audience surrogate.

Some antebellum wench songs were sung by the men playing the tragic mulatto, of course. Cross-dressed Dan Bryant "grieve[d] and repine[d]" because her beloved chose a sailor's life instead of her.[57] "I Dreamt I Lived in Hotel Halls" recalls a young woman's dream "dat buck niggers sought my hand/ . . . wid kisses dat no poor wench could withstand" even though she "lobed Coon still de same," demonstrating, according to Mahar, that love is "no less dear" among the working-class whites and free blacks than "any other New Yorkers."[58] Performance conventions, however, determined that wenches were the object rather than subject of the songs, and so female impersonators who sang and danced as well as looked the part were relatively rare.

In minstrelsy's second phase, after the Civil War, wenches became even more sympathetic and sentimental. Robert Toll remarks that these wenches were "hard to win and harder to hold. . . . Yaller gals . . . provided coquettish flirtations, happy romances, and sad, untimely deaths."[59] Just as on the antebellum stage, they were desirable but duplicitous. The most successful of the postbellum wenches was Francis Leon, who used blackface makeup to "give the appearance of a mulatto woman, and not a grotesque stereotype," becoming the "ideal subject for fantasy" and setting the template for wench (now usually referred to as prima donna) performance into the twentieth century. Heather May further explains that Leon and other prima donnas were remarkably virtuosic performers. Leon was able to credibly sing soprano parts and was a skilled dancer "capable of standing gracefully en pointe" who played heroines ranging from Bellini's operatic Norma to those of the sensational "leg show" *The Black Crook*.[60] This image of the mulatto, singing her own tragic songs and gracefully performing her own dances, largely replaced the silent wench for post–Civil War minstrel audiences.

By the early twentieth century, roughly a generation before Horne began singing and dancing in the Cotton Club's chorus line, according to May, white male impersonators like Leon were largely replaced by black female performers who "found that white minstrel images were so powerfully accepted . . . that they had no choice but to follow suit if they wanted to be successful."[61] At least until the 1920s, nearly all black performers, regardless of gender, genre, or venue, played in blackface, wearing the same flat black makeup, exaggerated mouths and eyes, fuzzy wigs, and white gloves as white performers in minstrel shows. These performers most directly influenced Horne's own reception in Hollywood films, as they were relatively familiar to both black and white audiences, whose parents or grandparents and even themselves might have attended black minstrel shows, either on white vaudeville stages or through the Theatre Owners Booking Association (TOBA) black vaudeville circuit at the turn of the century. The TOBA stars known as the Black Patti Troubadours, for example, toured the northeastern United States from the mid-1870s through the 1890s. Their "main attraction," claim the vaudeville historians Lynn Abbott and Doug Seroff, was the female minstrel Sissieretta Jones, "universally accepted as 'the greatest singer of her race,'" performing familiar operatic arias alongside traditional minstrel humor and variety acts, just as prima donnas like Leon had done a decade before. In 1902, Ernest Hogan and Billy McClain founded the Smart Set, a touring company that produced original musical comedies for both black and white audiences. By the 1910s, when S. H. Dudley had taken over the Smart Set, it combined minstrel farce, black vernacular dance, and the conventions of main-stream musical comedy.[62] As Jayna Brown chronicles, TOBA was simultaneously presenting charismatic female performers like Ma Rainey and Bessie Smith, sing-ing innuendo-laden blues numbers interspersed with raucous humor, clearly influenced by minstrelsy's early funny old gals. These numbers were co-opted by "coon shouters" like Fanny Brice and Sophie Tucker for white vaudeville audi-ences and early film.[63] Horne's Hollywood persona negotiated this ambivalent racial and sexual inheritance by casting Horne as the pure but doomed tragic mulatto from the minstrel stage, separating her from the sexualized blues women or grotesque comic figures, as I discuss below.

Thus, the movie musical that provided Horne's entrée to Hollywood is clearly rooted in a minstrel tradition, not least of which is the emphasis on spectacle over narrative movement and character development. At the same time, the peculiari-ties of the movie musical as genre are also linked to the naturalist conventions of Classical Hollywood narratives, especially naturalist performance. According to traditional accounts, Rodgers and Hammerstein's 1943 stage musical *Oklahoma!* introduced the integrated musical; its critical and commercial success spurred the rapid growth of integrated musicals on Broadway as well as in film. MGM in particular was associated with this genre and produced dozens of musicals every year that combined story and song. Sean Griffin's definition of integrated musi-cals clarifies their ties to naturalism: "the musical numbers . . . are 'integral' to the plot—either by revealing important character traits or by furthering the nar-rative itself. Thus, in integrated musicals, characters break into song when they should be talking, instead of only when they are 'putting on a show' . . . providing the sense of a unified and cohesive work in which all the pieces are in concert with each other."[64] Thus, not only *Oklahoma!* but also naturalism spurred the growth of integrated musicals.

Black performers are an especial problem for the 1940s and 1950s integrated musical: the Production Code forbade "miscegenation" and so kept black and white characters segregated on onscreen, making it difficult to develop narra-tives that featured both races in personal or professional relationships. There-fore, except for the all-black productions *The Duke Is Tops, Cabin in the Sky,* and *Stormy Weather,* Horne appears almost exclusively in specialty numbers (as when white characters visit a nightclub) in integrated musicals, or, more usu-ally, in unintegrated musicals. This no doubt led to her devaluation as a seri-ous performer capable of legitimate roles in musicals and especially other films. Of course, some musicals are hybrid, especially when nonwhite performers are shoehorned into the action. Carmen Miranda's first US film, *Down Argentine Way,* is an integrated musical except for Miranda's two nightclub numbers. In *The Duchess of Idaho,* for example, numbers like "Let's Choo Choo to Idaho" burst spontaneously from Van Johnson and Connie Haines; the black Jubilaires (playing Pullman porters, shoeshine boys, and other train workers) join in with their variation in song and dance. Other numbers, such as Esther Williams's water ballets, which open and close the film, and Lena Horne's nightclub song "Baby, Come out of the Clouds" occur when the main characters take in a show and are watched by audience members onscreen as well as in the movie theater. The integrated musical contrasts unintegrated or aggregate musicals in which the plot is interrupted by performance. Performers with little or no connection to the narrative appear, perform, and disappear. A 1944 review in the *New York Herald Tribune* condemned aggregate musicals as "a hodgepodge of specialty numbers decked out in garish color photography."[65] As this review indicates, integrated musicals were considered more artistic and legitimate. At the same time, integrated musicals are less realistic than aggregate musicals, as they do away with the fiction that performers are rehearsing for and presenting a professional performance. The aggregate or unintegrated musical allows for diegetic numbers, that is, those "that are called for by the book."[66] Backstage musicals, from Andy Hardy's adventures finding a barn and putting on a show, to classics like *The Band Wagon* and *Summer Stock*, only and always have diegetic numbers. In the integrated musical, on the other hand, performers burst into song for no plot-related reason. Rather, they sing in order to express emotion, a crucial distinction.

Integrated musicals may be fantastic (think of Esther Williams's water ballets in *Dangerous When Wet* or *Skirts Ahoy!*),[67] but they are critically understood (both then and now) as coherent, unified, and even natural. The rise of the integrated musical on stage and screen is often linked to the entertainment industry's response to the pressures of World War II. As Dyer argues, the integrated musical offers a utopic vision of the world, one that holds out hope for a rosy future and offers an escape from everyday problems.[68] Further, as Altman explains, in many integrated musicals, as in *Oklahoma!*, the musical numbers "absorb the individual into the group" in order to join onscreen players and offscreen audiences in this utopic community. In part, this community is achieved through the fiction that song and dance are "not art but the expression of emotion." Successful movie musical performers "are most often 'natural' singers . . . who seem to sing effortlessly, without training, in a manner which evokes not the opera or concert stage but the expression of personal emotion" so that the audience can easily put him or herself in the place of the singing character.[69]

Other scholars, such as Steven Cohan, stress the technical achievements of these musicals, arguing that the integrated narrative and performance justified the lavish spectacles.[70] Technology also played a part in the creation of "natural" singing, however. Invented in 1929, the playback system permitted manipulations of the recorded song, allowing orchestra and voice to be recorded separately from each other and from the filming of the musical performance segment. This technology, argues Altman, "contributed markedly" to the rise of singers "who, having left their physical efforts in the recording room, can act out the spiritual side of singing for the camera."[71] The focus of the songs then becomes the psychological motivations of the characters and their expression of emotion.

Scott McMillin, though arguing that integrated musicals operate on principles of difference rather than cohesion, admits that integrated musicals seem to deepen "the psychology of the characters, as though the way now [stands] open to the presentation of real people in real situations."[72] The songs are not interruptions of the narrative but instead offer crucial information, especially about the emotional lives of the characters. In *Guys and Dolls*, when Sarah Brown cuts loose like a ringing bell in Cuba, she reveals what the audience already knows: she's the perfect woman for Sky Masterson despite their surface differences. In fact, Arthur Knight points out that songs in the integrated musical are "an imitation or approximation" of what the characters would say, and "that, in consequence," music and story will seem to have a "'natural' or 'realistic' relation."[73] When characters erupt into song in integrated musicals, their songs are understood as a genuine response to stimuli from the events of the plot or relationships with other characters: to use a cliché of naturalist acting, the songs are *motivated*.

Traditional genealogies of the integrated musical gloss over other the theatrical and cinematic contexts in which *Oklahoma!* and Golden Age movie musicals developed. Integrated musicals, which suggest that song and dance are a "natural" expression of character emotion, is discursively as well as institutionally linked to American naturalism and even Method acting. The naturalist paradigm also facilitated the integrated musical's status as the jewel in the studio system's crown. By the 1940s, naturalism was understood as the most recognizable as well as most artistically and ethically legitimate style of acting, and the integrated musical's legitimacy was tied to naturalism's dominance as a performance as well as cinematic style. Though most histories of American naturalism locate it primarily within "serious" drama and tend to associate it with male performers like James Dean and Marlon Brando, this project demonstrates how actors of both genders and all genres used naturalist techniques, especially through Russell's, Williams's, and Gabor's case studies. All classical Hollywood actors, whether starring in serious drama, romantic comedy, or the movie musical, were produced by the same machine, which drew on discourses of naturalist acting in similar ways.

The movie musical is generically tied to naturalist drama as well. Steve Vineberg describes the typical naturalist play (drawing on examples from Anton Chekhov to Clifford Odets to Tennessee Williams) as driven by subtext: words and actions "make interior rather than narrative sense," and non sequiturs and unexpected actions are the product of hidden emotions. Individual actors use their bodies and voices (rather than dialogue or action) to communicate meaning not made explicit in narrative. Vineberg describes James Dean in *Rebel without a Cause* (a paradigmatic naturalist actor giving a paradigmatic naturalist performance): "Even the simple act of drinking milk focuses so much of his energy that it becomes emblematic: He swigs it from the bottle as if he needed to slake a thirst too deep to be merely physical."[74] I insist that songs in the movie musical serve the same function and communicate through similar registers. For example, Julie Andrews's outpouring of "The Sound of Music" as she runs through a mountain landscape is clearly framed as evidence of her emotional and physical passion. We know that this exuberantly singing woman is destined for romantic love, not the convent. When Laurey and Curly sing in *Oklahoma!* that "people will say we're in love," they are using the song to express emotions they are unable to articulate through dialogue. Songs in the integrated musical are the expression of inner emotion, even emotion that is hidden from the characters but is accessed through the performer's training and virtuosity.

Regardless of whether a song's naturalism derives from its relationship to narrative (as in the unintegrated musical) or its presumed expression of emotion (as in the integrated musical), it is always already marked as performance. Jerome Delamater explains that "acting in the musical includes a kind of performance that is not just an impersonation of fictional characters but is a presentation of the performer's singing and dancing abilities," further linking character and role.[75] Though Horne's appearances in unintegrated musicals do not require her to develop extensive characterizations (she generally plays a "singer" in a nightclub, as in *Duchess of Idaho*, or is one of dozens of other performers presenting a number or two, as in *The Ziegfeld Follies*), she must dramatize the song, embodying the lyrics and voicing their meaning as well as hitting the notes. In this way, Horne is clearly presenting an image or persona if not a character, one that is generally assumed to correspond with her own personality.

Of course, audiences know that actors are often lip-syncing during filming rather than recording live on the set. Further, most audiences are aware that other performers sometimes substitute for lead actors' voices. The plot of *Singin' in the Rain*, for example, turns on this convention: Debbie Reynolds/Kathy Selden speaks and sings for Jean Hagen/Lina Lamont in the film-within-a-film *The Dancing Cavalier*. Ironically, Reynolds's own singing voice was reportedly dubbed "because she could not reach high notes," and Gene Kelly "postdubbed the tap sounds for Debbie Reynolds' dance in the 'Good Morning' number" because she was out of sync with him and Donald O'Connor.[76] Even so, as Steven Cohan argues, because movie musicals employ direct address during production numbers, they heighten "the audience's sense of not observing the star play a character so much as witnessing her or his own authenticity, charisma, and talent without the mediation of fictional narrative or cinematic technology."[77] As with all Classical Hollywood films, movie musicals efface the means of production in order to seamlessly integrate narrative, character, mise-en-scène, and performance for maximum audience identification.

As Adrienne L. McLean's discussion of Rita Hayworth's dancing makes clear, however, these moments offer a kind of agency for performers who use their bodies or voices to intervene in narratives that otherwise limit their independence. Just as Esther Williams is really swimming and really undercutting a domestic female ideology that suggests women are vulnerable and dependent, Lena Horne is really singing, however that's been manipulated from initial recording to finished film. In Horne's case, her vocal performances intervene in a cultural (rather than movie) narrative of racial limitation that structures Hollywood policies and protocols, audience bias, and traditions of African American representation. Her voice and body, whether she's standing alone and singing with a flower in her hair or she's playing a character like Selina Rogers or Georgia Brown, challenge racist and limiting assumptions about black femininity.

THE REFINED, RESERVED, AND REAL LENA HORNE

Richard Dyer's simultaneous critique and celebration of movie musicals as "only entertainment" stresses that they show us, "head-on as it were, what utopia would feel like rather than how it would be organized." This utopia, he continues, is marked by the principles of abundance, energy, intensity, transparency, and community: their spectacular song-and-dance sequences offer lavish locales and animated performers overwhelmed by emotion, and their narratives depict sincere romantic relationships and a sense of belonging between characters as well as between performers and the audiences who idolize them. Both spectacle and plot coincide to produce pleasure through utopic vision. Of course, calling "attention to the gap between what is and what could be" engenders contradiction—within narrative and between narrative and spectacle—the films must "manage . . . [and] make them seem to disappear."[78] That musicals don't always succeed offers the potential for ideological intervention.

Dyer's strongest critique of the movie musical's utopianism is, of course, its disappearance of people of color, especially African Americans, from whom many of its musical and dance conventions were appropriated. Movie musicals, he explains, suggest that "bursting from the confines of life by singing your heart out and dancing when you feel like it" is the affective experience of utopia, though it is only "whites' privilege to be able to do this." Blacks are "nothing but entertainers," and their singing and dancing is for the express pleasure of whites. Unlike the white *characters*, who "have lives, especially love lives but also careers, vexatious relatives, personal problems of one kind or another," black *entertainers* have "no such wider life . . . which deprives [them] of the emotional resonances that the surrounding story and characterization give to numbers in musicals."[79] Though Dyer's argument is persuasive (and anecdotally introduced through Horne's appearance in *That's Entertainment III*), I want to reconsider it in light of Horne's all-black musical, *Cabin in the Sky*.[80]

Based on the 1940 stage musical starring Dooley Wilson as the gambling Little Joe whose soul is fought over by Lucifer Jr. and the Lawd's General, Ethel Waters as his long-suffering wife, Petunia, and the dancer Katherine Dunham as Georgia Brown, *Cabin in the Sky* was produced by MGM's Freed Unit in 1943 as a black-and-white, integrated musical starring Waters, Eddie "Rochester" Anderson as Little Joe, and Lena Horne as Georgia Brown. The film also includes cameos by Bill Bailey, Louis Armstrong, and the Duke Ellington Orchestra. Featuring a terrifying tornado, several nightclub numbers, and sentimental ballads ("Happiness Is a Thing Called Joe," "Love Me Tomorrow," and the title song), the narrative follows Petunia and the General's attempts to keep Joe virtuous while Lucifer Jr. and Georgia tempt him with money, music, gambling, and sex. At the end, Georgia repents, but Joe and Petunia are dead after a shootout—and the tornado— destroys the nightclub where much of the action takes place. On the stairway to the pearly gates, Petunia pleads one last time for Joe's soul, God relents, and the two ascend to heaven surrounded by black cherubs. Finally, Joe wakes up from what has been a dream all along, ready to give up gambling and live happily ever after with Petunia.

 Cabin in the Sky is understood as racist, then and now. Though its producer, Arthur Freed, promised a "dignified presentation of a peace-loving and loyal people," Hall Johnson, leader of the Hall Johnson Choir featured in the film, complained that an early draft of the script would be "immeasurably improved when [the language was] translated into honest-to-goodness Negro dialect" instead of the imaginary malapropisms of the scriptwriter's fantasy black language.[81] After its release, critical response ranged from the *New York Times*'s approval of its "inspiring expression of a simple people's faith in the hereafter and a spicy slice of their zest for earthy pleasures" to Ramona Lewis's charge in the *Amsterdam News* that it was "an insult masking behind the label of folklore."[82] Clearly, whether or not critics approved of *Cabin*'s depiction of black folk culture, they recognized its reliance on folk tropes. Further, the film itself seems to bolster its legitimacy through reference to folklore: the opening postcredit scroll explains that "powerful thoughts have been handed down through . . . the legend, the folktale, and the fantasy" and that *Cabin* should be understood as working in that tradition. James Naremore captures this representational ambiguity by pointing out that MGM mobilized "imagery of plantation-style darkies" but also allowed the film's characters "to behave like something other than minstrel-show caricatures."[83] The 2006 Turner Entertainment DVD includes a disclaimer that scrolls before the film (and its own disclaimer) to explain that the narratives and character presented "were wrong then and are wrong today" but insists it's an important document of the United States' aesthetic and racial past. This disclaimer points audiences toward a historical reading rather than a focus on narrative, character, or spectacle. Though the film is not without retrograde stereotypes, nor does it have the same high production values of other 1943 MGM musicals (which included the Esther Williams vehicle *Bathing Beauty*), it's worthy of more than a dismissal based on those faults or even recognition solely for its documentary value. In fact, *Cabin in the Sky* is remarkable for the way it negotiates racial stereotype through generic convention as well as Horne's "refined" depiction of temptress Georgia Brown.

In many ways, *Cabin in the Sky*'s depiction of happy, poor blacks singing on earth while hoping for glory in heaven is quite retrograde and even advocates a dangerous ideology for blacks to embrace: rather than working to improve material conditions now, they should simply wait for a heavenly reward. At the same time, however, its musical numbers are integrated into the narrative in much the same way as the numbers in other MGM musicals, share their vision of utopia, and are just as often anchored by consumption. For example, Little Joe surprises Petunia on her birthday with a washing machine—even though their home doesn't have electricity. At first Petunia cries because "ain't nobody got no right to be as happy as I am," but Joe soon asks her to sing, accompanying her with his own whistling and a small guitar. Now joyful, Petunia sings "Taking a Chance on Love," one of the musical's most memorable numbers. Tapper Bill Bailey, playing one of Little Joe's buddies, begins an exuberant tap dance in their small kitchen. Even Little Joe gets up to dance, clownishly landing in the sink before gently soft-shoeing with Petunia. The two are graceful and harmonious, and their dancing bodies project mutual love and respect. When Petunia begins the final chorus with a throaty growl, however, Little Joe's shocked "Petunia!" brings her back to the pleasant melody, and she trills the final lines wrapped in Joe's embrace and approval.

Though Bailey's tap-dancing echoes dozens of other similar dances performed by blacks in 1910s–1960s film, and though Little Joe's clowning, complete with popped eyes and wide grin, might bring to mind minstrel stereotypes, the joy they express by "singing and dancing when they feel like it" is no different than that of Hannah (Judy Garland) and Don (Fred Astaire) singing and dancing in *Easter Parade*. Dressed to the nines and about to become engaged, they don their chapeaux and celebrate the joys of fancy dress with "Easter Parade," the duet that closes the film. Hannah projects and gestures as though she's playing to the back of the auditorium, Don clowns and even sits on *her* knee, and the two joyfully dance out the door. Further, Hannah began the movie as a tomboyish and graceless dancer, but in this scene she's finally an elegant equal of Don, who approves of her refinement just as Joe approves of Petunia when she's sentimental rather than earthy. Of course, Hannah and Don's elegantly costumed, slender white bodies have different connotations than the casually dressed, fleshy Petunia and Little Joe. Even so, both couples (and Bailey) hyperexpressively sing and dance, the joy occasioned by a new hat or an unusable washing machine equated with their own love for each other and pleasure in their ability to participate in consumer culture. Viewed on its own, the sequence in *Cabin in the Sky* is uncomfortably clichéd, but when viewed within the context of other integrated musicals of the 1930s–1950s, it clearly participates in the genre's evocations of utopia. As such, the number is perhaps even subversive. If, as Dyer suggests, blacks in the movie musical are never allowed to sing and dance for themselves, this representation of distinctly black bodies citing the conventions of all-white musicals, female blues singers (through Petunia's throaty chorus), and even minstrelsy registers as an alternative to other such depictions. The song "bursts forth" from black narrative and characters rather than being staged for a white audience. Singing and dancing utopia with and through black bodies, *Cabin in the Sky* subverts traditional representations of both black characters and the movie musical itself.

Horne's performance continues this subversion. Her character, Georgia Brown, contrasts Petunia physically as well as morally. Georgia follows Lucifer Jr.'s orders to seduce Joe away from his wife and virtuous life. Dressed in a black skirt, a black-and-white dotted blouse tied into a halter, and a jaunty hat, she heads to Joe's home to tell him he's won a sweepstakes. She hesitates by the gate, plucks a magnolia blossom from a tree, tosses her hat away, and pins the enormous flower in her hair. Sauntering into the garden, she rests in a hammock, one leg bent and one arm curved over her head. When she tells Joe about the sweepstakes, he promises her a diamond bracelet, a fur coat, and her own nightclub. Georgia embraces him just as Petunia comes home. Furious, Petunia throws Joe

Figure 15: Glamorous Lena Horne, singing "Honey in the Honeycomb" in *Cabin in the Sky*, 1943, MGM.

out and he begins his descent to vice. Petunia is heartbroken, but Georgia seems indifferent to both her suffering and Joe's affection.

Everything about Georgia contrasts with Petunia—She tosses away her hat, something the frugal Petunia would never do; wears form-fitting, highly contrasting clothes; is slender and light-skinned; and speaks in a low and silky voice rather than Petunia's shrieks of anger. As Richard Dyer points out, "as a very light-skinned black woman, [Horne] was unplaceable except as the ultimate temptress in an all-black musical."[84] Her physical lightness results in Horne's typecasting as a version of the minstrel wench, desirable but untrustworthy and existing only as a foil to the virtuous mammy or funny old gal character recalled by Petunia's alternately maternal and screechingly angry behavior.

The Georgia/Petunia (or Horne/Waters) contrast is especially evident in the song "Honey in the Honeycomb" (see figures 15 and 16). As this number demonstrates, Waters's Petunia is earthier, more energetic, and more emotionally nuanced than Horne's Georgia Brown. "Honey in the Honeycomb" is part of Georgia's nightclub act at Jim Henry's Paradise Nightclub. When Georgia sings it, the raucous patrons are quieted by Jim Henry's (Ernest Whitman) piercing whistle. Dressed in a white satin dress and feather boa, and dripping in diamonds, Georgia sits on the bar with one leg gracefully crossed over the other throughout the number. Her bare shoulders, neck, and hands are visible, but the dress always covers her legs, and the feathers hide any hint of cleavage. The number is short: introduced with a muted trumpet wail, Georgia explains that her peculiar charm is that she has "love in me" just like there's always sugar in the cane, bubbles in champagne, sap in every tree, and honey in the honeycomb. As in *Stormy Weather*, Horne's arms are gracefully curved, never raised above her chest, and never fully extended. Despite the innuendo of the lyrics and the sparkle in her eyes, she's mildly flirtatious rather than sultry and seductive. Bathed in light, her skin glows and gleams, and her dress and diamonds sparkle. Because she's sitting on the bar and nearly always shot in close-up, she sings to the camera rather than Little Joe or the audience. Removed from them by camera framing, skin color, and attitude, Horne/Georgia seems infinitely desirable but also infinitely untouchable.

In the film's finale, Petunia arrives at Jim Henry's Paradise dressed in a dark sequined lace and satin dress with a lace mantilla to demand a divorce and half of Little Joe's sweepstakes winnings. After having a drink with Domino Johnson (John W. Sublett), she tells Jim Henry to instruct the orchestra "to put me in the mood so I can give out. . . . I suddenly feel a musical urge." Taking control of the audience and Little Joe (rather than relying on Jim Henry's signal), Petunia sings a jazzier version of "Honey in the Honeycomb." Her version is quicker than Georgia's and pitched about a third higher. Standing against the same bar and shot in close-up, Petunia sings casually without moving her arms but bobbing her head and shoulders in rhythm. She addresses the lyrics to Jim Henry, Domino,

Figure 16: Ethel Waters unglamorously singing (and dancing) "Honey in the Honey-comb" with John W. Sublett in *Cabin in the Sky*, 1943, MGM.

and Little Joe specifically, underlining key phrases to audience members with an eye roll or a murmured "uh huh." After finishing the chorus, Domino pulls her onto the dance floor for a modified lindy, including a back fall and high kick. Petunia grabs Domino's fedora and holds it over her head, high-kicking at it with both legs and then kicking out to each side. As the music slows for the song's final lines, Domino and Petunia execute a triple-step rock-step combo before Petunia turns with a full-body shimmy, backs Domino up against the bar, and presses back and into him. When the song ends, another immediately begins and the two slow-drag across the floor. Unlike Georgia, Petunia is eager and able to touch and be touched.

Waters is a charismatic performer, and she handily outsings and outacts Horne in *Cabin in the Sky*, but she doesn't look as good while she's doing it. Waters is full-figured, and her dress isn't as well-cut as Horne's: the satin bunches around her hips, and the bodice gapes over her relatively flat chest. Further, her dancing is sloppy, especially when contrasted with Sublett's smoothly intricate footwork, quick jumps, and fluid dips. Though Petunia's characterization as a Christian wife explains her poor dancing skills, the lack of abandon or propriety with which she throws her body across the screen is jarring, especially since her relationship with Little Joe has been framed as sentimentally romantic and even maternal rather than sensual and erotic. Appropriating Georgia's "coochie" number, Petunia is loose and unabashed about flashing her legs and shimmying her hips for the camera and the nightclub audience. Horne, on the other hand, looks glorious if a little stiff in her musical numbers. Though her face is animated, it remains pleasant; that is, the emotions of the song never disturb its gleaming and placid surface. Further, focusing the camera on her face rather than her body (a body that is already relatively still rather than shimmying across a dance floor) de-eroticizes her. She's not a body (certainly not a fleshy, messy body) but a voice and a face. Her movement vocabulary works together with the film's cinematography to deemphasize her sensuality and undercut her character's presumed seductiveness.

Critics noticed the misalignment between Horne's performance style and her character. In his admiring biography of Horne, James Haskins noted that "she infused the role with as much dignity as she could muster and . . . was not believable as a slut."[85] She is physically graceful and vocally pleasant when singing but stiff when delivering her lines. Her most seductive scene, singing "Ain't It the Truth" in a bubble bath, was cut before distribution, presumably to appease the MPPDA censors but with the further effect of keeping Georgia Brown a relatively virginal floozy.

Like her character in *Stormy Weather* and many of her "pillar songs," Horne's Georgia Brown is sophisticated and refined. Aloof instead of earthy, she is, says Gavin, "so different from the red-hot mama image of the black female entertainer."[86] Rather than activating a tradition of blues performance, Horne instead recalled the wench/tragic mulatto of the minstrel stage and subsequent film and theatrical productions. Further, comments about her sophisticated reserve reference Horne's biography as a member of the educated black middle class and NAACP as well as her singing. In this way (and because she was herself multiracial), Horne exemplified an authentic tragic mulatto, too cultured and polished to embody the sensuality supposedly natural to other black women as evidenced by their musical performances.

At the same time, Horne's "naturally" aloof performances in all-black musicals gives depth to her "pillar songs" in films like *The Duchess of Idaho, Words and Music*, and *Till the Clouds Roll By*. Separated from the other characters and from the narrative so that her segments could be cut for southern distribution, she is untouched and untouchable. These songs are equally linked to the wench songs of the antebellum minstrel show. Like most of those specialty numbers, Horne stands outside the story and embodies a stereotype rather than a character: the sad, pretty girl singing a sad, pretty song (see figure 17).

Figure 17: Lena Horne, leaning against a piano in a 1943 publicity shot.

In *Till the Clouds Roll By* (1946), Horne plays Julie in the *Show Boat* segment that opens this biopic of Jerome Kern.[87] Staged in a proscenium theater, the film opens with an African American chorus singing a particularly lighthearted version of "Ol' Man River" before being supplanted by an even larger white chorus singing the praises of southern beauties. Horne is introduced as "the beautiful Julie LaVerne." She dances next to (but not with) Kathryn Grayson (playing Magnolia Hawks) before exiting stage right. Magnolia dances with Steve Baker (Bruce Cowling), Julie's husband, instead. The spectacular and abridged musical rushes through its major numbers, one seguing into the next, until Julie's heartbroken "Can't Help Lovin' Dat Man." The film jump-cuts to Julie sitting on bales and boxes in a medium close-up, dressed in a lavender dress with purple flowers in her straight and silky hair. Though the song is written in "Negro" dialect, Horne's diction is nonetheless perfect; for example, she bites off the *t* in "dat." She looks dreamy throughout, especially as she elegantly reclines to promise that "He can come home as late as can be/Home without him ain't no home to me." The segment ends with a shot of the enthusiastic audience before again jump-cutting to Caleb Peterson reprising "Ol' Man River" surrounded by the black chorus, the white chorus ranged behind and above them. The extended musical number ends and the film proper begins.

"Can't Help Lovin' Dat Man," according to Horne's biographer James Gavin, "reveals the continued emergence of a mesmerizing actress-in-song." Three years after her leading roles in *Stormy Weather* and *Cabin in the Sky*, Horne's voice has considerably more range and power, and she'd worked with Kay Thompson on her breath control, which "really extended" her range and allowed her to hit "the notes [she] didn't know [she] could."[88] Her facial expressions include sadness, confusion, satisfaction, and defiance in addition to her earlier repertoire of "pleasant," "less pleasant," and "more pleasant." Her number in the finale, "Why Was I Born," is less emotionally rich than her characterization of Julie, however. Wearing a white Grecian dress and standing on a platform with a backdrop of gold leaves, she's part of a medley of Kern's greatest hits sung by Lucille Bremer, Kathryn Grayson, and Frank Sinatra (reprising "Ol' Man River" in the song's original "Negro" patois). It's a mournful song, and Horne barely moves her body, keeping her feet in place. Her elbows remain close to her sides, and she waves her lovely, curved hands in front of her torso and to her side. Her arms never fully extend; rather, they reach tentatively to the side before curving back again toward her body. In general, her arms encircle her body, and she seems to be retreating from the audience rather than reaching toward them with either her body or voice. This movement vocabulary, interestingly, echoes representations of wenches as engraved on nineteenth- and early-twentieth-century sheet music. While I'm not suggesting that Horne (or her producers and directors) consciously modeled her gestures on these images, the parallels are undeniable. In fact, the repetition of particular gestures instead suggests that Horne performatively cited a minstrel heritage that continued to govern how black bodies were represented and interpreted.

Though Lena Horne specialized in ballads, some of her films did have up-tempo numbers. Even so, these extended her dignified persona through costuming, gesture, and mise-en-scène. For example, Horne sings "Love," a torchy bossa nova, in *The Ziegfeld Follies* (1945), a biopic like *Till the Clouds Roll By* and offering as many opportunities for specialty numbers.[89] The sequence opens in a "Caribbean" saloon, filled with black male and female dancers and drinkers, candles in beer bottles, several parrots, and a love triangle. Two light-skinned, flashily dressed women fight over a darker-skinned man in work clothes, pulling hair, startling the birds, and knocking over drinks before one runs up a curving staircase in tears. Horne walks through the door, rests languidly against the wall, and begins explaining that "love" can be "a sweet endeavor or a dirty shame" but "love is almost never, ever the same." Horne is terrific in this Latin-inspired number, infusing the lyrics with passion and humor and moving freely through the bar setting. Unlike the rest of the working-class patrons, she's dressed brightly in a pink and green blouse with sleek green skirt, purple flowers in her hair, gold jewelry, and her requisite perfect manicure. Her clothing is more stylish than everyone else's in the bar, even the two battling women. All the patrons look at her with a mixture of interest, weariness, and confusion, sitting perfectly silent and still as she sings and salsas among them. The lyrics of "Love" demonstrate that Horne understands the complexities of love and desire. Her singing, which is energetic and knowing rather than admonitory, signals that she's above the raging jealousy that leads other women to fight over men; she can even mock their passion. She is separated from the black patrons through her clothes, certainly, but most clearly through her attitude, which oozes sophistication and energy while the others seem backward and exhausted.

"Brazilian Boogie," from MGM's 1944 *Broadway Rhythm*, operates under similar principles of separation, reinforcing Horne's dignified persona despite the number's Latin rhythm and Brazilian-inspired costuming and mise-en-scène.[90] The number, set in a nightclub, begins with a dark-skinned man in red striped pants and a vest over his bare chest beating bongo drums before it pans to another man's feet in yellow spats tapping the rhythm. The camera pans across three identical pairs of feet and up to Horne, dressed in a yellow halter and a long purple silk skirt (it matches her manicure) slit up both legs, with yellow flowers over both ears and gold earrings and bracelets that match the trim on the deep V of her neckline (see figure 18). The trim attaches her halter to her skirt in order to keep it above her navel, modesty the censors insisted upon for Horne and other actresses in "Latin" dress. She sambas with the yellow-spatted dancers and sings that the "new Brazilian boogie" is a "half-breed" because "its mammy was a samba and its pappy was swing." Backed by a singing and dancing chorus of light-skinned black women dressed in flowered halters with short red skirts or gold loincloths with lamé turbans and off-the-shoulder halters trimmed with "bones," Horne performs her most complicated movie choreography, but it's the same as or less complex than the chorus's dancing. Surrounded by male and female dancers and singers, she doesn't interact with them and barely acknowledges their presence. And though the chorus choreography emphasizes shimmies, pelvic thrusts, and hip rolls, Horne dances primarily by quickly moving her feet and gracefully waving her lovely, curving arms. In addition, her diction is perfect, and her face is relatively still, especially when compared to the wide grins and bright eyes of the chorus. The drums suggest a primitive jungle setting, and the chorus is especially exuberant (performing shimmies, buck-and-wings, and hip rolls) and underdressed (in loincloths, bare chests, and skimpy halters), but Horne remains sophisticated and poised.

Lena Horne rarely played a character, but she created a role, "Miss Lena Horne," the nightclub entertainer par excellence. This character remained

Figure 18: Lena Horne and chorines in "Brazilian Boogie" from *Broadway Rhythm*, 1944, MGM.

relatively stable and identifiable through the early 1940s into the mid-1950s, as evidenced in one of her last films, made after MGM had dropped her contract and she'd returned to recording and cabaret singing. *The Duchess of Idaho* (1950) is a spectacular if largely forgettable Esther Williams vehicle.[91] (She sings! She swims! She falls in love! She skis!) Horne sings in a nightclub visited by two supporting characters, Douglas (John Lund) and Ellen (Paula Raymond). Introduced as "Miss Lena Horne!" she enters to applause, bows her head to the crowd, and smiles before launching into "Baby, Come out of the Clouds." Her lips are very red, and her teeth are very white, matching the enormous pearls in her ears and the collared white silk crepe blouse she wears buttoned to her neck. Her hair is short and wavy, her manicure is flawless, and she wears a sea-foam green organza full skirt with a high waist and slightly darker green ribbon. As usual, she slowly walks down a staircase toward the audience before gracefully moving back and forth with her arms mostly waist high and curved inward for the majority of the song. Nearly a decade after her film debut (and after years performing mainly in cabarets), she is, however, a more energetic performer. She gestures gracefully to the heavens when begging her lover to "come out of the clouds" and love her on earth, crosses her arms to pout a bit, and even sits on a padded banquette. She waltzes introspectively on the line "if you're like an angel" and hides her face in embarrassment when she hopes it's not "just my imagination" that her lover is willing to "drop down to earth and say you'll be mine." She finishes the song with a long and drawn-out final plea for him to "come out of the clouds," her head thrown back and her mouth opened very wide. Even though she's successfully signaling the lyrics with her gestures and face, and even though her movement vocabulary has increased (she frequently rolls a wrist when raising that arm over her head), she is still the pleasant, refined singer of *Stormy Weather* or "Why Was I Born." If her body is freer, her costuming keeps her contained, with only face, hands, and glimpse of satin-shod foot visible. This is her only appearance in the film, and it repeats and even cites her performances in films during her MGM contract years. As in those films, her performance only hints at inner emotional turmoil while presenting her as naturally reserved, refined, and sophisticated.

Horne's performance style is rooted in her training at MGM. Because the studio was ostensibly grooming her to be a star like its other ingénue actresses, she was given the same makeover processes and charm school treatment as white starlets. Further, MGM's publicity and the black press stressed the studio glamorizing process and drew parallels between Horne's makeover and similar efforts on behalf of other actresses.[92] Emily Torchia, who worked in MGM's publicity department, remembered that the press loved her and that her blackness didn't present any problems in terms of placing stories about her in fan magazines or other outlets.[93] Like the other women I discuss, Horne was also featured in fan magazines and the mainstream press, though black-identified magazines and newspapers (such as *Ebony* and the *Chicago Defender*) were more likely to feature stories about her. Even so, as Megan E. Williams points out, these stories tended to follow the format of more mainstream fan outlets, focusing on Horne's "out-of-the-spotlight roles" and stressing her domestic activities and the challenges she faced as a working mother. At the same time, *Ebony* and *Crisis* (the NAACP's press organ) also highlighted her commitment to civil rights, particularly notable because most Hollywood stars were presented as resolutely apolitical. Of course, Horne's relatively liberal politics were assumed to be a rallying point for most of her black fans; Esther Williams's politics, on the other hand, had the potential of alienating large segments of her heterogeneous mass audience, who presumably held a variety of political and social viewpoints. Finally, like Jane Russell, Horne was mobilized as a World War II pinup, albeit one directed exclusively at black servicemen. According to Williams, *Ebony* magazine asserted that Horne's "most enthusiastic fans" were GIs and named her "the champion pinup girl of Negro America."[94] In many ways, Horne's experience under an MGM contract paralleled that of white starlets, and her publicity tended to focus on similar points of identification for her audiences.

Like other aspiring stars, Horne was also subject to MGM's exacting (and exactly homogeneous) beauty standards. According to her biographer James Gavin, her "slightly crooked front teeth . . . [and] pug nose with flared nostrils" were corrected by cosmetic surgery by MGM doctors. Like many other writers,

Gavin reports that Horne's contract specified that her weight had to remain below a certain number (122 pounds), and when she gained weight, "the M-G-M physician prescribed weight-reducing amphetamines" just as studio doctors were doing for Judy Garland.[95] Though these practices were common, Horne remembered the lessons in etiquette and deportment as well as the makeovers as indicative of the white ideal under which MGM operated, suggesting that they were all attempts to tone down her blackness and turn her into a "bronze swan" who swam happily with MGM's other graceful, white stars. In addition, she recalled in *The Lady and Her Music* that studio directors continually exhorted her not to open her mouth so wide when she sang, presumably to counter the big-lipped, wide-mouthed caricature of the minstrel stage.

Horne had certainly been raised with a sense of propriety appropriate to a child of the black middle class, but her MGM training also influenced her performance style. Gavin echoes many critics and other biographers when he notes that "everything M-G-M had taught her about how to dress, move, and command the spotlight" was evident in her films and later cabaret performances. Horne credited her glamorous appearance to the lessons in makeup application she'd learned at MGM. She also admitted that she'd learned how to play to an audience at MGM, transferring its lessons in singing for a camera to singing in an intimate cabaret setting. Despite being part of the MGM star-making process, Horne recalled that her classes didn't include much dramatic coaching. In the early 1940s, "hoping for substantial roles, she found an acting coach, while wishing that M-G-M would enroll her in the drama school on the lot." It's crucial to note that Horne remembered MGM as having a school in which one might enroll, which contradicts Lillian Burns's and others' testimony that MGM didn't hold formal acting classes. This discrepancy suggests how Horne (and others) might have felt excluded from a system that purported to treat all stars equally. Further, Horne's dramatic acting is often criticized. James Gavin describes the radio play *You Were Wonderful* as her attempt to demonstrate to MGM that she was "a gifted and neglected actress"; instead, it "exposed Horne's weakness at delivering lines."[96] If Horne was denied—whether through neglect, oversight, or outright racism—the kind of naturalist acting training in which the studios specialized, MGM was better able to justify its claims that it was nearly impossible to cast her in integrated musicals or as characters within narrative. She could certainly sing, but she just couldn't act.

Negative appraisals of Horne's acting ability erase her virtuosity at crafting a persona through song. Kristin McGee remarks that Horne's "elegant and confident stage presence reinforced her expert theatrical and musical skills," underscoring how Horne used her MGM training to express the emotional meanings of her songs in both cabaret and film.[97] Stella Adler classed Horne and Judy Garland as "the greatest singing actors" and noted that Horne in particular was exemplary of self-control.[98] In general, Horne was aloof in performance, separate from the audience and from the other performers with whom she shared the stage. In 1948, she explained that "most of the time I'm not singing to the [audience.] I'm singing to myself."[99] Horne employs what Shane Vogel suggests is a "strategic mode of black performance" that "distance[s] her from traditions of early-twentieth-century black women's performance."[100] Singing to herself rather than to the audience perhaps offered Horne some measure of dignity and self-respect within the racist institutions in which she performed—not only Hollywood films but segregated cabarets.

As I demonstrate above, movie musicals borrow the discourses of naturalist acting to suggest that songs are the expression of inner emotion, even emotion that is hidden from the characters. Horne described her singing style in these terms. Recognizing that songs were vehicles for expressing emotion but at the same time wary of overexposure (perhaps because she wanted to refute a stereotype of black excess; perhaps because MGM insisted she contain her blackness), Horne remained relatively detached, especially during performances of ballads and love songs, which were most directly descended from minstrelsy's wench songs. "It was a self-absorbed kind of performance," she said. "I was there to be had, but not too much."[101]

This self-absorption, of course, associates Horne's singing with discourses of naturalist acting. Naturalism, as Lee Strasberg's emphasis on Stanislavsky's principles describes, posits that "the basic problem in acting is to learn to be private in public."[102] As George Kouvaros demonstrates in *Famous Faces Yet Not Themselves*, being private in public is productively understood as a kind of absorption that mediates between a focus on the emotional reality the actor creates and an awareness of the camera or audience.[103] By appearing to hold back some of the inner emotion called up by such dramatic songs as "Stormy Weather" or energetic "Latin" numbers, Horne suggests an inner life that remains tantalizingly out of reach for her audience. Further, because this aloof performance style describes her characters in narrative films and her "pillar songs" as well as links to her biography as a member of the black bourgeoisie, audiences likely associated these performances with an authentic self. The discourses of naturalist performance combine with Horne's biography as exemplary (and mixed-race) black woman to suggest she is refined and reserved, just like the idealized wench of the minstrel stage. The authenticity assumed by minstrel audiences watching white performers blacked up is assumed once again when Horne, wearing Light Egyptian, sings sad songs in melancholy self-absorption.

CHAPTER 4

CARNIVAL!

CARMEN MIRANDA AND THE
SPECTACLE OF AUTHENTICITY

In 1936, Carmen Miranda was featured in the film *Alô Alô Carnaval*, singing the solo *marchinha* (march) "*Querido Adão*/Dear Adam." Though *Alô Alô Carnaval* is no longer extant, Miranda's *marchinha* is available on YouTube, thanks to a dedicated Brazilian fan.[1] The number is staged for the camera on a facsimile of a nightclub stage, but the band and singers accompanying her are not visible. Her voice is light and her diction crisp. Using her body to underscore both the comedy and the theme of the song, she gestures with curving arms and fluttering hands, and punctuates key lines with rolling eyes, wriggling eyebrows, and pointing fingers. During the instrumental bridge, she marches in time to the music, grinning impishly at the camera and swaying her hips.

José Ligiéro Coelho suggests that like her performances in Hollywood musicals, "*Querido Adão*" "captur[es] the idea of the best moments of a live performance," though the audience to whom Miranda directs her lively performance is the camera.[2] In many ways, the Carmen Miranda of *Alô Alô Carnaval* is nearly indistinguishable from the Carmen Miranda of *The Gang's All Here* (1943), the Fox musical directed by Busby Berkeley that solidified her US iconicity, which in turn is nearly identical to her performance in *Doll Face* (1945), a lesser, later film.[3] The sinuous hips, flashing eyes, and pitter-pattering vocalization that make Miranda such an imitable entertainer are evident in this early Brazilian performance. Of course, there are differences. Miranda is not dressed in the towering turban and midriff-baring *baiana* costume in which she always appears in US films.[4] She's wearing light-colored, loose satin pants and a short-sleeved, darker sequined blouse with attached cape and large satin collar and tie; it's a rather masculine costume. Her chin-length, dark hair is set in marcel waves, and her eyebrows are pencil thin rather than thickly drawn. But her wide, dark mouth is the same, as is her repertoire of gestures. Most importantly, the sexy, flirtatious, energetic Miranda persona is identical whether she sings the Portuguese "*Querido*

Adão" in 1936, the burlesque "Chico Chico" from *Doll Face* nearly a decade later, or "The Lady in the Tutti Frutti Hat" in between (*The Gang's All Here*, 1943). The performances are always excessive, spectacular, and carnivalesque.

Alô Alô Carnaval also demonstrates how easily Miranda's performances were transferred to Twentieth Century–Fox musicals, where Miranda plays entertainers (or former or aspiring entertainers). "*Querido Adão*," a comic lament about Adam's expulsion from the Garden of Eden, is typical of the music of *chanchada*, which José Ligiéro Coelho defines as a "popular style of cinema . . . loosely structured around musical numbers."[5] The *chanchada* is similar to the backstage musicals in which Twentieth Century–Fox specialized but is also rooted in Brazilian *filmes cantantes* (sung films).[6] Further, according to Robert Stam, *chanchadas* are "intimately linked to the cultural universe of carnival, in that they were timed to be released around the carnival, featured carnival songs, and had an imaginary deeply imbued with carnivalesque values." Of course, as Stam himself argues, even Hollywood movie musicals are "two-dimensional carnival[s]" that stylize, choreograph, and mythically transcend the "oppressive structures of everyday life."[7] Though not as lavishly produced as their Hollywood counterparts, *chanchada*'s links with carnival ensure that the same values (of spectacle, of hyperexpressivity, of consumption, and of frivolity) are marked in both, transcending if not always subverting the strictures of daily existence.

The performative similarity between *Alô Alô Carnaval* and Miranda's US films bespeaks the peculiar authenticity of her performances. In the same way that Esther Williams cites athleticism and independence, and Lena Horne cites dignity and reserve, Carmen Miranda cites *Latinidad*, which Mary Beltrán defines as the "construction of a collective, imagined 'Latin-ness'" that reiterates energy, sex, the exotic, and rhythm for cultural intelligibility.[8] Miranda plays herself, or a character very like her public persona, in her US films. She always sings "samba," accompanied by the same band; she always wears the same towering platform shoes, midriff-baring dress, and soaring hats; she always lapses into Portuguese when she's excited. Further, she's usually surrounded by the same group of actors: Alice Faye or Betty Grable, John Payne or James Ellison, Don Ameche or Cesar Romero, Charlotte Greenwood, Leonid Kinskey, and Edward Everett Horton in her first six Fox films; with Vivian Blaine, Phil Silvers, and Perry Como taking over the ingenue, comic sidekick, and romantic lead roles in her last three. The links between her films' narratives, characters, and costars allow her performances to build on each other, concretizing a persona that seems real and true.

Despite their performative authenticity, Miranda's performances of self are unnatural: they are not quotidian and everyday; they do not traffic in absorption; they are not intelligible as what's generally understood as Method acting. Miranda is always spectacular and excessive, even when she's playing a wartime machinist like Chiquita Hart in *Something for the Boys*.[9] In that film, though playing one of her most three-dimensional characters, she still sings samba, wears platform shoes and turbans to breakfast, speaks charmingly to an old army colonel in Portuguese, *and* receives radio broadcasts through her teeth. Nor are her performances steeped in emotional truth. Unlike Lena Horne in her heartfelt "pillar songs," Miranda mugs her way through comic numbers and slinks through sexy sambas. She never sings ballads, and because her songs are often in Portuguese and thus unintelligible to US and non-Brazilian Latino audiences, they express a sense of joy in rhythm and music alongside an exotic sensuality but little else. Miranda thus demonstrates the ambivalent relationship between "authenticity" and "naturalism" in movie musical performances. In short, Miranda seems authentically indicative of *Latinidad*, if only because she's the only major Latina performer in Classic Hollywood film, but remaining "unnatural" as I've been using the term throughout.

Instead, I explain the essential duality of her performance through the lens of Bakhtinian carnival. Many critics agree with Shari Roberts's assessment that Miranda's "parodic text . . . allow[s] for negotiated or subversive readings by her fans,"[10] but I tie her grotesque parody of femininity and Brazil specifically to the carnivalesque in order to explain how her performance works within but also explodes a naturalist frame. In particular, Miranda's spectacular performances in US films are grotesque. Her extravagant costumes and excessive facial expressions, vocalizations, and gestures offer a body and voice threatening to explode off the screen. For Bakhtin, the grotesque "is looking for that which protrudes from the body, all that seeks to go out beyond the body's confines."[11] Her eyes roll and pop as her wide mouth carefully articulates speedy lyrics, her tongue flicking out as she sings. Miranda dominates the film space, and in her US films, her ubiquitous turban frequently exceeds the frame, transforming into cornucopias of the real fruit its decorations suggest (see figure 19). Further, as a singer from "down South," Miranda is always already a Bakhtinian "low other," a designation supported by her body in performance. Her hips never stop moving in the samba's modified bump and grind. Both her typical costume with its bared midriff and her movements invert the conventional dominance of head/rationality to privilege the belly/emotion, presenting a grotesque (if also spectacular and compelling) body.

Because the Latino carnival tradition that Miranda embodies is markedly different from European carnival, it inflects her body with particularly freighted representations of race and sexuality. Lizabeth Paravisini-Gebert insists that unlike European carnivals, which indicate the calendar of planting, growing, and harvesting, Caribbean and other Latin carnivals are "rooted in the experience of slavery and the commemoration of emancipation." Latin American carnival, though clearly indebted to European traditions, is focused on inverting race rather than class, and symbolically reenacts seminal moments in the trajectory from enslavement to independence. When Miranda invokes Rio's Carnival in her US films and her persona, she's invoking a racial mythology

Figure 19: The Bando da Lua and Carmen Miranda, "The Lady in the Tutti Frutti Hat," from *The Gang's All Here*, 1943, Twentieth Century–Fox.

that solidifies Brazilian national identity. Latin American carnival and the carnivalesque, Paravisini-Gebert continues, articulate "resistance to the dominant culture's tendency to regard its own principles [such as the separation of the races] as eternal truths."[12] Carnival's status as a populist festival (a meaning expressly promoted by President Getúlio Vargas and others eager to trumpet Brazil's racial utopia during Vargas's first presidency, 1930–1945) celebrates the process by which the disenfranchised, marginalized immigrants and formerly enslaved might constitute the nation.

Priscilla Peña Ovalle explains how "Miranda embodied an in-betweenness; her body, image, and persona existed between the representational poles of blackness and whiteness,"[13] capturing specifically Brazilian attitudes toward race as expressed in that country's 1930s revival of its carnival tradition. Further, by bringing together representatives of the US and Latin America through production numbers like "Pan-American Jubilee" from *Springtime in the Rockies*,[14] Miranda's dancing body is a point of contact for multiple ethnic and national identities. At the same time, Peña Ovalle argues, the contrast as well as the kinship between Miranda and her white counterparts allows US audiences to "disavow [their] own black-white racial tensions by creating a fantasy of hemispheric unity in her films."[15] The finale of *Down Argentine Way*,[16] with its combination of samba rhythms, Tin Pan Alley melodies, and energetic tap-dancing, for example, presents a Latin American fantasy of members of at least three different ethic groups (Anglo, Latino, and African American) sharing music, dance, and the same social space, something not generally sanctioned in most of the United States.

The "exotic" rhythms of samba coupled with her bejeweled and beturbaned body mark Carmen Miranda as categorically different from the other characters in her films, even when those characters (like Alice Faye/Edie Allen in *The Gang's All Here* or Vivian Blaine/Blossom Hart in *Something for the Boys*) are also nightclub entertainers. Her embodied ethnic Otherness (based on the Bahian musicians, singers, and dancers who originated samba as well as her roots in Brazil's Portuguese immigrant community) stabilizes the white, American women in her films, symbolically sealing their performing bodies within the film frame and their characters within the narrative. Where Miranda nearly explodes, the white women are safely contained. Though carnivalesque musical numbers and characterizations temporarily taint the hegemonic narratives of her films, those narratives—of race, class, and sexuality—are reinscribed, usually through the romance between white characters.

In the same way that Esther Williams's natural body allows her characters to challenge the conventional narratives in which they act, Miranda's grotesque body inverts the emphases of her films as well as audience assumptions about authenticity in performance. Ultimately, however, the carnivalesque elements of Miranda's persona and performance style suggest as much about Classical Hollywood discourses of naturalist acting as they do ethnic representations. In this chapter, I tease out Miranda's dual performances of authenticity and antinaturalism, exposing the multiple and conflicting ideologies inherent in her films. On one hand, she's a spectacular performer, her body, voice, and face charismatically holding camera and audience attention and supporting ideas of movie musicals as "only entertainment." On the other, she's a guarantor of ethnic harmony and a living symbol of the United States' World War II Good Neighbor policy. Finally, and perhaps most crucially for my project, her antinaturalist performance style highlights the more conventionally naturalist acting of her white costars, making their characters and stories seem more realistic and inviting audience identification with the narratives and ideologies of her films.

I begin with a brief biography, focusing especially on Carmen Miranda's adoption and use of the *baiana* costume in Brazil and the United States, before turning to her embodiment of carnivalesque *Latinidad*. Here, as well as in the work on Gabor that follows, I foreground the Cold War political context of spectacular female performance in the Classical Hollywood era. I pay close attention to Hollywood's promotion of the Good Neighbor policy, suggesting how discourses of naturalist acting influence the narratives, characters, and visual spectacle of those films. Hollywood in general and Twentieth Century–Fox in particular developed film narratives that stressed the United States' benign but necessary role in South American culture, economy, and politics. Certainly,

both Brazilian and US audiences read Miranda as central to this project: Roosevelt sells international policy, naming Miranda an official Good Neighbor;
Miranda sells an ideal Brazil, and its consumer goods. In important ways, Miranda's films produce a Foucauldian archive of the Good Neighbor policy, especially because of their interchangeability of plot, cast, and location—not least
of which is Miranda's constant playing of herself. I also read *The Gang's All Here*
and *Something for the Boys*, two similar films about the role of entertainment
in the war effort. Both posit a rural utopia as a haven from battlefield crises as
well as a space to invert but then restablize the performances of race and class in
which their characters engage.

Constructing Carmen Miranda

As with many Classical Hollywood stars, especially those who died young,
accounts of Carmen Miranda's life are more hagiography than academic biography. Even José Ligiéro Coelho, whose "Carmen Miranda: An Afro-Brazilian
Paradox" is his dissertation for NYU's PhD in performance studies, borrows
the narrative tropes of Miranda's popular biographies.[17] These accounts stress a
few key points: Miranda's incredible work ethic was forged by her impoverished
childhood; she felt a natural connection with Lapa-district Afro-Brazilians and
their music; and she created the "Carmen Miranda" persona in order to protect
her family's privacy and her own sense of honor. The emphasis on the separation
between "Carmen Miranda" and "Maria da Cunha" (her given name) is especially
relevant to my understanding of Miranda's performance style. In important
ways, Miranda was always "onstage," and she merged her nightclub and movie
persona with her "real," offscreen personality as much as any of the women I consider here. But because she was always already understood to embody *Latinidad*,
she and her studios were especially invested in demonstrating the authenticity of
this persona. Thus, her performance is forcefully constructed as "real" despite its
constant foregrounding as performed.

Maria do Carmo Miranda da Cunha was born in Porto, Portugal, in 1909.[18]
Less than a year after her birth, her father, José Maria Pinto da Cunha, immigrated to Rio de Janeiro, Brazil, in order to make a better life. A few months later,
his wife, Maria Emília Miranda da Cunha, followed him with their daughters
Olinda and Maria. Da Cunha had worked as a barber in Porto, and he continued
that profession in Rio, but his dreamed-of wealth never materialized. In 1915,
the family (which now included Mário, Cecília, and Aurora; baby Oscar was
born in 1916) moved to the Lapa district near Rio's waterfront. Depending upon
the biographer, Lapa in the 1910s and 1920s was either a "raucous meeting place
for sailors and prostitutes" or a melting pot of recent Portuguese immigrants,
former African slaves, and the mixed-race poor that offered Miranda "the freedom of expression" enjoyed by "the destitute peoples" who create a rich culture

from their voices and bodies rather than their material goods.[19] Maria and her siblings attended the Escola Santa Tereza, run by nuns who educated Lapo's poor but worthy children. Maria and her older sister, Olinda, left school around 1925 in order to work as milliners and dressmakers; their struggling parents also opened a Lapa boardinghouse in a final attempt to move out of poverty. According to her biographer Martha Gil-Montero, Maria "took on her young shoulders the responsibility of delivering pots filled with the food prepared by her mother" to hungry customers in the neighborhood in addition to making hats at Maison Marigny and La Femme Chic, two downtown stores that catered to a solid middle-class clientele.[20] Friends and relatives noted that Maria was creative and fashionable: her younger sister Aurora remembers that she was a successful salesperson because she wore hats with such flair herself. Her talent and work ethic were extremely important to the family; when José "left home and went to live with another woman, Maria became the head of the household," according to Gil-Montero.[21]

While making and selling hats in downtown Rio, Maria da Cunha began working as a singer. Many of the family's boardinghouse residents and restaurant customers were musicians, and Maria used those connections to start performing. In 1928, she met Josué de Barros, a Bahian composer and guitarist, who recalled for Gil-Montero that he knew from their first meeting that she was special. "I was in front of someone who had an original message in her eyes, her smile, her voice . . . a voice impregnated with grief and anguish—I could not help but imagine her singing our music, our samba, our moving, sensual Brazilian music."[22] When she began performing publically with de Barros, Maria used "Carmen Miranda" as her stage name, combining "the passionate Spanish name of Carmen" with her mother's family name of Miranda.[23] Eventually, Oscar and Aurora, who followed her into show business and the United States, adopted the Miranda surname as well. After successful public recitals together, de Barros took her first to Brunswick Studios and then RCA Victor in Rio de Janeiro to record some of his songs. She recorded with RCA until she left Brazil for the United States in 1939, working with de Barros and a number of other Brazilian and Afro-Brazilian musicians.

RCA Victor was anxious to promote Miranda as a Brazilian (not Portuguese) singer, insisting that she sing only typical Brazilian music such as *marchinhas* and samba. These songs, generally very quick, rhythmic, and energetic, are carnival music originating in Bahia, where many freed African slaves settled both before and after emancipation. Miranda was very successful in these genres, and over the next decade she released nearly three hundred records, played several nightclubs in Rio, and toured Brazil, Argentina, and other South American countries. She became very wealthy and was able to purchase a home for herself and her family in one of Rio's most desirable neighborhoods.

Priscilla Peña Ovalle attributes Miranda's success in part to her "professional and performative hybridization of race and class." As a Portuguese immigrant,

Miranda was a white European; as a samba singer, she was Brazilian if not actually native or black, embodying both cultures. Peña Ovalle explains how samba in general and Miranda in particular became national symbols for Brazil's presumed racial equality. After the 1888 emancipation of its African and Native slave populations, "Brazil addressed the so-called problem of blackness by attempting to hybridize the racial identity through whiteness," promoting interracial marriage, removing race from the 1920 census, and encouraging European immigration.[24] The Brazilian anthropologist Gilberto Freyre published *The Masters and the Slaves* in 1934, arguing that Portuguese, Native, and African Brazilians were living in a racial democracy, and Robert Stam asserts that President Getúlio Vargas promoted a populist, racially flexible Brazilian national identity by transforming "'ethnic' practices—samba, carnival, capoeira—into national symbols."[25] As the "Ambassadress of Samba" and a close friend of Vargas,[26] Miranda was uniquely positioned to participate in the rebranding of Brazil as a racial utopia, both within and without its borders.

Carmen Miranda launched her US career in June 1939, appearing in the Broadway revue *The Streets of Paris*, produced by the comedy team Chic Johnson and Ole Olsen (who wrote and produced several revues under the Hellzapoppin' trademark) and the Shubert Theatre Organization. According to the *New York Times* theater critic Brooks Atkinson, most of the musical numbers "ap[e] the tawdry dullness" of genuine Paris revues, and "the chorus girls, skin-deep in atmosphere, strike what Broadway thinks a Paris pose ought to be." Atkinson continues, "South America contributes the most magnetic personality" of the revue. Carmen Miranda, singing "rapid-rhythmed songs in Spanish to the accompaniment of a Brazilian band, . . . radiates heat that will tax the Broadhurst [theater] air-conditioning plant this Summer." Though Atkinson finds the bulk of the musical numbers forgettable (and seems not to recognize the difference between Spanish and Portuguese), he tells his readers that Miranda makes the show.[27]

Atkinson wasn't the only who noticed that Miranda was a major talent. Twentieth Century–Fox quickly signed her to a multiyear, multifilm contract, and she made several films set in Latin American and the Caribbean (*Down Argentine Way* [1940], *That Night in Rio* [1941], *Week-End in Havana* [1941], *Nancy Goes to Rio* [1950]), as well as others in which she played a Brazilian (or half-Brazilian) entertainer (*Springtime in the Rockies* [1942], *The Gang's All Here* [1943], *Greenwich Village* [1944], *Something for the Boys* [1944], *Doll Face* [1945], *If I'm Lucky* [1946], *Copacabana* [1947]). Because her image was increasingly static and seemed to capitalize on exotic stereotypes (and because Miranda seemed willing to be a symbol for the Good Neighbor policy, despite its limitations), many Brazilians rejected her in the 1940s. In July 1940, she returned to Brazil for a vacation and a short engagement at Casino da Urca, where she had had her first Brazilian success and where Lee Shubert had first seen her perform and offered her a US contract. Miranda's missteps at her first concert are legendary: she spoke in English rather than Portuguese, she only wore *baiana*, and she sang "South American Way" from the Fox film *Down Argentine Way*. Roundly criticized by the Brazilian journalists and critics who'd been invited to the performance—they accused her of forgetting how to sing samba and of parodying a specific Brazilian folk costume—Miranda canceled the engagement. Two months later, she returned to the Casino, opening her show with "*Disseram que Eu Voltei Americanisada*/They Say I Came Back Americanized." She asked her audience, "How can I become Americanized/I who was born with samba ... /I always say 'eu te amo' and never 'I love you." According to José Ligiéro Coelho, by "sharing the stage with ... her old partner Grande Otelo, the greatest black Brazilian actor of all time, she reinforced the idea that ... her American success had not changed her." For the most part, this show was successful; her audience forgave her supposed transgressions against Brazilian culture, and she enjoyed a popular and sold-out run. Even so, Miranda didn't return to Brazil until her 1954 treatment for depression, and she never performed there again.[28]

Like the film careers of all the other women I consider, Miranda's was relatively short but incredibly successful. She made thirteen films in the 1940s (her final film appearance was as a Mexican tortilla seller in the Martin and Lewis 1953 vehicle *Scared Stiff*), appeared on several radio and television variety shows, made dozens of US records for RCA Victor, and performed in nightclubs, promoting samba and her own personality. Her coworkers, like Alice Faye, Don Ameche, Irving Cummings, and the producer William LeBaron, remembered her as an especially hard worker. That hard work paid off. In 1945, she was the highest-paid woman, and the ninth-highest-paid person, in the United States.[29] But by 1950 her film career was virtually over. Limited by the persona she'd so carefully created in a decade of movies, television and radio shows, and theatrical engagements, Miranda was unable to play romantic leads or character parts that didn't capitalize on *Latinidad*. According to Peña Ovalle, when "Hollywood's enthusiasm for an exotic, international Latin American fantasy declined," so did Miranda's film career.[30] Postwar, post-studio-system reductions in film budgets also explain her declining popularity. *Down Argentine Way* and *The Gang's All Here*, for example, are Technicolor explosions stuffed with major stars and familiar character actors. It's nearly impossible to resist their visual appeal, and Miranda's bright costumes, elaborate production numbers, and flashing dark eyes and bright red lips play a major part. Miranda's later films, shot in black-and-white, mute her charismatic presence; the fact that they're made with lesser stars, fewer production numbers, less elaborate set pieces, and shakier plots also diminishes their attractions.

In 1947, while filming *Copacabana*, a silly and overcomplicated film, this one costarring Groucho Marx, Miranda began a relationship with one of its producers, David Sebastian. The two married that March. Though they remained married until her death in 1955, it wasn't a happy marriage, and they were often separated. In 1948, Miranda had a miscarriage, which further strained the relationship. As her career declined, Miranda became depressed and more dependent on drugs and alcohol. In 1953, she and Sebastian embarked on a disastrous European tour; according to Gil-Montero, though the star was "mobbed by ardent fans," she was "downhearted" and "melancholic." She became hypochondriac, addicted to pills and alcohol, and terrified of getting fat. In 1954, she left Sebastian for the third time and spent several months "resting in paradisiacal Rio de Janeiro" and healing her body and soul. In April 1955, she met David in Miami and the two returned to their Hollywood home. In August 1955, she began rehearsing for a guest appearance on *The Jimmy Durante Show*. Filming the live show in front of a studio audience, she stumbled and dropped to one knee, apparently suffering a minor heart attack. She continued with the show, celebrated with friends and family until early in the morning of August 5, and then died of a second heart attack, alone in her bathroom on her way to bed.[31]

Miranda's family and Sebastian held a Hollywood funeral; over four thousand friends and fans swarmed into the Church of the Good Shepherd on Saturday, and a smaller requiem mass was celebrated the following day with only her family and close friends in attendance. Though the expressions of Hollywood grief were tremendous, they were nothing compared to the Brazilian response. Her body was flown to Brazil, and on August 13, 1955, more than a million people filed past the casket to pay their respects. Miranda was buried in São João Batista Cemetery in Rio de Janeiro.[32]

The public outpouring of grief seems genuine, despite Miranda's complicated relationship with her home country. According to Gil-Montero, her death compelled "a desire to rethink Carmen's legacy" for both the Brazilian government and the Brazilian people.[33] Certainly Rio has honored her in the last fifty years. In the late 1960s, "the cutting-edge multi-field" political and artistic movement *Tropicalismo* "appropriated her as one of its principal signs."[34] As Caetano Veloso, one of the movement's founders, remarks, she "was at once a disgrace and a deity. She was also, finally, an artist."[35] In August 2005, on the fiftieth anniversary of her death, the Carmen Miranda Museum in Flamengo Park opened a major new exhibition of Miranda memorabilia and held a weeks-long "carnival-like celebration" with singing, dancing, and Carmen Miranda fans dressed as their idol.[36] As Shari Roberts points out, "Miranda's image still holds great emotional power for Brazil and still influences Brazilian self-perception and Brazilian identity."[37] For Brazilian as well as US and European fans, Miranda is emblematic of Brazil, especially in the Good Neighbor era.

There is no greater symbol of Miranda, and by extension Brazil, than her physical image, which depends largely on her modification of the traditional *baiana* costume, first worn in Brazil in 1939 (see figure 20). In fact, according to James Mandrell, she reached iconic status in the United States "by performing

a persona known as bahiana . . . a figure associated with Brazilian Carnival."³⁸
Though Miranda became successful singing samba in evening clothes (as did
most of RCA Victor's samba artists, whether European- or Afro-Brazilian), she
adopted the *baiana* costume as her signature in the United States. Miranda's first
performance in *baiana* is as mythologized as any of the other seminal moments
in her career. According to Gil-Montero, Miranda was looking for a production
number about the Bahia region for what was her last Brazilian film, *Banana da
Terra*. Dorival Caymmi, a young Afro-Brazilian singer and composer, had written and recorded *"O Que é Que a Baiana Tem?"* ("What Does a Bahian Girl
Have?"). Miranda initially didn't like the song because of its rhythm but agreed
to listen to Caymmi sing it live. This time, says Gil-Montero, "she could not help

Figure 20: The imitable Carmen Miranda in a publicity shot for *Copacabana*, 1947,
Republic Pictures.

but fall in love with it." The song was included in the film, and Caymmi stood
off-camera and "mimicked for Carmen the gestures and movements she was
supposed to make while singing."[39] The filmed song includes Carmen with what
became her regular band, the Bando da Lua, on a soundstage meant to invoke
a village square. The song repeats the title question, and Miranda answers by
naming and pointing out the elements of the costume: a turban, large earrings,
many necklaces, a scarf, bracelets on each wrist, and a full skirt. By the second
verse, Aloysio de Oliveira, a Bando member (and Miranda's longtime lover and
collaborator), points out the costume elements on her body as Miranda gently
sambas in place. During the musical bridge, she dances in a circle, swaying her
hips. The last verse of the song attests to the Bahiana's "grace like nobody else,"
her hypnotic hips, and her sexual appeal, and the number ends with several fad-
ing repetitions of "*O que é que a Baiana tem?*"[40]

Though both the film and song were commercially successful, Miranda's
decision to adopt the *baiana* costume was also controversial. Bahia is one of
the twenty-six Brazilian states, and the region most associated with the Brazilian slave trade. Not only did African slaves work on its sugar plantations from
the early sixteenth century on, but Bahia was the port of entry for Yoruba and
other Africans into Brazil. In the generation before slavery was abolished, Bahia
was also home to many freed African slaves who achieved their status through
individual manumission for loyal service as well as the purchase of their freedom and that of their family members.[41] The women of Bahia, freed or enslaved,
were famous for their beauty and sensuality as well as their distinctive dress,
especially the gold and silver jewelry they presumably received from wealthy
white and mixed-race lovers and then sold to obtain their freedom. From the
mid-nineteenth century onward, these heavily jeweled women participated in
the Catholic processionals that were the prelude to Carnival, reportedly "attract-
ing a large audience with their lascivious dances executed during the intervals
between prayers and hymns." Bahiana also worked as street vendors, selling pastries and fruit.[42] Thus, the Bahiana was especially visible on Brazilian streets, her
gender as well as her costume making her stand out among the other citizens. As
a white, aspirant middle-class, European immigrant, Miranda crossed significant
race and class lines in her appropriation of Afro-Brazilian traditional dress. Of
course, the costume further links Miranda to carnival. Not only were the Bahiana
important members of traditional Rio Carnival parades, but Miranda inverts
expectations of bourgeois femininity by wearing clothing associated with black
women who sold food (and often themselves) on Rio's streets.

There are, of course, other explanations for Miranda's adoption of the *baiana*
costume. Most biographers agree that Miranda carefully crafted a persona, first
in order to protect her family from the presumed shame of having a daughter
who worked as an entertainer, and later to "keep her personal self hidden," says
Coelho, which may explain her reliance on the *baiana*, especially in the United

States. The *baiana* that Miranda made her signature differs from the traditional dress in several ways. First, Miranda's costume generally included a halter that bared her shoulders, arms, and midriff, rather than the loose, three-quarter-sleeved peasant blouse worn by the Afro-Brazilians. Second, rather than wearing a starched skirt with petticoats, Miranda wore what Coelho describes as a "tight, wraparound satin skirt [that] outlined her body contours. It gave more emphasis to her hips and more sensuality to her leg movements."[43] Her skirts were usually made of light fabric (lamé, satin, rayon) that swirled around her body, often puddling at her ankles, and with a long center or side slit. In many ways, Miranda's costume was racier and more erotic than the traditional Bahiana's. At the same time, its outlandish, even grotesque elements tempered her sexuality; seemingly weighted down with hundreds of pounds of jewelry and negotiating enormous turbans and trains, winking and cutting her eyes as she sang of the lust that destroyed Adam or the erotic charms of Bahian women, she was as much soubrette as siren. Miranda's adaptation of the *baiana* also enabled her to create a more commanding physical stature. Just over five feet tall in her bare feet, she used the towering turbans and skyscraper platform shoes (neither of which was part of a Bahiana's everyday costume) to add several inches to her frame. Miranda seems larger than life in her films—she takes up a tremendous amount of actual, physical space—and most of that is due to her costume rather than her actual, physical body. In every way, then, the *baiana* created the Miranda persona, emphasized elements of the grotesque, and signaled a kind of carnivalesque racial inversion.

It's important to note that although "*O Que é Que a Baiana Tem?*" was a major hit for Miranda, it was not her most popular or best-selling samba recording for RCA in Brazil. And, though the wide release of *Banana da Terra* ensured that many Brazilians saw her in the provocative *baiana*, they did not expect her to wear it always. Miranda was a Brazilian star before this particular song, and it's logical to assume that her popularity would have continued without this particular recording or costume. But in the United States, the *baiana* costume defined Miranda. It made her immediately recognizable and marked her as different, exotic, and spectacular. Because Miranda freely adapted the costume and used it with an uninformed audience, its nonspecificity enabled her to transfer her persona across geographic and cultural borders. Instead, the costume and persona were read as generically "Latin American." In her US films, she never performs in anything but its turbans, jewels, platform sandals, and swirling skirts. Even when she plays a character integrated into the film narrative (rather than merely appearing as a nightclub entertainer), her street clothes echo the lines of the *baiana* costume, and she generally retains her turban and platform shoes. Further, few US audience members would have connected the slit skirt, halter, jewelry, and turban with Afro-Brazilian street vendors, making it an adaptable signifier.

In the United States, controversy around Miranda's costume centered on its threat of indecent exposure rather than its cross-racial implications. James Mandrell explains that the Production Code specifically addressed costumes, especially costumes worn by dancing bodies. These costumes should not highlight "male and female organs and the breasts of a woman"; should not be "cut to permit indecent actions or movements or to make possible during the dance indecent exposure," especially of the breasts or "intimate parts of the body"; nor suggest nudity. Like Lena Horne's first Georgia Brown costume, Esther Williams's bathing suits, and Marilyn Monroe's "Heat Wave" ensemble, Miranda's costumes also always cover the navel, a body part not mentioned specifically by the Code but clearly hidden from cinematic view. Of course, many of Miranda's costumes are quite revealing. Her *baiana* for *Down Argentine Way*, for example, has cutouts along the waistline that reveal the skin of her stomach, hips, and buttocks. Dancing and singing "Batucada" with Harry James in *If I'm Lucky*, her very high-cut slit skirt and twisting legs reveal what appear to be her sequined panties several times. In all her films, says Mandrell, Miranda is "extravagantly sexual" and "couldn't be more different from the remote ice queens of the US, who are . . . buttoned up" against Miranda's open sexuality.[44] Though her performances are often parodied for what Roberts calls their "nonsexual camp female grotesque," watching her in her early films is a stunning reminder of how beautiful, sexual, and nearly naked Miranda often was.[45]

In one infamous photograph, Miranda was more than nearly naked (see figure 21). In a publicity still for *Week-End in Havana*, Cesar Romero spins Miranda in the air. The studio photographer shoots up her skirt to reveal that she's not wearing panties. Though the photograph was never published, according to Gil-Montero, it was widely circulated.[46] The photograph puts Miranda's pubic hair at the exact center of the image, making explicit what her sexualized *baiana* and exotic persona only imply. Analysis of the photograph as well as the dance sequence it supposedly represents demonstrates how Miranda's body was simultaneously carnivalesque and grotesque, spectacular and compelling, Latin and Americanized.

In *Week-End in Havana*, Romero and Miranda play the feuding Cuban lovers Rosita Rivas and Monte Blanca, secondary characters to John Payne and Alice Faye's American romantic leads, Jay Williams and Nan Spencer.[47] In the photograph, Romero is in the white dinner jacket he wears in much of the film, and Miranda is dressed in the turban, ruffled *baiana*, and tiny bandeau with enormous puffed sleeves from the production number "The Ñango." "The Ñango" is typical of Miranda's production numbers in presentational style as well as theme. Miranda doesn't dance much but sings energetically, and the number concludes with presumably white nightclub patrons joining "Latin" dancers onstage. Like most of these production numbers across numerous films ("Chica Chica Boom Chic" from *That Night in Rio*, "Batuca Nega" from *Something for the Boys*, and

Figure 21: The carnivalesque but unused publicity photo of Cesar Romero and Carmen Miranda for *Week-End in Havana*, 1941, Twentieth Century–Fox.

Doll Face's "Chico Chico"), the Ñango is described as an authentic Latin song and dance but is composed and choreographed specifically for the film. Rosita begins the number alone on a huge nightclub stage, moving across the floor and into the audience, promising that "even though you can't pronounce it," dancing the Ñango gives "señors" especially eloquent powers of seduction. She leaves the stage and is replaced by a dozen light-skinned women in *baiana* with maracas and peacock turbans shaking their stuff until a chorus of men in loose pants and puff-sleeved shirts joins them for a short example-cum-dance-lesson. The Ñango, according to the production number, is a combination of rumba, tap-dancing, and the jitterbug. It begins with the women facing front and encircled by their male partners from behind. They rumba in place, turn a circle, and split apart to roll their shoulders and torsos toward each other in time to three thumps of a bongo drum. The music shifts to emphasize a strong 4/4 beat, muted trumpets and a jazz percussion set take over the music, and the dancers execute a series of simple tap combinations before launching into a modified jitterbug. Rosita returns to the stage and invites the audience to dance, pairing them with the professional dancers. She sees Nan sitting alone at a table, finds a dinner-jacketed young white man for her partner, and sends them to the dance floor. The camera pans across the presumably Latin- and US-integrated dance floor, focusing first on a young redhead dancing with a "Cuban" who barely touches her even as they rumba together, a society matron ecstatically leaning into her professional, darker-skinned partner, and an old, overweight, business-suited white man and his sexy "Cuban" partner. His hand slides up her torso toward her haltered breasts before she forcefully replaces it on her hip. As in the early modern carnival balls mythologized by writers, dramatists, and visual artists, sexual mores, class distinctions, and racial hierarchies are overturned in the nightclub's Ñango. Through carnival, old, white, conservative, and conventionally unattractive dancers can experience the exotic pleasures of youthful, dark-skinned, licentious Others. At the same time, conventionally attractive but cross-raced couples are kept apart, reinforcing carnival's only temporary displacement of the status quo. The carnival spirit moves from Miranda's single body to all of the chorus bodies and finally into the social body of the audience. Order is restored at the end, of course, as Jay enters looking for Nan and claims her for a more Western foxtrot.

The unpublished publicity still representing "The Ñango" was available to many in the 1940s and to anyone with an Internet connection now. According to Gil-Montero, the photo immediately "appeared . . . on a bulletin board where Fox's stars and employees pinned their memorabilia." Stars, studio employees, and even the studio head, Darryl F. Zanuck, saw and commented on the photograph.[48] As with the backstage photographs taken by Ed Clark during the filming of Gentlemen Prefer Blondes, these candid shots' unpublishability doesn't mute their power or influence. In fact, this hidden photograph and the multiple narratives it contains are crucial to understanding how Good Neighbor audiences understood Miranda. Though Rosita dances with Jay, and Monte with Nan (though not in "The Ñango"), in the actual film, Rosita and Monte never dance together. Their dance is dance staged for the publicity cameras and underscores Peña Ovalle's "emphasis on physical mobility" and its connotations of sexual abandon to which Latinas and Latinos in Hollywood film were subject.[49] Second, some "suspected that the scandal was just a publicity stratagem of the International Bahian." Gil-Montero denies this claim as soon as she acknowledges it, explaining that Miranda (who in fact had several lovers before and after her marriage) was too "virtuous, untainted, and generous" and "never wanted or needed the kind of publicity that lewd photographs might bring" to have participated in its staging or circulation. That some assumed Miranda might have staged the photograph suggests that she was relatively suspect in Hollywood, in terms of both her morals and her hunger for fame. Further, some, including Zanuck, believed that she never "wore pants when she danced. . . . It was a matter of her freedom of body movement." Miranda and Romero, however, asserted that her pantless state was accidental. Hardworking professionals, both decided to ignore this "wardrobe malfunction" in order to quickly to finish the shoot.[50] Finally, the photograph is shockingly graphic, and Miranda's fleshy thighs, labia, and thick, dark pubic hair dominate the frame. Even if the photograph wasn't staged, it's a well-composed shot, and its sexual impact is considerable.

Though Miranda's persona is often understood to parodically signify female sexuality,[51] the photograph offers inarguable proof that there's a real, sexually available woman beneath the image. Miranda's skirts usually offer tantalizing glimpses of her hips, buttocks, and crotch, especially as she twists, jumps, and turns. Though none of these are as explicit as the unpublishable photograph, they clearly highlight what the PCA referred to as "the intimate parts of the body," which of course correspond to the body's grotesque, carnival elements. The photograph makes visible what Miranda's costumes (barely) hide. As the photograph clarifies, Miranda's ethnic dress associates her with a sexualized *Latinidad*. At the same time, the *baiana* (and the photograph) indicates her mutual performances of the authentic (truly Latin, truly female) and the unnatural (overexposed and overdressed). Miranda's *baiana* marks her as always inverted and doubled but also always sexual and grotesque, contaminating the narratives of her films with her carnival body as much as her ethnic identity.

Being a Good Neighbor

Miranda left Brazil in 1939 with a contract with the Shubert organization and the full support of the Brazilian government. Lee Shubert reportedly signed Miranda after seeing her perform in February at the nightclub Casino da Urca. President Getúlio Vargas piggybacked this contract to include Miranda in Brazil's pavilion at the World's Fair and to ensure that the Brazilian musicians Bando da Lua played at both venues as her musical accompaniment. According to Gil-Montero, Vargas believed that Brazil needed to make a splash at the fair in order to expand into US markets, especially in coffee and other food exports.[52] Miranda and samba enabled Vargas to position his country as the United States' best Good Neighbor for Brazil's own economic benefit.

Thus, Miranda and the US Good Neighbor policy were inextricably linked from Miranda's first appearance on Broadway throughout her film career. Both *That Night in Rio* and *The Gang's All Here* specifically mention the policy, and film after film opens or closes with an elaborate production number in which Miranda is joined first by her white costars and then by the white audience watching the floor show in a symbolic enactment of neighborliness. The policy, President Franklin Delano Roosevelt's rearticulation of US interests in foreign countries, focused on propaganda rather than armed intervention and was increasingly important for the film industry during World War II. As Cynthia

Enloe points out, "Latin American movie stars replaced the marines as the guarantors of regional harmony."[53] With European markets relatively inaccessible, the United States looked to Latin America for audiences.

Further, according to Philip Swanson, Roosevelt's administration pursued a policy of hemispheric unity, regularizing "cultural relations across the Americas" to "ensure a united front against the Axis."[54] In 1940, he created the Office of the Coordinator of Inter-American Affairs (CIAA), which had its own Motion Pictures Division, headed by John Hay Whitney. Whitney used provisions in the 1934 Production Code meant to censor depictions of violence and sexuality in film, applying notions of offensiveness to ethnic representations.[55] At the same time, the US armed forces were strengthening their ties with Hollywood. In 1942, the newly formed Office of War Information, a government unit consolidating the various public messages and images about the war, opened a Bureau of Motion Pictures, which read nearly all studio scripts (Paramount was the lone holdout) and placed information officers on the sets of relevant US films.[56] According to Ana M. López, the nearly one hundred Good Neighbor films produced from the late 1930s to the mid-1940s were films starring North American stars but set in Latin American (such as the Bette Davis vehicle *Now, Voyager*), B and lower movies that featured low-level US actors and Latin entertainers (such as *Carnival in Costa Rica*, with Dick Haymes, Vera-Ellen, and Cesar Romero), or lavish musicals starring major US and Latin stars.[57] This latter category was the most overtly Good Neighborly, and not coincidentally dominated by Carmen Miranda. Without Miranda, it would have been difficult for Hollywood studios to marry the demands of the CIAA with their commercial interests. Though it's true that Miranda's career benefited from the Good Neighbor policy, her carnivalesque screen presence also ensured the policy's cinematic intelligibility.

From the vantage point of seventy years later, the results of Whitney's oversight seem simplistic at best and stereotypic at worst. According to Brian O'Neil, he advocated, first, including more Latino/a actors in Hollywood film, and second, an end to films that "create a bad impression of America or Latin America." Though both are worthy goals, more Latinos in film doesn't guarantee that they'll be represented carefully, and the urge to avoid controversy often results in sentimental, banal depictions of people, places, and events. Whitney urged Will Hays, the head of the Production Code Administration, to appoint a Latin American specialist, Addison Durland, to oversee Hollywood's growing Pan-American output. Ultimately, as O'Neil argues, Durland's tenure enabled "the Latin America imagined by Hollywood" to become "more prosperous and modern than ever before" but to relegate its citizens to "subordinate entertainers."[58] There were more Pan-American-themed films and more Latino/a stars in the early 1940s, but their representations tended to privilege narratives that proposed US intervention (whether in matters of politics, economics, or love) as always already beneficial to the countries and peoples depicted. During the war, however, Hollywood praised its own attempts to be sensitive to Latin American and Caribbean audiences. In Hedda Hopper's article about the filming of *Week-End in Havana*, she reported that the Cuban consul had read the script. Hopper was especially proud that when Miranda, "who's cast as a Brazilian, not a Cuban," objected to a word because it "might be misunderstood in Brazil," the word was removed, "without argument." Hopper warned that it was important to be careful about Latin representations because "German propagandists down south are twisting every slip . . . to disrupt the good neighbor policy." She concluded that if the studios had "gone to their Latin-American actors for advice on Latin-America . . . Hollywood wouldn't be sitting on a powder keg today."[59] In all, Hopper suggests that film is a crucial component of the Good Neighbor policy, especially when handled correctly and with Latino/a input.

Despite Hopper's laudatory commentary, *Week-End in Havana* and the rest of Miranda's World War II films absolutely reinforce imperialist assumptions. In *Down Argentine Way*, for example, Glenda Crawford/Betty Grable falls in love first with a beautiful racehorse and then with its owner, Ricardo Quintana/Don Ameche, a wealthy Argentinean. She follows him down to Buenos Aires, with her Aunt Binnie/Charlotte Greenwood, in order to get her horse and her man. Complications ensue, and Glenda discovers that long ago her father nearly ruined Ricardo's father's business. Of course, Glenda is able to set things right, "presenting a positive view of U.S. intervention in . . . the affairs of Latin America," says Shari Roberts, by romantically and financially rescuing the Quintanas.[60]

In *That Night in Rio*, Don Ameche plays a dual role as Brazilian baron Manuel Duarte and American actor Larry Martin, who solves the baron's marital and financial crises by impersonating him for forty-eight hours. In one of the only films in which Miranda's character is romantically paired with a white American (albeit one who personates a Euro-Brazilian like herself), Ameche also successfully romances the baron's wife, the American-born Cecilia (Alice Faye).[61] Though these and many other Good Neighbor films contrast US national identity with its Latin Good Neighbors, the dual romantic and financial problems of Latin American characters are neatly resolved through a union with a US character. The "natural" solution for Latin Americans, then, is romance and rescue by North Americans. If love can bloom between characters as different as feisty, independent Glenda and tradition-bound Ricardo or macho Manuel and WASP-y Cecilia, then surely the United States and its neighbors to the south can become political allies and economic partners.

Miranda's films, especially those produced by Twentieth Century–Fox in the early 1940s, use dance to transmit cultural hierarchies and concretize the identities of "Good Neighbors." Dance transfers between Latin and Anglo bodies in interesting ways. In *Down Argentine Way*, Miranda's first US film (and Betty Grable's first major Fox film, after taking over for Alice Faye), Grable, the almost preternaturally white Fox Blonde, performs "Latin" dances better than "native" dancers. In the song "Two Dreams Met," she and Don Ameche trade verses in Spanish and English before Glenda (not the Latino character, Ricardo) teaches the white nightclub patrons to cha-cha. In Buenos Aires, Glenda visits the Club Rendezvous with her guide, Tito (Leonid Kinskey). There, a presumably Argentinean (though very light-skinned) couple performs a "hot conga" that Tito promises is unlike anything Glenda could see in New York. When Tito compliments them in Spanish, the two explain that they are from Syracuse and don't speak the language. Americans, including the black Nicholas Brothers, who transform the film's "Down Argentina Way" theme song into a flashy tap number, can dance to Latin rhythms better than those who originated them.

Even the Argentinean characters are eager to see the visiting Americans show off their talents. When Ricardo takes Glenda to a village fiesta to see the "true Argentine," a dancing group of very light-skinned peasants (several blond or auburn-haired, including an uncredited female featured dancer who performs a modified tango) quickly begs Aunt Binnie to sing for them. Greenwood obliges with "Sing to Your Señorita" and is able to work in her trademark windmill kicks. As Philip Swanson notes, on one hand Aunt Binnie stands in for US audiences as she enjoys the "thrill of getting down with the locals" while "becoming (literally in terms of framing) the centre of attention."[62] As usual, the North American perspective supersedes the South American, even when US characters are out of place and outnumbered. The film's finale celebration, set to a medley of the film's songs, including the third version of "Down Argentina Way," features the same villagers. After the female dancer performs a spirited cha-cha, Glenda, dressed in a magnificent red and gold, midriff-baring and leg-displaying *baiana*, does a similar though less complicated version while singing Miranda's "*Mamãe Eu Quero*" in English. Of course, the native Argentines applaud her abilities with twice the gusto they offered their own dancer. The Nicholas Brothers are back, too, and do a quick version of their previous tap dance.[63] The finale ends with Glenda and Ricardo embracing under the pampas moon. Though song and dance literally unites Argentineans with US-Americans, a strong hierarchy that equates special skill with whiteness/Americanness remains. Further, the Latino/a ethnicity presented is clearly a fiction; though I'm not suggesting that no Argentineans have light skin or auburn hair, it's surprising to see a whole village so populated.

In Miranda's second film, *That Night in Rio*, she rather than the American female character, Baroness Cecilia Duarte (Alice Faye), uses song and dance to integrate the nations. The film opens with fireworks exploding in front of Rio's Sugar Loaf Mountain and then cuts to a chorus of white-seeming, *baiana*-clad women holding sparklers as Carmen/Carmen Miranda launches into the Portuguese "Chica Chica Boom Chic." The stage (with Sugar Loaf as its backdrop) is flanked on both sides with these women, who perform the torso-twisting *rebolado* movement that generally signals Latin dance in Hollywood film. The Bando da Lua, dressed in white pants, turtlenecks, and straw hats, is center stage, and light-skinned men and women dressed in attractive and well-cut street clothes fill in the space. When Carmen finishes the final chorus, a convertible driven by a swarthy man in peasant dress brings Don Ameche/Larry Martin dressed as a naval officer and accompanied by three sailors onto the stage. The music slows, and Larry sings his good-byes: "May we never leave behind us/all the common ties that bind us./ . . . Come on and sing the Chica Chica Boom Chic!" Larry takes over the lyrics, now sung in English; the tempo is considerably slower; the instrumentation shifts from the onstage Bando da Lua to an offstage big band; the white backup dancers take over the steps; and Carmen's contribution is reduced to several nonsensical "chica chica booms" accompanied by shaking hips and shoulder thrusts. Clearly, in order to bring Latin rhythms and Latin culture to US audiences, the tempo must slow down, the instruments must be Western, and the words must be in English. Later in the film, Carmen performs (one song in Portuguese and the other, "I-Yi-Yi-Yi-Yi-I Like You Very Much," in English) at a party given by the baron, now being impersonated by Larry. Her energetic performance transfixes the guests, impresses Larry, and motivates the usually reserved Cecilia to dance a sensual rumba. The finale is a medley of the film's major songs performed by Miranda, Ameche (in both roles), and Faye. The spirit of Rio has inspired all of them to love honestly and passionately, and has successfully realigned the Brazilian baron and his American wife as well as Miranda and her American lover, Larry.

Because *That Night in Rio*'s romantic pairings reverse some conventions of Good Neighbor narratives, it is a particularly good example of how Miranda's films traffic in the carnivalesque. In this, her first US film in which she played a character, Miranda is aggressively Other, not only to Americans Cecilia and Larry but also to Baron Duarte. Unlike Duarte, she has little command of English, and most of her lines are in Portuguese, especially when she is angry—and she's angry a lot. At the time, Miranda didn't know much English, so the script allows Larry to translate for her. She speaks very quickly in Portuguese, and he incorporates her content back into his responses; her point of view is filtered through his, and the overall effect is to make her seem especially emotional and silly. When she learns that Larry isn't available for their show, she tears apart his dressing room, smashing glasses and trampling his clothes, gesticulating wildly and unleashing a torrent of furious Portuguese. When she speaks to Larry's dresser, Alfonso (played by US actor Eddie Conrad) to confirm her suspicions that Larry's with another woman, she does use English, but it is so heavily accented that she's nearly incomprehensible. As always, much of the meaning is conveyed by her body language and facial expressions. But despite Miranda's grotesque vocalizations and movement vocabulary, she is attractive, both in the film and to the audience. Larry leaves rich, white Cecilia to finally marry Carmen, and the baron wants to make Carmen one of his many conquests. In this way, Carmen, who is represented as culturally, socially, and intellectually lower than the other characters, not least because she's so sexually compelling, transgresses class boundaries. Larry does so as well, obviously, playing the American but uncultured nightclub performer and the aristocratic but Latin Duarte. Of course these class transgressions are only temporary, and everyone ends up with the correct class (if not ethnic) partner. In a film that advocates hemispheric unity, this resolution is unsurprising.

During World War II, Miranda's Fox films were overtly Good Neighborly, and many plots (such as *The Gang's All Here* and *Something for the Boys*) revolved around the war. After the war, her films were less likely to reference FDR's policies, though they still featured narratives of benevolent US intervention. These later films (*Doll Face, If I'm Lucky, Nancy Goes to Rio*) incorporate Miranda more completely into the narratives; that is, she's not there to exemplify *Latinidad* but is a bona fide supporting player and good friend to the white female leads. At the same time, these films also blunt her presence. Without the gorgeous nightclubs and lavish parties of *Springtime in the Rockies* or *Down Argentine Way*, Miranda has little to do beyond offering wisecracks to the men and racy but sage advice to the women.

AUTHENTICITY AND THE ARCHIVE

Miranda's spectacular performances signal a kind of ethnic and geographic authenticity at the same time that they are fantastically unnatural. Thus, because they are both real and unreal, Miranda's performances illuminate how carnival bodies signal transgression while stabilizing a status quo. In important ways, Carmen Miranda's carnival persona naturalizes the narratives and other performances in her Hollywood films. The vision of exotic (and disparate) locales like Havana, Rio, or Buenos Aires is authenticated by both her musical performances and her ultimately generic *Latinidad*. Her costars thus seem "natural" when compared with her, regardless of how stilted or melodramatic their characterizations might otherwise be. Miranda, a grotesque and excessive carnival fool, stabilizes the white, heteronormative, upper-middle-class primary narrative of her films by representing the inversion of those norms.

Many critics (rightly) see in Miranda's characters a dangerous stereotyping of excess that flattens all Latin American identities into one through the supposed authenticity of her image, but I shift focus from the effect of that "authenticity" to its causes. First, the Good Neighbor films themselves engaged in a project of authenticity in order to naturalize their narratives. According to Brian O'Neil, this project was largely in the hands of Addison Durland: the PCA combated offensive representations by stressing authenticity. Durland reviewed scripts, pointing out errors in geography, food, music, and language. Recognizing that Latino/a actors played a variety of nationalities and ethnicities, many not consistent with their biographies, Durland insisted "the script had to be modified to explain any inauthenticity that might result."[64] Esther Williams, for example, recalls that though her swimming bullfighter in *Fiesta* was twin to Ricardo Montalban, their difference in accents (as well as appearance) was officially attributed to the fact that their mother was American and their father Mexican: one twin took after each parent physically as well as linguistically.[65] Durland also regularly visited film sets and "supplied the producers and directors with books and pictures" in order to enhance the film's visual authenticity. At the same time, as O'Neil explains in his important exegesis of Durland's PCA tenure, his "quest for authenticity" was "subservient" to the larger demand that the representations in Good Neighbor films offend neither Latin American nor US audiences, and of course US audiences were much larger and financially more important.[66] In general, whether biopics, musicals, or dramas, these war-era movies present Latin America as a group of nations united through their similarities to American and European cultures as well as their obvious dependence on the United States.

In important ways, Durland's emphasis on the visual and aural markers of authenticity glossed over the grosser inauthenticities of Good Neighbor films. Promotion of a specific, pro-US ideology aside, the Good Neighbor films tended to depict Latino/as as light-skinned and European-looking. As O'Neil points out, both *That Night in Rio* and *Week-End in Havana* feature all-white casts, including the background extras who populate the films' nightclubs, casinos, hotels, and offices.[67] Of course, this is true of most Hollywood film in the 1940s. Because Good Neighbor films are especially preoccupied with "authenticity," however, the absence of black, mestizo/a, or dark-skinned characters is particularly striking. Further, given Brazil's imagined status as racial utopia, the lack of racial integration in films set there is especially troubling; like Brazil's unofficial policy of intermarriage in order to lighten its national complexion, these films present an ideal of integration achieved by forcefully whitening the population.

Second, Miranda herself promoted "authenticity" through her voice and body. According to José Ligíero Coelho, she relied on African and *sambista* (samba singer) traditions in her performances. In particular, she used call-and-response with her band (as in the examples of "*O Que é Que a Baiana Tem?*" and "*Batuca Nega*") and supporting singers, though she took on the traditional role of male singer (the call) and her male band frequently provides backup (the response). Usually staged in the center of a circle of musicians, singers, and other dancers, Miranda appropriated African circle dance patterns in performance. Further, she used her eyes, face, hands, and body to demonstrate the lyrics of her songs, "just as . . . in the African oral tradition."[68]

Miranda's use of samba steps and traditional dances supported her films' claims to authentic representation of Brazilian or Latino culture. José Ligíéro Coelho's PhD dissertation details how thoroughly Miranda incorporated these traditional movements into her Brazilian and US film and stage performances.

He characterizes samba as requiring "three-dimensional body movements in time to a syncopated rhythm characteristic of Bantu culture. . . . Loose hips and legs, not too straight and not too bent, keep the body in constant balance." It directly contrasts Western European dance styles, which emphasize the vertical and horizontal planes. Though Coelho suggests that Miranda was "completely unaware of the cultural significance of the dance patterns and poses" she used, she understood "in a general sense" that they came from an authentic samba tradition. He specifically links her movements to the rural *pastoras*," Afro-Brazilian female samba singers and dancers. *Pastoras* use "*ginga, miudinho,* [and] *rebolado* accompanied by pointed movements of the shoulders and arms" and tend to remain in place zigzagging their arms in front of their bodies rhythmically. These female singers generally stand in the center of the musicians and audience, sometimes twirling around. *Ginga* is basically stylized walking, with arms and hips in opposition to the legs. Miranda incorporates these movements in her film performances, often adding twisting jumps to her mostly stationary singing. She also includes *miudinho,* where the feet glide while the knees remain bent; for both men and women this is a traveling move. The *rebolado* is a female-only movement, twisting the hips while the torso remains upright, or reversing the movement so that the torso moves in a circle on a stationary base. This is a particularly sensual move, and one that Miranda uses almost exclusively during the musical bridges of her songs. Finally, says Coelho, Miranda "embraced and embodied . . . bahiana styles in her performance" by using traditional Kongo storytelling poses in order to put across the meaning of her songs (see figures 22 and 23).[69] These are incorporated into her usual choreography and are key components of her gestural vocabulary, whether she is singing and dancing, interacting within narrative, or posing for publicity photos.

Like Miranda, US audiences were probably largely unaware of the racial and cultural traditions on which she drew. At the same time, because Miranda incorporated these samba movements and African oral traditions into all her performances, whether she presents a conga ("Chica Chica Boom Chic") or samba ("*Mamãe Eu Quero*"), as in *That Night in Rio,* audiences may have associated her movements with a specific and fixed dance tradition. Further, Miranda's dances connect with other African and African American dances in 1940s movie musicals. For example, as Constance Valis Hill demonstrates in *Brotherhood of Rhythm*, the Nicholas Brothers' exciting jazz tap routines evolved from West African *gioube* and transformed "black vernacular dance, with its stomps and buck-and-wing tapping, into a modern black expression."[70] Katherine Dunham, whose heralded Dunham technique integrated her ballet and modern dance training with the African flexible torso and spine, articulated pelvis, isolated limbs and general polyrhythmic strategy of moving,[71] choreographed or danced in at least nine films in the 1940s, as well as appearing on Broadway six times. Some film-goers would certainly have recognized correspondences between Miranda's

Figure 22: Publicity photo of Carmen Miranda in a Kondo pose for *The Gang's All Here*, 1943, Twentieth Century–Fox.

movements (especially as they are linked to Dunham technique) and those of African American performers; all might well have seen similarities between "ethnic" performers, regardless of their race or nationality. For different kinds of audiences (for example, black vs. white, dance aficionados vs. casual fans), the intertextuality and repetition of Miranda's movements solidify her performances as capturing something authentically non-US, enabling her status as a Latin American Good Neighbor.

This is especially evident in Miranda's production number for the black-and-white *Doll Face* (1945), "Chico Chico (from Porto Rico)." The film itself is notable for its lack of Miranda performances, despite the fact that it's a typical backstage musical: she plays burlesquer Chita Chula, best friend to Vivian Blaine's "Doll Face." Though Chita often appears in showgirl costumes, she doesn't sing or dance until the finale, the premiere of the Broadway musical based on Doll Face's

Figure 23: Publicity photo of Carmen Miranda in a Kondo pose for *That Night in Rio*, 1941, Twentieth Century–Fox.

life.[72] More than any other number from her Fox films, "Chico Chico" stages Brazilian Carnival, complete with Bahianas carrying platters of pastries and fruit on their heads and men selling carnival masks, broad-brimmed hats, and chickens. "Chico Chico" is a comic samba, very like the numbers Miranda performed in Brazil (though it's sung primarily in English), and clearly meant to evoke Brazilian street performance (though it references Puerto Rico). Chita wears large earrings and a richly sequined turban, slit skirt, and halter, but she's barefoot and bereft of her usual layers of jewelry. Her costume is a Hollywood designer's interpretation of simple and blends with the peasant costumes of the chorus men and women. The men wear blanket ponchos, capri pants, and sandals, and the women are dressed in traditional *baiana* costumes with peasant blouses and starched skirts; they too are barefoot. Shots of the tuxedo-clad and bejeweled, white-gloved audience members are intercut with the peasant men and women onstage.

Like the *pastoras* Coelho describes, Chita stands at the center of a circle of musicians and backup dancer/singers, making fluid gestures and shaking her shoulders in rhythm. After completing the verses and chorus, Chita dances over to her band, now singing rapidly in Portuguese before dancing a quick rumba with the dancers and a donkey. Chita watches her feet and lifts her skirts so that the audience focuses on her feet stomping into the floor rather than the lines of her body. After a second chorus and verse, Chita spits out "boom chica chica tum baba tum" as the drums take up a rapid samba beat. Chita spins and leaps before pulling a sleeping dancer out from underneath his blanket to join her in the carioca. Some US filmgoers (and most in Latin America) would have recognized this Brazilian dance, made famous a decade earlier in *Flying Down to Rio*, starring the Mexican idol Dolores del Rio and Fred Astaire and Ginger Rogers. (Their first onscreen dance was in fact the carioca.) Miranda and the uncredited specialty dancer (probably Ciro Rimac) twist and twirl in the center of sambaing Bahianas. The two first circle in *rebolado* and then touch foreheads as they samba across the floor. Though this dance features more "fancy footwork" than Miranda usually employs, it signifies folk rather than concert dance. The movement originates with the pelvis, and the energy moves toward the floor rather than up and out as in Western ballroom or ballet. The effect is of a raucous peasant celebration rather than a highly choreographed and stylized production number.

From the costumes to the choreography to the intertextuality of the carioca, the number demonstrates Miranda's authenticity as a Brazilian performer. Miranda's performance of Brazil (rather than pan-*Latinidad*) combined with her relative integration into the narrative makes *Doll Face*, an otherwise forgettable film, crucial to understanding her labor to create a Brazilian persona even within narratives (or songs) that denied her specificity. Even more, its staging of carnival enlivens an otherwise dull finale sequence and duller film.

Along with the *baiana* costume and sinuous gestures, Miranda's voice is crucial to the construction of her persona. Miranda's use of Portuguese throughout her US career (both in her singing and her acting) kept her linked to Latin America, demonstrating her non-Americanness through the incomprehensibility of her language. Martha Gil-Montero recounts Miranda's attempts to improve her English, including working with a dialect coach: "Eet is very, very seely. . . . Wot kind of dope dey tink I am? Een Holleewood where I joos make two peecture dey geeve me some songs I should seeng in English. So I stoddy very hard and seeng in good English. Den wot? Dey holler at me and tell me to seeng in Souse American like I talk! Dey must be nutts."[73] Coelho reports that Miranda had a solid command of English by 1941,[74] but her accent remained strong, clearly because it suited her persona as well as Good Neighbor demands of authenticity. Miranda's performance English improves slightly from her initial Fox movies to her later films, though her sung English is generally quite clear, especially after *That Night in Rio.* Miranda needed to retain a strong foreign accent in order to authenticate her pan-Latina characters.

Her accent and fractured English were not necessarily dictated by Fox but were central to her own comedic persona. As part of her efforts on behalf of American soldiers, Miranda participated in several USO shows as well as news-reels. An undated film held at the Radio, Film, and Television Archive at UCLA shows Miranda in "Sing with the Stars," hosted by Richard Lane.[75] Dressed in elaborate *baiana*, which she changes three times during the eight-minute short, Miranda appears on a facsimile of a nightclub stage, complete with cardboard palm trees and the Bando da Lua. She sings "Chica Chica Boom Chic" and then greets the film audience with "Hello mes amigos" before lapsing into Portuguese to deliver an effusive monologue presumably praising the war effort. Lane asks her to please speak English, because she's speaking to Americans. They trade lines in pidgin English (Miranda) and Spanish, not Portuguese (Lane), and then Lane suggests they sing a few songs. Miranda replies, "That's what I thought you said," nudges him, and asks, "Now what did you say?" before launching into "I-Yi-Yi-Yi-Yi-I Like You Very Much." Lane asks the film audience to sing along and "follow the bouncing ball." Miranda mimes listening, and the soldiers presumably sing, their part supplied by postrecorded sound. Then Miranda tells them they'll sing in Portuguese, and produces a bouncing "chapple" and then a bouncing banana from her turban. She begins "*Mamãe Eu Quero*," but Lane stops her about halfway through, complaining that no one can under-stand her songs and that they make no sense. They banter some more, then sing "K-K-K-Katy" together, and Miranda reprises "I-Yi-Yi" before bidding the film audience "A Deus." This film demonstrates that Miranda is comfortable lam-pooning her accent, but she also insists on teaching the soldiers a bit of Portu-guese, as well as reminds Lane that English songs (like "Mairsy Doats") don't make much sense either. It demonstrates how early in her US career Miranda effectively manipulated language in order to establish *Latinidad.*

Finally, Miranda and her costars formed a gang of Good Neighbors. Like many other stars of 1940s movie musicals, Miranda worked with the same actors across several films. Steven Cohan explains that studio-era "musicals in large part derived their coherence from their leading players."[76] Developed to promote spe-cific personae and highlight stars' specific talents, musicals used star personae and production numbers in lieu of plot or nuanced characterization. Star image was a kind of shorthand for character, most effective when the same kinds of characters and the same stars interacted in film after film. Miranda's cohort (Don Ameche/Cesar Romero as the Latin lover, Betty Grable/Alice Faye as the Ameri-can ingenue, Leonid Kinskey as the bumbling foreigner, Charlotte Greenwood/ Everett Edward Horton as the chaperones, and James Ellison/John Payne as the romantic hero) make a Foucauldian archive of Good Neighbor musicals, sedi-menting representations, performance styles, and narratives until they become taken for granted. The Russian-born Leonid Kinskey is an especially interesting addition to the group. He appeared in four films with Miranda (*Down Argentine Way, That Night in Rio, Week-End in Havana*, and *Nancy Goes to Rio*) playing, respectively, an Argentinean tour-guide-cum-gigolo, a French diplomat in love with Cecilia/Alice Faye, a Cuban bellhop, and a Russian playboy. Kinskey thus counterpoints Miranda's pan-Latina characters with his own performances of pan-ethnicity, and like Miranda plays comic supporting roles.

The performance of pan-ethnicity seems to be specifically gendered in the 1940s, especially in the Good Neighbor films. While Miranda never played European or Anglo-American characters, her male costars often did. Cuban American Cesar Romero (like Fernando Lamas, Esther Williams's husband and frequent pan-ethnic costar) was able to move between ethnicities, playing roles ranging from Cubans and Mexicans to Italians, South Asians, and Anglo-Americans. Romero was a B movie star, headlining as the Cisco Kid (1939–1941), as well as a supporting player in A pictures. Of course, Italian American Don Ameche became a leading man because he was easily pan-ethnically cast, playing Frenchmen (*The Three Musketeers*), Latinos in Good Neighbor films, Russians (*Midnight*), and assorted Anglo-Americans (including Alexander Graham Bell and Stephen Foster). Ethnic women, as Miranda's and Lena Horne's experiences make clear, were unable to play nonethnic roles.

According to Ameche, he had success in these varied roles because he was an actor with a particular talent and technique. Others, like Miranda, were personalities. In 1977, he told interviewer Ron Davis that "I always thought that performers were always in two categories in pictures—personalities and actors. And there weren't very many actors out there. Most of them, the majority of them, were performers."[77] Though Ameche credits his success to his acting ability, it is equally likely that gender played a role. It seems as though men were more easily able to move between ethnic categories, whether they were European or Latino (though African American men remained in place). As Ameche's remarks about personality indicate, stars who were strongly identified with a particular type and understood to be playing themselves were more likely to have limited career opportunities and play a narrower variety of roles. As I have demonstrated throughout, actresses were especially linked to their characters, understood to be playing themselves rather than calling upon talent or technique. Undoubtedly, spectacular performers like Russell, Williams, Horne, Miranda, and Gabor, who created a specific and strong persona (regardless of their labor to develop as actresses), were cast and recast in the same kind of role. When these personae overlaid a specific and visible nonwhite ethnic identity, they "naturally" played characters stereotypic of their ethnicity's presumed salient characteristics.

Though Miranda's characters are virtually interchangeable, the same is true of her costars. Faye and Grable are both perky blondes, differentiated only by

Figure 24: Perky dancer and Fox Blonde Betty Grable in *Down Argentine Way*, 1940, Twentieth Century–Fox.

their primary talent of singing (Faye) or dancing (Grable). Ellison and Payne have the same dark hair and lantern jaw, and both are flummoxed by Miranda's "Latin" passions before returning to their blond, American love interests. As in most of her films, Greenwood is a dancing spinster looking for romance and excitement. This interchangeability allows audiences to read intertextually and may offer more nuanced (or perhaps merely more logical) motivations, especially for Miranda's one-dimensional characters. For example, in *Springtime in the Rockies*, audiences might understand Miranda/Rosita's sudden attraction for Horton's stuffy McTavish because their characters flirted in *The Gang's All Here*.

While most movie musicals follow a generic romance plot, and many musical stars played the same character type in multiple films (*pace* Esther Williams), because Miranda was one of the only Latina actresses working in 1940s Hollywood, her representations are especially important. Her characters cannot be subtly compared the way that Grable's and Faye's might be, with some fans appreciating how Faye's husky voice and earnest candor ground her more working-class characters and others relishing Grable's feisty, fun-loving celebrities and heiresses. Further, Grable and Faye have markedly different performance

Figure 25: Pensive, singing Fox Blonde Alice Faye in *The Gang's All Here*, 1943, Twentieth Century–Fox.

styles: Faye is a more introspective actress, often staring into the middle distance to connote emotional turmoil, while Grable uses her mobile mouth to signal happiness, confusion, or anger (see figures 24 and 25).

Instead, Miranda is a singular performer, with a spectacular ethnicity. As Shari Roberts argues, Miranda was frequently "ideologically linked and filmicly paired with Betty Grable, the feminine, all-American 'norm' posited by Twentieth Century–Fox."[78] Whether she served as a foil to Grable or Faye (or, later in her career, Vivian Blaine), Miranda's difference solidifies the American heroines' position as the yardstick against which female behavior can be judged. By inverting standard depictions of femininity, Miranda disrupts her films. As Dave Kehr explains, Carmen Miranda "radically expanded the range of options available to actresses in American movies":[79] as a nonnative English speaker, physical comedienne, singer/actress, and pure spectacle, she defied convention.

CARMEN MIRANDA AND THE CARNIVALESQUE

The film scholar Sheldon Wigod describes Busby Berkeley's *The Gang's All Here* as "completely audacious in its bizarre and imaginative production numbers and cavalier attitude toward plot."[80] Miranda's second number, "The Lady in the Tutti Frutti Hat," offers her most iconic image, surrounded by vulvic strawberries and phallically waving bananas as a fruit salad seems to sprout from her head. *The Gang's All Here* is also a remarkable document of dance, music, and performance styles during World War II. Its overly complicated plot follows three nightclub entertainers—Edie Allen (Alice Faye), Dorita (Carmen Miranda), and Phil Baker (as himself)—from their successful Club New Yorker, where Edie meets and falls in love with Sgt. Andy Mason (James Ellison), to a war-bond benefit in upscale Westchester, New York. The benefit is organized by Andrew Mason Sr. (Eugene Pallette) and held at Oakwood, a nearby estate owned by Mason's friend and business partner Peyton Potter (Edward Everett Horton). His daughter Vivian (Sheila Ryan) is Andy's presumed fiancée, and Mrs. Peyton Potter (Charlotte Greenwood) is a former dancer who, unbeknownst to her husband, worked with Baker in Paris. Dorita figures out that Andy, a war hero on his way home in time for the benefit, has been professing his undying devotion to both Vivian and Edie and schemes to help Edie find true love. In the end, Vivian decides to pursue a dance career in New York, and Edie and Andy presumably reunite. (In a striking reversal of movie musical convention, their reunion is unfilmed; instead, the entire cast joins in a reprise of "Journey to a Star," their disembodied heads suggesting stars in the suburban sky.)

Three principal elements mark *The Gang's All Here* as especially carnivalesque: Berkeley's surreal dance sequences highlighting abundant food, bodies, and pleasure; the narrative movement from urban to rural settings; and the romantic relationship between rich, upper-middle-class Andy and working-class entertainer Edie (echoing the union between Blossom and Peyton Potter). As Robert Stam points out, the "abundance," "energy," and "community" that characterize movie musicals as utopic for Richard Dyer are analogous to Bakhtin's feasts, celebration of the life force, and "collective *jouissance*" of carnival.[81]

In many ways, *The Gang's All Here* also documents different Classical Hollywood acting techniques. Though Miranda obviously represents a hyperunnatural style of acting, hers isn't the film's only antinaturalist performance. Horton's and Greenwood's pratfalls and mugging and Baker's autobiographical nightclub emcee demonstrate how film acting during the 1940s continued to operate within frameworks of live variety performance, especially vaudeville. For example, Greenwood/Blossom Potter is dozing with *Variety* covering her face when Ellison/Andy Jr. calls her from the Club New Yorker to let her know that Peyton will be home late. Rather than picking up the telephone, Blossom picks up a white Persian cat, repeating "hello" impatiently until she realizes the phone is still ringing. She pushes the cat away from her face with a moue of disgust, does a quick double take, and answers the phone with belated dignity. This kind of playing to the audience (for whom is the double take performed if not for an audience?) is of course characteristic of the variety stage. Performers like Greenwood and Horton, who began in vaudeville, carried their personae and performance style from one venue to another, becoming successful character actors by transforming their live acts. Horton's characterization is full of the twitchy fussiness that made him a successful character actor for over forty years. Like Greenwood, Horton specializes in the double take, especially when interacting with Miranda and Greenwood. On one hand, these double takes, obviously directed at the audience in order to telegraph the joke, vividly break the narrative frame. At the same time, however, they support Miranda's own antinaturalist shenanigans. Though she stands out, she's not as out of place as she might be in other genres or with other performers. When filmed with physical comedians like Greenwood, Horton, and Phil Silvers (in several later films), her grotesque body and carnivalesque humor occupy the far end of a continuum of excessive performance, filled in by former vaudevillians and contrasted by the performances of the white, contained romantic leads.

Those romantic leads perform in a notably naturalist style. Though the *Variety* review noted that Ellison was "generally ineffectual in the acting department," he certainly seems to be trying for emotional depth, especially in the short sequence of him on patrol in the South Pacific. With his face artfully smudged and his gun gripped firmly at his side, Ellison projects the kind of earnest courage moviegoers presumably associated with US soldiers. He often seems to be actively thinking: for example, when he "remembers" the star he and Edie wished upon the night before, his brow furrows in concentration in order to suggest internal emotional and intellectual processes. It's not especially subtle acting, to be sure, but it is indicative of the interiority that marks naturalism on stage and screen. Faye perhaps works hardest at naturalism, telegraphing her emotions with bitten lips, brimming eyes, and shaking hands. While both Faye and Ellison might seem to be indicating rather than experiencing their emotions, in comparison with Miranda (and even Greenwood and Horton), they seem authentic. In fact, the *Variety* reviewer noted that "Faye *underplays* as usual, but always clicko,"[82] demonstrating the different registers in which film performance can be received.

The Gang's All Here is also a smorgasbord of 1940s dance styles. The Benny Goodman Orchestra, billed as itself, plays signature swing in concert, at rehearsals, and at the benefit finale. Goodman and the band are introduced at the Broadway Canteen, where Andy and Edie first meet. While Goodman sings "Minnie's in the Money," he and his band travel through the USO club, spotlighting three jitterbugging couples. The jitterbug here is relatively virtuosic, especially when the army private crouches in a backbend while twirling his partner around him before leaping up and swinging her onto his hip. Another version of the jitterbug is danced at a pool party at the Potters' given for Andy and Vivian. The teen-aged Beezy (Charles Saggau, appearing uncredited) has heard that Mrs. Potter loves to dance—since she's played by Charlotte Greenwood, she does indeed. They begin gently waltzing before he breaks out into a raucous jitterbug. At first reluctant and seemingly confused, Mrs. Potter quickly picks up the steps and indulges in her trademark windmill kicks, allowing Beezy to twirl her around by her ankle until her outraged husband interrupts them. The jitterbug, of course, is an appropriation of the Lindy Hop, a black virtuosic and vernacular dance devel-oping out of tap, the cakewalk, and the steps performed in the nightclubs and on the dance floors of Harlem in the 1930s and 1940s. Transformed to the jitterbug, it's just barely acceptable in Westchester and other upper-middle-class locales. Peyton Potter's alarm at his wife's enthusiastic dancing undoubtedly registers the crossing of racial and class lines this dance signals.[83]

Other numbers include an uncredited dancer, probably Miriam LaVelle, per-forming an extremely acrobatic dance (little more than gymnastic tricks, albeit ones requiring prodigious flexibility and strength) during a rehearsal for the war bond benefit. Mrs. Potter does a parody of the apache that made her and Baker famous in Paris in the '20s. Finally, Tony DeMarco, a frequent Twenti-eth Century–Fox featured dancer, performs a Viennese waltz with his partner Marie at the Club New Yorker, an exhibition foxtrot with Vivian at the benefit, and the salsa version of "Paducah" with Dorita/Miranda. Importantly, DeMarco outdances her, adding several kicks, leaps, and turns while Dorita remains faith-ful to more traditional samba movements. In all, *The Gang's All Here* includes a comprehensive repertoire of World War II era dance. This abundance of dance, often signaling community and borrowing from vernacular styles as well as spot-lighting virtuosic bodies (LaVelle is especially notable in this regard), further underscores the carnivalesque potential of the production numbers, and their "festive undoing" of the class and race hierarchies the film presumably supports.

The buffet of dance and musical styles offered by *The Gang's All Here* contrasts Dorita's several samba numbers. In general, nonsamba numbers are danced by a soloist or a couple. The audience is invited to admire the elegant lines of Tony and Vivian's foxtrot, thrill to the athleticism and balance of the jitterbug, or mar-vel at LaVelle's flips and spins. In all cases, the film audience mirrors the onscreen audience. When Dorita dances, she is always accompanied at least by her band but usually by scores of chorines as well. Though it's difficult not to focus on Dorita—Miranda is a charismatic performer—the effect is less a virtuoso than an entertainer enjoying herself with her audience. Second, the musicians in Dorita's numbers seem less skilled and virtuosic than those for Tony DeMarco's dances or the Broadway Canteen jitterbug. Goodman, of course, but also other members of the band are singled out, and both the foxtrot and jitterbug have extended musical sequences that spotlight the band. The Bando da Lua, though certainly no less skilled, is neither granted this kind of cinematographic focus nor offered solo opportunities. Further, their instruments, especially the tambourine and maracas, seem relatively easy to play: one need only shake them in rhythm. Of course, ethnomusicologists have decried the presumption that more technical skill is required by Western as opposed to African instruments; certainly the way that the Bando is framed in this and other Good Neighbor musicals contributes to this perception.

The dance numbers in *The Gang's All Here* thus stage the split between high, virtuosic Western dance and low, ethnic folk dance. Most importantly, they suggest that everyone can samba and therefore play at *Latinidad*, inverting ethnic markers and crossing class lines. At the Club New Yorker, for example, Phil brings out Dorita, the Bando, Edie, and a bevy of "beautiful dance instructors specially imported to teach you that brand-new South American dance sensation, the Uncle Samba." Though the dance instructors are costumed in midriff-baring *baianas*, both Edie and Dorita are in evening clothes.[84] Edie dances with Mason Sr., and Dorita teaches Peyton Potter the steps. He's not a good dancer but masters the steps enough to enjoy himself enormously—until he's caught by paparazzi. Returning to his table with Masons Jr. and Sr., he refers to Dorita as a gypsy and a South American savage. And, though insisting that "what I was doing out on the floor wasn't Peyton Potter at all," he's very pleased when Mason Jr. tells him he was "sensational." It's important to note that the frame is crowded with old, white, American men learning to samba with the club's chorines. Despite the claim that they've been imported, the dance instructors appear to be Caucasian, many with light hair and all with very light skin. As this sequence demonstrates, anyone (even stuffy old men like Peyton) can learn to samba; when they do, they get to hold a gorgeous young woman in their arms. Taken as a whole, the dances in *Gang* are a metaphoric carnival, where "exotic" South American bodies can be tried on (but ultimately discarded) by the white nightclub audience members as well as the white leading players.

The Gang's All Here presents several different dance styles, but Miranda does very little dancing herself. As Wigod points out, Berkeley's production numbers are notable for "how little dancing they actually contain."[85] Instead, their spectacular pleasures come from production design (including excessive, erotic, and even grotesque fruits, limbs, and disembodied heads) and cinematography (traveling shots and the novelty of neon light). Despite its enormous chorus, "The Lady in the Tutti-Frutti Hat" has no "dancing" beyond Miranda's simple samba and the drill-team-style choreography of undulating giant bananas manipulated by the chorines. Edie's final number, "The Polka Dot Polka," is similarly bereft of movie musical dance moves. This ode to the erotic power of a polka-dotted glove features at least a hundred female dancers dressed in turquoise unitards manipulating neon hula hoops and then pink and green or gold and silver discs over their heads and around their bodies. This surreal number shifts to a reprise of Edie's "Journey to a Star" love song, with each principal's disembodied head appearing on a floating polka dot as she or he sings a line. The finale is a staid number that forecloses the kind of community through dance in which most Classical Hollywood musicals traffic and the cross-cultural exchange of dancing bodies undergirding most of Miranda's films. Berkeley offers audiences visual excess rather than utopic community, disrupting the narrative structure and generic conventions of the movie musical in a final subversive, carnivalesque move.

Something for the Boys's cross-cultural exchange is predicated on an impossible trio of cousins, Blossom (Vivian Blaine), Harry (Phil Silvers), and Chiquita Hart (Carmen Miranda), who look and act nothing alike. The three (who have never met) inherit a decrepit Texas plantation, Magnolia Manor, and turn it into a home for wives of the soldiers stationed at nearby Camp Dixon. The soldiers chip in money and labor, but Magnolia Manor is falling down and its taxes are overdue. Sgt. Rocky Fulton (Michael O'Shea), who was a big-band leader before joining the war effort, suggests they put on a show to raise the remaining funds. Blossom, a nightclub singer, happily agrees. She and Rocky fall in love, but his fiancée, Melanie Walker (Sheila Ryan, again), shows up and tries to take over the show, the home, and Rocky's life. A furious Blossom and her loyal cousin Chiquita make the show a success and impress Colonel Grubbs, who runs the camp, but Lt. Ashley Crothers discovers Harry's illegal gambling operation (housed in an upper bedroom). Crothers (who has conveniently fallen in love with the brittle Melanie) declares Magnolia Manor off-limits for all army personnel . . . unless they're on maneuvers. Maneuvers begin, and Magnolia Manor is at the center of the war games. Rocky, taking the opportunity to plead his case to Blossom, is captured by the opposing Red Army. Though all seems lost—he and Blossom won't forgive each other, and Rocky faces disciplinary action—Chiquita saves the day with her radio-receiver tooth fillings. Rocky first translates the Morse code coming through and then uses Chiquita's teeth to send a message to the Blue Army, which surrounds Magnolia Manor and captures the flag. When Colonel Grubbs shows up, Chiquita explains everything to him, in Portuguese, which he understands perfectly. The two flirt a bit, and Colonel Grubbs reopens Magnolia Manor to his troops. Rocky is sent to officer training, Blossom forgives him, and they all put on another show.

Most reviewers agreed with the Los Angeles Times's Philip K. Scheuer that "Something for the Boys IS." "Tall girls, small girls, fair girls, red-heads and raven brunettes," enthused Bosley Crowther for the New York Times, were filmed in brilliant Technicolor. The "tempestuous Miss Miranda" was "still rather fearful to behold" but sang and danced with "superb snap."[86] Though Crowther and other reviewers focus on Miranda's singing and dancing, Something for the Boys is one of her richest acting roles, even if she is stuck playing the radio through her fillings. As the daughter of a Brazilian who married the American Fuller Brush salesman Jake Hart, she's portrayed as a proud US citizen rather than a transplanted Latin American. Except for her explanation to Colonel Grubbs, she speaks in English throughout, wisely counsels both Rocky and Blossom, goes by the Americanized nickname "Chicky," works hard and efficiently to renovate the plantation, and makes jokes at Harry, Rocky, and Melanie's expense rather than being the object of ridicule herself. Miranda plays a character with a history and fierce loyalties, albeit one who brings down the house with her energetic "Samba Boogie" and *"Batuca Nega."* And if *Something for the Boys* "seems to mean a generosity of girlish pulchritude," as the *Boston Globe* review asserts, it also celebrates feminine friendship.[87] Blossom and Chiquita band together to outwit (and outsing and outdance) their cousin Harry, stuck-up Melanie, and the army officers who get in their way, inspiring a legion of army wives to stand up for themselves and their husbands.

In the move from the city to a rural paradise, *Something for the Boys* is structurally similar to *The Gang's All Here*, but this move is more central to the overall meaning of *Something for the Boys*, which suggests a timeless locus of pleasure and ease amid the trauma and tension of military training. The Hart cousins are all resolutely northern and urban: Harry peddles stockings on gritty city streets, Blossom sings in a third-rate nightclub revue, and Chiquita works as a machinist in a war parts factory. All are clearly marked as working-class—Blossom isn't a star but a featured player in a struggling club, Chiquita is a blue-collar worker, and Harry is always one step ahead of the police and his creditors. At Magnolia Manor, the three are on top, giving orders, offering help, and enjoying the respect of the local community rather than struggling to get by in low-paying jobs. Harry in particular inverts his status and even his identity, shifting from a fast-talking northern flim-flam man to a drawling southern gentleman. As John Docker points out, Bakhtin "conceives carnival as folk, rural, and local," situating its transgressive potential in its geographic location on the margins of commercial, urban life.[88] After a brief scene in the office of their small-town lawyer, Colonel Calhoun, the Hart cousins remain at Magnolia Manor, surrounded by cypress trees and creeping kudzu that threaten to swallow the crumbling plantation. At Magnolia Manor, the Hart cousins sort out their financial, romantic, and even physical troubles: Harry is finally successful, Blossom is in love and promised a spot as a singer in Rocky's band after the war, and Chiquita's radio teeth help the army with tricky battlefield communications. This rural utopia allows the Hart cousins, especially Blossom and Chiquita, the opportunity to take charge of their lives and their fortunes. Of course, as is the case in Bakhtinian carnival, this inverted space is only temporary. At the end of the film, Blossom settles down to love and marriage, and Chiquita moves into a maternal relationship with the young army wives and hapless Harry: order is restored on all fronts.

Like the Latin American Carnivals that rework Bakhtinian tropes of class crossing, Magnolia Manor's carnivalesque inversion rehearses a complicated racial history, specifically trafficking in stereotypes of the Deep South. The production numbers, part of the two talent shows the Harts and Fulton produce to support Magnolia Manor, showcase Blaine and Miranda. The first show opens with "80 Miles outside of Atlanta," introduced by Rocky, his band, and a barbershop quartet. Blossom/Blaine takes over the lyrics about the bucolic life in small town Georgia, celebrating its innocent joys. The number is far from innocent, however. Dressed in a very short green sequined dress with a tulle parasol, Blossom is joined by about a dozen female dancers dressed in a pink polka-dotted bow and a figure-eight-shaped bodice over a flesh-toned sequined bodysuit.[89] The costumes are quite racy, with the illusion of nudity highlighted by the dancers' twisting pelvises and swinging hips. As Blossom sings, she gently shimmies her shoulders, and her hips remain still throughout, visible in the medium shots that frame her in the center of the chorines. When these chorines take over the dancing, they execute a burlesque walk, bumping and grinding as they move slightly forward and back. For the dance's signature choreography, when the women press their right hips and tap their right feet in a four-beat circle, the lights go down on their upper bodies. As their legs and hips kick and fan, the cameras focus on their lower bodies, their polka-dot-covered crotches in the center of the shot. As Rick Altman, Lucy Fischer, and especially Nadine Wills explain, "the convention of the crotch shot" in movie musicals stereotypes and stylizes femininity. Multiple crotches in motion, as in dance numbers like this one, actually problematizes the female body and "draws boundaries around femininity as a performance."[90] The excess of signifiers of female sexuality make visible the anxiety these signifiers engender. Thus, "80 Miles outside of Atlanta" is particularly carnivalesque in its inversions: the innocent lyrics juxtaposed with the revealing costumes and burlesque movement vocabulary, the supposed laziness of rural southern towns contrasted with the women's energetic singing and dancing, and the ambivalencies of the costumes and cinematography.

Chiquita/Miranda's "*Batuca Nega*," sung entirely in Portuguese, immediately follows "80 Miles outside of Atlanta." Chiquita enters to the male chorus (probably the Bando da Lua) wailing the same "initial melodic gesture" used in "Brasil" in *The Gang's All Here*. The ethnomusicologist Walter Aaron Clark points out that this is an "an ascending major sixth, an interval that has an enduring history signifying longing and desire."[91] The effect here is to imaginatively transport audiences even farther than the previous number, and to keep them moving farther south. As she emerges from a pergola flanking the house-right side of the stage, Chiquita begins singing the up-tempo samba, complete with waving arms, stomping feet, sinuous hips, and flashing eyes. Chiquita remains on the far right of the stage (though shot in the center of the camera frame) throughout the song, never taking a spot in its center. She motions for her band to join her, and she sings flanked by them, gesturing with her arms and marching her feet in quick samba steps, using the authentic *pastoras* style described above. Throughout, Chiquita/Miranda is shot in medium close-up, her full body visible. She wears a relatively refined green sequined fruit basket filled with peaches on her head, and a green and white *baiana* with exposed midriff and shoulders. Working in a foreign language and dressed in an "ethnic" costume—at least in contrast to the racy polka dots of the "80 Miles" chorines—Chiquita is an especially low other.

"*Batuca Nega*" offers the film and talent show audience what Clark calls an image of Brazil as "a zone of tropical splendor and insouciant languor."[92] Chiquita, who hasn't previously been described as an entertainer, is dynamic and virtuosic, perhaps even more than Rocky and Blossom, who have worked professionally. This exotic image of race and ethnicity, juxtaposed against the brilliantly white Blossom and her backup dancers, further inverts a racial and geographic hierarchy. Those women, whose movements include the shimmy and tap vocabularies appropriated from black dance, of course offer an inversion of their own. The audience is invited to access a carnival and utopic Brazil specifically through their already activated nostalgia for the slow and simple life of the Deep South.

Chiquita's other production number, "Samba Boogie," opens the final talent show with loud, syncopated "Brazilian" drumming accompanying the samba-stomping feet of about two dozen chorines. The camera focuses on their quick steps and swishing legs before picking out three men with hand drums attached to their hips. The music is a quick and sexy samba and entirely percussive. The big-band instrumentation begins, and Chiquita is silhouetted behind a curtain. Chiquita sings in English about the new musical style, samba boogie. Her costume for this number is eye-popping: an enormous purple, green, and gold sequined hat, a high-necked, long-sleeved turquoise halter with a heavy gold collar, and a pair of purple sequined hot pants with a long, ruffled white train like a peacock tail (see figure 26). As always, her platform shoes give her another four to five inches in height. The tempo for Chiquita's lyrics is much slower—as in "Chica Chica Boom Chic," samba is translated for US audiences by a more relaxed and gentle beat. She explains that to samba boogie, one must "Move it, groove it/Keep the jive alive and you'll improve it," which seems to mean adding the blues to samba. A samba boogie, then, is slinkier, sexier, and more reminiscent of a burlesque bump and grind than the storytelling gestures of a Brazilian *sambista* singing for a local audience. Chiquita/Miranda traces lazy figure eights with her hips in time to the music before ceding the stage to the female backup dancers. The women shift between energetic, quick samba steps and stomps and slower "boogie woogie" shimmies, incorporating the hip-thrusting, toe-tapping turn of "80 Miles." When the male dancers take the stage, Chiquita returns to beat their drums before they execute several barrel rolls in rapid succession. The song ends with Chiquita and the dancers rapidly switching from boogie to samba style but ending in a samba flourish that incorporates Kongo poses from Miranda's repertoire on all the dancers' bodies.

Figure 26: Carmen Miranda's sexy, strutting "Samba Boogie" from *Something for the Boys*, 1944, Twentieth Century–Fox.

In *Something for the Boys*, female bodies generally merge tropes of African American dance, samba, and contemporary movie musical choreography. Harry Hart/Phil Silvers also embodies racial contradiction. Harry transforms himself into a southern gentleman, one worthy of owning a plantation. He shows up at the lawyer's office in a white suit with a ribbon tie and a thick accent, his loud plaids and brash voice left up north. More than his female cousins, Harry embraces an aristocratic manner, aping the gentility he supposes the plantation's original owners expressed and falling comfortably if comically into his new role. And, in a comic tour de force, he embodies the history of African American slavery and spiritualism, offering a squirm-inducing spectacle of contemporary movie musical minstrelsy.

In this remarkable set piece, contrived to stall the Red Army, led by Lieutenant Crothers, until the Blue Army can capture them, Harry/Silvers traffics in multiple representations of blackness, dexterously merged through his own comic persona. Harry begins by proclaiming himself a true son of the "southland," segues into "Dixie" and then the protest spiritual "I Got Shoes," and insists that he knows and loves all the Souths: South America, South Dakota, South Brooklyn, and South Africa. Rocky begins beating a "tribal" rhythm on his helmet, which Blossom and another army wife pick up. Harry stomps his feet and begins chanting "hanga hanga ying goo yah," "ooga ooga chatanooga chooga" and other "African" nonsense. He leaps about the room in a reasonable facsimile of African dance, pelvis contracted, torso and hips moving oppositionally, and energy pressing into the floor. When Lieutenant Crothers makes a final attempt to take his troops and go, Harry stops him with another list of all the things the South has: "cotton pickin', fried chicken, molasses thicknin', magnolia blossoms, eatin' possums, and shortnin' bread." This last nostalgic utterance segues into an energetic version of "Mammy's Little Baby Loves Short'nin' Bread." Harry waltzes around the room before pratfalling into the fireplace, standing up with his mouth outlined with soot in the familiar minstrel caricature. He finally leads the entire company in the spiritual "Climbing Up Dem Golden Stairs," complete with call-and-response and rousing "Hallelujahs!" In just over five minutes, Harry puts on various versions of blackness, inverting his own assumed position as upper-class white man to a comic representation of those he might have enslaved and oppressed. Of course, as the discussion of Lena Horne makes clear, movie musicals employ minstrel conventions, one of which is white working-class men blacking up for the entertainment of other men. *Something for the Boys* is not necessarily reflexively commenting on a minstrel tradition or advocating class and race reversal (however temporary). At the same time, this set piece, Silvers's only opportunity to show off the comic persona he developed in vaudeville and burlesque as well as dozens of movies in the 1930s and 1940s, does offer a carnivalesque inversion of race that acknowledges the heritage of slavery on which Magnolia Manor was built as well as renders it comic. The exuberance of Harry's

singing and dancing, the mass of chorines and soldiers tramping up and down
the plantation stairs, the commingling of officers and enlisted men through song
and dance, and the festive version of army training as war games briefly upend
the hierarchies structuring the world of the film.

Carmen Miranda, instantly recognizable as the performer most likely to
wear fruit-studded turbans, developed a persona founded on the precepts of
Latin American carnival. Certainly comic but infused with a carnivalesque life
force and an undeniable eroticism, Miranda's characters—of course based significantly on her "natural" body and personality—are taken as authentic representations of *Latinidad*. At the same time, her grotesque body and unnatural
performance style stabilize the white American characters and legitimates their
"naturalist" performances. Securing Miranda's authenticity as well as that of her
costars was particularly important because most of her films were consciously
produced in order to further the US Good Neighbor policy with Latin America.
If Miranda seemed authentic and her cohort seemed natural, so too would the
narratives positioning the United States as benevolent friend to South American
countries and Brazil as a logical trade partner to the United States. As this case
study makes clear, naturalism is often mobilized to support enabling fictions of
authentic nationality, ethnicity, and gender. Further, political positions are often
implicitly and explicitly addressed in movie musicals, where their outcomes
can be naturalized by performance conventions. The temporary disruptions
of carnival, however, also destabilize the class, gender, and racial hierarchies of
Miranda's films. Not only a symbol of *Latinidad*, Miranda is thus also a symbol
of carnival—defined by Robert Stam as "a liberating explosion of otherness"[93]—
that offers a symbolic victory over the traumas of World War II and the Cold War
tensions that follow.

CHAPTER 5

FAMOUS FOR BEING FAMOUS

PERSONA, PERFORMANCE, AND
THE CASE FOR ZSA ZSA GABOR

In 1958, Universal Pictures released *Touch of Evil*, written and directed by and starring Orson Welles.[1] This film noir, famous for the incongruity of all-American Charlton Heston playing a Mexican, its three-minute opening tracking shot, and especially Welles's struggle with the studio over final cut, is now recognized as a classic of US cinema. Universal hired Harry Keller to reshoot some scenes and add new material, then edited the film to a lean ninety-three minutes but left much intact, including Zsa Zsa Gabor's cameo appearance (see figure 27).

Gabor appears on a staircase in the "strip-teasers" club she manages, walks down a few steps, and lounges there to explain that she didn't know Zita, the stripper who's just died in a car-bomb explosion at the US-Mexico border. She has one line and is onscreen for about ten seconds. She looks lovely, but no lovelier than any of the other women at the club; she is certainly not as visually striking as Marlene Dietrich as Welles's old flame Tana or Janet Leigh, playing Charlton Heston's Philadelphia bride. In a film with memorable, naturalist performances from Heston, Welles, Leigh, and Joseph Calleia as Welles's partner, Pete Menzies, Gabor is especially stilted. Even so, posters for the film proclaimed her appearance, and she's fifth billed, appearing on the same "guest-starring" title card as the legendary Dietrich, who played a much larger and more pivotal role. Gabor's part in *Touch of Evil* perfectly captures her negotiation of performance and celebrity in Classical Hollywood. She doesn't do much, but she makes the most of what she does.

Zsa Zsa Gabor is famous for being famous. She's been alternately blamed and celebrated for contemporary celebrity culture, with the Hilton sisters, Paris and Nicky (who are her step-great-granddaughters), and the Kardashian clan often cited as following in her high-heeled footsteps.[2] Though she's now a figure of either pity or parody, Gabor was once a familiar member of the Classical Hollywood celebrity pantheon. The popular culture scholar Neal Gabler refers

169

Figure 27: Zsa Zsa Gabor's brief appearance in *Touch of Evil*, 1958, Universal Studios.

to "the Zsa Zsa Factor" as "fame that required having to do no work to get it, save gaining media exposure."[3] Gabler's dismissal of Gabor and other similar celebrities, however, ignores the labor they undertake to gain media exposure, and the work staying in the spotlight demands.

It's not coincidental that contemporary celebrity culture developed its salient characteristics at the same time that naturalist acting, and especially the Method, gained currency within the film industry as well as for audiences. The paradox of naturalism, a technique to be learned and perfected while simultaneously dependent upon actors' authentic personalities and experience, justifies Don Ameche's smug claim that some performers are just personalities and others are true actors.[4] Celebrities, then, are those who trade on their personality and persona for fame. They are not actors in any traditional sense. But at the same time, naturalism's collapse of self and role foregrounds the significance of authentic personality to felicitous film performance, which in turn suggests that personality is as much a part of acting as it is of celebrity. It's also not coincidental that many celebrities accused of more fame than talent are women; the assumption that women are presenting themselves rather than crafting performance reverberates through the careers of Russell, Williams, Horne, Miranda, and countless others. But as Gabor's case study makes clear, the professional presentation of self is a performance, one carefully calibrated, continuously revised, and dependent on social context and narrative frame as well as performer agency and intent.

Gabor's show business beginnings were quite humble. In 1951, when she was married to her third husband, the Hollywood actor and recent Academy Award winner George Sanders, she appeared as a last-minute replacement on the Los Angeles CBS affiliate program *Bachelor's Haven*. The show featured a rotating panel of celebrities who offered romantic advice to lovelorn singles, both men and women, who wrote letters and called in questions. *Bachelor's Haven* mobilizes the war between the sexes, suggesting in its animated opening credits that women nag, scold, control, chase, and trick men into marriage for their own amusement. Whether Gabor molded her early persona to fit the program's needs or (more likely) was cast for her perceived natural fit, *Bachelor's Haven* was a perfect springboard for her unique talents. According to her biographer Peter Brown, Gabor's glamour, accent, and quick wit made her an immediate hit. On the first show, when the host, John (Johnny) Jacobs, introduced her by complimenting her diamond bracelet and enormous ring, Gabor fired back, "Oh, *dahlink*, these are just my working diamonds."[5] On this program, Gabor established her Hungarianness, sexual desirability, and willingness to laugh at herself, three constituent components of her persona that concretized into her "natural," "authentic" self through repetition across a variety of media.

As is the case with much early television broadcast live rather than recorded, few episodes of *Bachelor's Haven* still exist. The UCLA Film and Television Archive holds the October 17, 1951, episode, featuring Gabor, Eve (Mrs. Van) Johnson, the B-actor Richard Greene, and the *Los Angeles Daily Mirror* columnist Paul Coates.[6] Though the show is filmed live, it's clear that the panelists have rehearsed their advice and banter with each other. Coates and Gabor are regular panelists, and their relationship is combative. On this episode, the two argue about feminism, finances, and female power:

COATES: The feminist movement among women, they say we'll have a woman president someday, and I've never believed that and never will because to be president you must be 35 and there's no woman in the world who's 35.

GABOR: I want to be serious on this one—why do men always think they have better brains, when it's so obvious that ours is better. . . . Seventy-five percent of [America's] fortunes are in women's hands, which is well put there, because women know what to do with money.

COATES: They close their hot little fists around it and that's the end of our money.

At this, Gabor sniffs and carefully settles her fringed, sequined velvet scarf further down her shoulders to expose her dark, strapless tulle dress and its multiple diamond brooches, ending the argument by calling attention to her own wealth as well as her physical beauty. (Gabor is stunningly attired and perfectly coiffed; Jacobs, Coates, and Greene wear tuxedos; and Johnson is in a light-colored, sleeveless satin dress with a diamond brooch fastened at her deep-V décolletage.) Gabor is clearly the star of the show: most of the questions are directed to her first, and the camera tracks her more than other performers. At the same time, she's not in control of the discussion in the way she is for later appearances on, say, *The Tonight Show* or *What's My Line*. Even so, she's very aware of her self-presentation. Throughout the show, she makes subtle adjustments to her clothing and hair. Her accent is very thick, and she seems very young, though she's in her early to midthirties. She frequently performs confusion at references to carpooling, the magazine *Field and Stream*, and javelins. When they're defined she pronounces the first two "not chic" and the latter "terribly chic," the French adjective she uses at least a dozen times in the twenty-two-minute program and which seems to be her trademark.

Gabor's run on *Bachelor's Haven* was quite successful and quickly moved her into a national spotlight. The October 17 episode was bookended by John Jacobs's highlighting that week's *Life* magazine, which featured Gabor on the cover. In a light-colored strapless satin dress, satin stole, diamond bracelet and necklace, and large pearl and diamond earrings, Gabor is shot from the waist up, her chin lifted to meet the viewers' gaze with her own. Fresh flowers are pinned to her bodice, and her breasts are on creamy display, a dark shadow suggesting deep cleavage running between them. The accompanying text contrasts Zsa Zsa with her more famous sister. The photographer, Philippe Halsman, enthused that comparing the sisters was like comparing "a fine white wine—Eva—with a fine champagne—Zsa Zsa" but continued that Zsa Zsa's "brain exudes more sex appeal" than anyone he'd ever met.[7] The article, "Another Gabor," is illustrated with a two-thirds-page, full-body photo of Gabor dressed in a strapless white-eyelet sundress and matching parasol walking in her Bel Air garden with her toddler, Francesca, dressed in a dark dress and white pinafore. Another photo, from the *Bachelor's Haven* set, shows Gabor flanked by Jacobs and Amanda Blake, another panelist (who went on to star as Miss Kitty on *Gunsmoke*). Here, Gabor is dressed in a very low-cut, strapless, dark dress with jeweled brooches, earrings, bracelets, and necklaces, gesturing animatedly. The final photograph shows Gabor rehearsing choreography from *Lovely to Look At*, the Mervyn LeRoy film in which she's just been cast. Dressed in a low-cut black leotard with shorts, fishnet tights, and strappy high-heeled sandals, she's bent gracefully at the waist, arms in a balletic pose and eyes focused on her dance coach.

The text explains that Gabor is "the biggest new hit on West Coast TV" on account of "her beauty, ripe Continental accent and the Hungarian *savoir-faire* with which she tosses off her advice to the lovelorn." Gabor claims that she's popular because "men have always liked me and I have always liked men," foregrounding her desirability and gesturing toward her notoriety. The article includes several of her zippy one-liners, like her advice to a woman who had received lingerie, a ring, china, a stove, and a bed from her fiancé but had broken off their engagement: "She should give back the stove."[8] *Life*'s assessment of Gabor's popularity was prescient. She was nominated for a regional Emmy, up against her fellow TV personality Betty White. According to White, Gabor was the Emmy favorite: "They were going to announce the name, and Zsa Zsa got out her purse, and she powdered her nose and put her lipstick on, and they said my name." Both women were shocked.[9] White, of course, continues to be a beloved television comedienne, but Gabor struggled to develop a legitimate acting career.

Gabor's time on *Bachelor's Haven* demonstrates that she started at the very bottom rung of the celebrity ladder and built her career from there. In the early 1950s, she was commended for her beauty and wit, presenting a glamorous, worldly persona on which her early casting drew. Her beauty and persona were compelling enough that she was offered an MGM contract and cast in three big-budget Technicolor musicals, *Lovely to Look At* and *Moulin Rouge* in 1952 and *Lili* in 1953. In the 1950s she made fifteen films and appeared on television as characters in over a dozen programs and as a guest on another dozen variety and talk shows. Gabler's "Zsa Zsa Factor" separates "fame" and "achievement," arguing that Gabor "had the greatest fame with the least achievement"[10]—in short, she didn't *do* anything to deserve her celebrity. The narrative of Gabor's early career, on the other hand, suggests that she did quite a bit, first to get noticed and then to develop as a performer.

Gabler is correct to distinguish Gabor from other 1940s and 1950s actresses. Importantly, her start in show business was as a television personality. Unlike Russell, who trained with Maria Ouspenskaya, Williams, who swam competitively, or Horne and Miranda, who established singing careers before signing a Hollywood contract, Gabor became famous for being herself, or at least being someone who seemed to be an authentic representation of a multiply married Hungarian refugee with a passion for men and diamonds named "Zsa Zsa Gabor."

The women in this book occupy a continuum of performance based on playing themselves. Jane Russell, appearing in film noir, musical comedy, and Westerns, was perhaps the most versatile, able to play a variety of roles if not always a variety of types. Williams is an extremely engaging and quite competent performer, but she's always a swimmer, and that identity defines her characters. Horne, limited by institutionalized racism to versions of the tragic mulatto, and Miranda, embodying *Latinidad*, were equally tied to their personae in their film roles. These four women, however, began with an especial talent, skill, or appearance and created a persona that linked those qualities with their roles. But Gabor made a career playing herself, reversing the process. First she created a persona and then parlayed that into a film and television career, using her performances as a springboard to greater celebrity and concomitantly a stronger persona.

In this chapter, I make a case for the importance of Gabor in considerations of postwar naturalist acting, arguing that she epitomized the collapse of self and role through which naturalism was often understood. Because I take for granted that Zsa Zsa Gabor is an antecedent of contemporary celebrity culture, her case study also illuminates links between the naturalist paradigm and the performance of self that often defines contemporary performers, whether they are legitimate film stars or reality television personalities. Using Gabor's appearances on domestic sitcoms, I demonstrate how naturalism transferred to television acting in the early days of the medium. Further, her television roles reveal how playing herself undercuts the naturalist paradigm while subverting the narratives of her television plots. I begin with Gabor's biography, paying particular attention to her efforts to create a distinctive persona, one with a remarkably long shelf life predicated at least in part on her willingness to parody her own image. I turn to early descriptions and debate about television acting as distinct from both theater and film in order to place Gabor's performances in context as well as expand my interrogation of the naturalist paradigm. Finally, I read Gabor's performances on *December Bride, Mr. Ed*, and *The Joey Bishop Show* as indicative of the limits of naturalist (television) performance when confronted by deliberate performances of self.

Spectacular Persona, Spectacular Performance

Zsa Zsa Gabor's performances of self were also performances of excess. Accentuated with tight gowns, opera gloves, and ostentatious jewels, Gabor's voluptuous body promised sensuality commensurate with her notorious marriages and love affairs. A familiar figure across a wide range of Classical Hollywood media, she made a spectacle of her body, ambition, wealth, and commitment to marrying (frequently) for money as much as for love and lust. Gabor's persona epitomized excess: she wasn't merely curvy, she was pneumatic; she didn't wear a wedding ring, she dripped in diamonds, emeralds, rubies, and pearls; she was dressed not merely attractively but in recognizable haute couture; she wasn't titillating, she was overtly sexual. Performed for a scandalized but fascinated audience, her excessive persona set her apart from even the spectacular women I consider above.

Gabor established a biography that naturalized her claims to perennial youth, fabulous sexuality, and ostentatious wealth, enlarging familiar tropes of femininity to perform a self that was always already spectacular and bigger than life. Even without her physical appearance, and even with a skeptical eye toward some of her embellishments, Gabor has a rather remarkable personal history. She was born Sari Gabor sometime between 1917 and 1923 in Budapest to upper-middle-class parents with strong connections to the Hungarian military and financial networks.[11] Her father, Major Vilmos Gabor, was nearly twenty years older than her mother, Jolie Tilleman, the daughter of a successful Budapest jeweler. Jolie had longed to be an actress,[12] and she passed her ambitions on to her three daughters, Zsa Zsa, Magda (two years older) and Eva (two years younger and famous from *Green Acres*, a 1960s television program costarring Eddie Albert). The Gabor marriage was always rocky, and all three sisters were sent to Madame Subilia's School for Young Ladies in Lausanne, Switzerland. When she was fifteen, Gabor claims in her autobiography, she entered the Miss Hungary Pageant and won, though she was disqualified because the winner had to be sixteen. As consolation, her mother took her to Vienna, where the famous tenor Richard Tauber discovered her; he had written and was about to produce an operetta, *The Singing Dream*, and cast the teenager as Violet, the soubrette, despite her singular lack of talent.[13]

After her Austrian debut (when, according to her first autobiography, she took her first lover, "Willi" Schmidt-Kentner, a married German composer), she returned to Budapest determined to leave her family's suffocating ambitions and petty jealousies. She proposed to a Turkish diplomat, Burhan Belge, and the two were quickly married.[14] Gabor moved to Ankara and had an affair with Mustafa Kemal Atatürk, the first president of Turkey and founder of its republic (according to her second autobiography, he rather than Schmidt-Kentner or Belge took her virginity).[15]

Gabor left Belge to visit her parents in Budapest in 1940 and never saw him again. She fled her husband and the Nazis in a months-long trip to the United States via the Orient Express to Bombay. In Bombay, she boarded the SS *U. S. Grant*, and scandalized her fellow passengers when "dancing in the ship's ballroom, [her] sari unraveled—leaving [her] nude."[16] When she joined Eva in Los Angeles in 1941, the *Los Angeles Times* reported that "Sara" Belge was thrilled to be in the United States because of "the absence of oppression."[17] Her parents (now divorced but still close) and sister Magda were trapped in Budapest, and Eva and Zsa Zsa tried to help them immigrate. The final three Gabors finally arrived in the United States in 1946 after spending time in Portugal; one of Magda's lovers was the Portuguese ambassador, and he organized their escape from Hungary.

In April 1942, Gabor married Conrad Hilton after her first marriage was annulled. Like Belge, Hilton was several decades her senior; the two remained married until 1946.[18] During that period, they were separated for months at a time; Gabor often lived at Hilton's Plaza Hotel in New York City while Hilton was based in California. Despite their separation, and Gabor's hospitalization for depression they had a daughter, Constance Francesca (called Francie), in 1947, after their divorce was finalized.[19]

On April 2, 1949, Gabor married George Sanders, whom she usually called the great love of her life. Even so, the two had a difficult marriage and frequently fought bitterly only to reconcile briefly.[20] The marriage wasn't helped by Sanders's focus on his career (he won his Academy Award in 1951 for playing Addison DeWitt in *All about Eve*), Gabor's growing fame after *Bachelor's Haven*, or her long love affair with Porfirio Rubirosa. Sanders filed for divorce in 1953. Also in 1953, when Gabor was preparing for her first Las Vegas sister act, Rubirosa blacked her eye because she refused to marry him.[21] Rubirosa married Barbara Hutton instead, but he and Gabor continued their affair. When her divorce from Sanders was finalized in 1955, the *Los Angeles Times* announced that she and Rubirosa would marry soon (and gave her age as thirty-four), but the two never did.

In the late 1950s and early 1960s, Gabor worked regularly, appearing in small roles in films, on television, and in Las Vegas in solo nightclub acts as well as with her two sisters. In 1962, she married Herbert L. Hutner, a wealthy industrialist. She told the *Los Angeles Times* that "I have known heem for a long time. . . . And then, four weeks ago, we see each othair and we fall een luff."[22] Two days after divorcing Hutner, on March 6, 1966, Gabor married the Dallas petroleum executive Joshua S. Cosden Jr. Though she planned to live in Texas with him, she also hoped to continue her career.[23] Apparently her career, which was mostly appearances on talk shows and variety programs, was more important, and the two divorced a little over a year later. Gabor was single for the next eight years, living mainly in Palm Springs and working sporadically until she married the "millionaire industrialist" Jack Ryan on January 22, 1975. That marriage lasted about eighteen months, and she married Michael O'Hara, her divorce attorney, on August 27, 1976; they divorced in 1982. She almost married Felipe de Alba in April 1982, but her divorce from O'Hara wasn't yet final, and so the marriage was invalid. Though she and de Alba planned a wedding for that July, Gabor backed out because "he bored me. . . . He's a playboy and I'm a hardworking actress."[24] Despite her claim, Gabor rarely acted or even appeared on television in the late 1970s and 1980s. She married Frédéric Prinz von Anhalt on August 14, 1986, in a small ceremony at her Bel Air home. Eva and her mother, Jolie, "boycotted the ceremony" because they believed that Prinz von Anhalt was "a convicted con man who bought his German title," but the close family soon reconciled.[25]

In 1989, Gabor had her last real moment of fame. Driving in Beverly Hills, she was stopped by Patrolman Paul Kramer. She slapped him, and he arrested her. Gabor was sentenced to 72 hours in jail and 120 hours of community service. Though initially the butt of jokes, Gabor turned the arrest to her advantage, appearing in commercials, on talk shows, and in films that parodied the incident until the late 1990s.[26] In 2002, she was in a car accident that left her partially paralyzed, and she had a stroke in 2005. Since 2010, she's been in and out of hospital after complications from a fall.[27] Her husband (who claimed to have fathered Anna Nicole Smith's daughter, Dannielynn) and her daughter, Francesca, have been battling for conservatorship and for access to her fortune.[28] Gabor's sisters and parents are dead, she remains married to Prinz von Anhalt, and she is frequently estranged from Francesca.

Styling herself after the mythic courtesans of the nineteenth century, Gabor manipulated her personal narrative in order to present herself in the most desirable light. She focused on three constituent components of her biography to authenticate her persona: her Hungarianness, her sexual desire and desirability, and her parodic self-presentation. These three of course overlap, were carefully manipulated, and shifted throughout her long career. In important ways, Gabor's excessive but "authentic" persona provided key alternatives to more traditional ideologies of femininity circulating in the 1950s and 1960s, at the height of her fame. At the same time, Gabor's persona was flexible enough to adapt to changing definitions of the feminine and especially female sexuality, keeping her pop-culturally relevant into her old age.

Gabor presented herself as a proud Hungarian, especially during the Cold War. In October 1956, Hungary briefly rebelled against the Soviet regime, but on November 4, the Soviet army invaded Hungary and overwhelmed the revolutionary forces. In January 1957, *Time* magazine named the "Hungarian Freedom Fighter" Man of the Year; the cover image showed a grim-faced, gun-toting young man with dark hair, a sharp nose, and determined eyes shadowed by an armed peasant woman and a young, slender man with a rifle of his own. The text profiled four revolutionaries and explained that they "gave to millions, and specifically to the youth of Eastern Europe, the hope for a foreseeable end to the long night of Communist dictatorship."[29] Thus, Hungary symbolized another front in the cold war against communism, and its citizens were figured as impoverished, desperate, but determined revolutionaries. Zsa Zsa Gabor, however, challenged this understanding of Hungary.

Drawing on notions of Old World aristocracy, Gabor separated her persona from the grim-faced freedom fighter, articulating Hungary as sophisticated, opulent, and glamorous rather than dispossessed. For example, the Foreign Press Association publicized its second annual awards event with a one-third-page photograph of Gabor in a low-cut, strapless gown, opera gloves, a huge diamond choker, and a diamond and feather tiara—an ensemble that was luxurious as well as oddly exotic. The event, described by an FPA spokesperson, Henry Gris, as "reminiscent of the days before World War I," was intended to remind Hollywood studios that the aesthetic and cultural standards of foreign markets could influence film success.[30] While her contemporary blond bombshells Marilyn Monroe, Mamie Van Doren, and Jayne Mansfield were all-American, Gabor's thick accent, passion for all things European and chic, and "continental" attitude toward love and marriage were constitutive elements of her persona. In her personal life as well as her many public appearances, she identified herself as Hungarian and used her national background to distinguish herself.

For example, in 1952, the *Los Angeles Times* style columnist Lydia Lane wrote a two-page feature about Gabor's secrets for success. Gabor credited her appeal to her European sense of chic and focused on the difference between American and European style. "It is easy to be chic if you choose simple clothes and simple colors. I find the American woman is inclined to be too fancy," she claimed, and went on to explain that Americans, unlike Europeans, had so many options at such bargain prices that they might "go wild" and buy everything that appealed to them, a mistake she made when she first arrived in the country. She counseled Lane's American audience: "If you can afford just a sweater and a skirt have a good cardigan and a skirt that fits well. You can change around with a scarf, flowers or pearls at your throat."[31] Here Gabor deploys fashion advice familiar to any reader of any woman's magazine—shop for quality, not quantity—but clearly highlights her own chic by suggesting jewelry or fresh flowers to add variety. Further, her criticism of American women simultaneously notes the "marvelous" consumer choices available to US shoppers. Capitalism was obviously superior to European economic systems but needed to be balanced with the kind of good taste a European upbringing offered.

Gabor also used her Hungarianness to demonstrate that she was just a regular gal, despite her fabulous diamonds and décolletage. When Hedda Hopper interviewed her in 1953 at her Hollywood Hills home, Gabor invited her in for goulash and girl talk. Gabor and Sanders had been having marital difficulties, and Gabor used the interview to explain that she and Sanders were once again happily living together. Hopper—who appended "Hungarian" or "Budapest" to nearly every mention of Gabor—approved of her traditional Old World wifeliness and portrayed her as happiest taking care of her husband. Further, Gabor spiced up married life with paprika (and presumably other, less family-friendly Hungarian tricks).[32] The Gabor family reportedly maintained their Hungarian heritage as well as their connection to each other through traditional family parties, featuring that ubiquitous goulash (see figure 28). In 1958, for example, Gabor phoned Hopper to tell her about the party she was throwing for her sister Eva and Noël Coward: "I expected it would be for our intimate friends, but everybody wants to come. Mamma is flying out from New York to prepare Hungarian goulash."[33] Ten years after the Hopper interview, Gabor was still plugging goulash. She appeared on *The Steve Allen Show* in a low-cut taffeta evening gown with lacy apron and diamond and pearl jewelry to prepare champagne goulash with sauerkraut, a "very Hungarian" dish, offering several facts about Hungarian cooking, Hungarian women, paprika, Hungarian hunting dogs, and "gypsies" during her thirty-minute segment.[34] Like her focus on fashion and glamour, Gabor's definition of "Hungary" as family and goulash rearticulated it within Cold War discourse.

Figure 28: Three generations of Gabors posing in Vienna, Austria, on October 29, 1958. From left are Zsa Zsa, Papa Vilmos Gabor, and Francesca Hilton, Zsa Zsa's daughter. Standing behind are Magda, Mama Jolie, and Eva. (AP Photo)

Gabor's comfort in the United States was contrasted with the circumstances of friends and family members she left behind. In 1954, the *Los Angeles Times* ran two articles, six months apart, about Gabor's father, Vilmos, who had returned to Hungary after living in the United States with his daughters. It's unclear why these articles ran, as they're not especially newsworthy, but they are notable for how they position Gabor and her family within narratives of communist repression. For the first, Endre Marton interviewed Vilmos Gabor at his home, a one-room apartment in the Budapest suburb of Budakeszi. The article reports that Vilmos fled Budapest with Jolie and Magda in 1944 when "the Hungarian version of the Nazi movement began a short but bloody Reign of Terror," returning alone in 1947 to reclaim his real estate holdings and jewelry business. In 1950, he was "dispossessed by the Reds and exiled from Budapest." His financial holdings were nationalized, and he and his second wife were ordered out of Budapest as undesirables; they spent the next two years in the Jewish asylum in Nyireghaza. His current situation is contrasted with his life before World War II and communism:

> Budapest old-timers recall the way the Gabors swanked around the city in the relaxed 1930s. Although the Hungarian capital had a rigid caste system which excluded shopkeepers and their families from really top-drawer society, Mama Jolie and her three beautiful daughters flashed around in expensive cars, had foreign tutors and their own stable, patronized the exclusive and fashionable restaurants in the company of members of the diplomatic

corps and generally raised the eyebrows of the city's Old Guard, which never did let down the bars to admit the family.

Marton reports that Vilmos's daughters, grateful for their earlier life of luxury, support their father by sending him the limit of US$40 in gifts and cash each month. The article ends by noting that Vilmos was a decorated World War I hero who was now "patiently" waiting to rejoin his daughters in the United States. "And next times," he says, "I won't be tempted to return."[35]

Though Gabor touted her aristocratic national heritage, she also underscored her identification with democracy. In 1952, the *Los Angeles Times* television reporter Walter Ames reported on Gabor's addition to the March 17 *Congressional Record*. Ames congratulated Gabor on her citizenship and reprinted much of her entry. "You, as Congressmen," she wrote, "can speak out if you see something happening in our government that you believe is wrong. If I think you are right, I can say so. If I think you are not right, I can say so, too. People like me, who have come from countries that are not free and who now have this privilege that native-born Americans take for granted, know that it is the basis of all freedom."[36] As repression in Hungary intensified, Gabor continued to champion her countrymen and women. In 1956, Hopper reported that Gabor phoned to say she'd checked in at the Plaza. "Zsa Zsa is out raising money for the Hungarian war relief; says she can't think of anything else. 'All our relatives are there,' she told me."[37] In 1957, she cohosted an all-star benefit for Americans for a Free Hungary featuring Danny Thomas, Frank Sinatra, and Dean Martin as well as a Hungarian troupe performing authentic dances.[38] Though Gabor's self-promotion of her charity work may undercut its sincerity, it does demonstrate how thoroughly her persona depended on Hungarianness for intelligibility.

Gabor's performance of Hungarian and US national identities further refigured Eastern European immigrant identity for US audiences, and especially erased any connection to the Holocaust. She always insisted that she immigrated to the United States in 1941 in order to escape her stifling marriage to the Turkish diplomat Burhan Belge, whom she married to escape her stifling relationship with her father. Importantly, Gabor framed her World War II emigration as fleeing from men, rather than from the ravages of war.

Obviously, Gabor plots a different narrative from the Jews who fled Hitler's Nazis and their extermination policies, one that may have offered multiple identificatory positions for other recent immigrants. Gabor never claimed (or admitted) she was Jewish, but she explains in her first autobiography that she flung champagne in a man's face because he'd made an anti-Semitic remark about Charles Isaacs, Eva's second husband.[39] In both autobiographies, she makes approving remarks about Jewish men in particular. Further, her family background in jewelry, their exclusion from "really top-drawer" society, the attention paid to her dyed blond hair, and speculation about a nose job suggest that elements of her persona incorporated stereotypes of Jewishness.[40] Some audiences might have read these anecdotes and identified her (as well as identified with her) as Jewish. Recently, the gossip columnist Cindy Adams, a longtime family friend and the author of Jolie's biography, claimed that the family was genuinely Jewish. Jolie, claims Adams, told her, "Eva's new about-to-be-husband hates the Jews, so in this book make us Catholic."[41] Regardless of her ethnic and religious affiliation, Gabor mobilized her Hungarian identity to locate herself outside narratives that figured European immigrants as victims or refugees, insisting on her status as a freedom-loving femme fatale. Finally, that some immigrants might have modeled themselves in her image (whether Jewish or not), demonstrates how flexible her persona could be, and how authenticity can be differently read depending on audience experience and cultural context.

Zsa Zsa Gabor certainly was a femme fatale. Her sexual desire, and the desire she incited in others, was legendary. "If she didn't have a husband, she had a lover, because that's the only way a Gabor knows she's alive," Adams said.[42] Her autobiographies detail affairs (or at least one-night stands) with Sean Connery, Frank Sinatra, Richard Burton, Aly Khan, Charlie Chaplin, her stepson Nicky Hilton, and near misses with John F. Kennedy, J. Paul Getty, and Henry Kissinger. Gabor's sexuality is another marker of her authentic self, made to seem natural. As Richard de Cordova argues, the "sexual scandal is the primal scene of all star discourse, the only scenario that offers the promise of a full and satisfying disclosure of the stars' identity." Because Gabor offered up her sexual scandals, sometimes hinting at her sexual appetites and at other times, as in her affair with Rubirosa, offering photographic and verbal evidence of unbridled passion, she seemed especially "real." If, as de Cordova explains, "the popularity of stars has always been linked with their 'sex appeal,'" then Gabor's self-exploitation is unsurprising.[43] Not having many screen characters with which to build an identity and endear herself to movie audiences, Gabor used what she had—her fabulous and well-documented sex appeal—to craft a persona. Following from Foucault, sexuality is an especially privileged sign of authenticity and truth, and Gabor (despite her evident self-manipulation of her image) was thus an especially authentic star, one who voiced and embodied female sexuality at a time when it was largely hidden from view.

In 1959, as she prepared to write her first autobiography with Gerold Frank, *Life* magazine ran a cover story, "Zsa Zsa Gabor and Her Famous Ghost." Again photographed by Philippe Halsman, the cover foregrounds Gabor's ripe sexuality; Frank stands behind her, shrouded in mist. Gabor's blond hair is in loose short curls around her upturned face, and her lips are especially full and barely parted. She wears a strapless, rhinestone-studded white gown that reveals a daring décolletage including the bottom curve of the right breast, accessorized with a sparkling diamond necklace and earrings. In the accompanying nine-page article, Frank explains that he writes so that readers can discover what it's like to "actually, literally roll in the gutter . . . to know ecstasy that most of us never know—to be transfigured by love." *Life* told its readers to expect an exciting narrative because "Frank turns out major best-sellers by helping ladies reveal sensational pasts." Frank himself compares Gabor to Madame de Pompadour and Madame du Barry, surviving the conservative mid-twentieth century "undamaged by the PTA."[44] The article promises scandal and sexual titillation.

Indeed, the book frames Gabor's life as a series of love affairs, with both husbands and lovers. Reviews noted that she "shared a bird, bottle and bed with some of the biggest male celebrities of the mid-20th Century" and that "her morals are not conventional," suggesting that the book would shock many readers.[45] The book promises a glimpse at the "true" Zsa Zsa Gabor, with her sexual exploits uncensored. Of course, given the book's 1960 publication date, her affairs are described euphemistically: "I was Eve, the first and last woman in the world, without name, without history; he was Adam, the first and last man in the world, without name, without history. . . . I went to him each dawn like a grateful dog who goes to his master."[46] This purple prose, with its metaphors of the Garden and suggestions of domination, certainly indicates Gabor's enthusiastic enjoyment of physical intimacy with men, even those she doesn't know or love. This lover, for example, was an anonymous, rugged, and silent fisherman she met on the beach in New Jersey while recovering from her mental breakdown.

Zsa Zsa's most famous relationship wasn't with any of her husbands but with Porfirio Rubirosa, a Dominican playboy who married nearly as often and as well as she. Rubirosa, who wed the Dominican dictator Rafael Trujillo's daughter Flor de Oro in 1932 but divorced her five years later, was named ambassador to Argentina in 1947 while married to the tobacco heiress Doris Duke. Those two soon divorced, and by 1953, he was romancing Gabor.[47] Rubirosa's reputation for his sexual prowess was based in large part on his large part. Doris Duke rhapsodized that "it was the most magnificent penis that I had ever seen . . . six inches in circumference." His biographer Shawn Levy repeats the chestnut that Parisian waiters nicknamed their largest pepper mills "Rubirosas" in his honor.[48] Though Gabor and Rubirosa were both married to other people (Sanders and Barbara Hutton), they had a passionate, transatlantic affair (see figure 29).

In December 1953, as Zsa Zsa was preparing for her Las Vegas debut with her sisters, Eva and Magda, Rubirosa apparently punched her in the eye because she refused to marry him. Gabor premiered in a black eye patch and reportedly contemplated suing her lover for $1,000,000 in damages. Phoning Hedda Hopper with this scoop, Gabor explained that Rubirosa hit her "for one single reason. He loves me and couldn't understand I don't want him."[49] According to Gabor, her refusal sent him to Barbara Hutton, and the two immediately eloped; in his own attempt at image management, Rubirosa claimed that Gabor's black eye was nothing more than a publicity stunt.[50] Gabor was a hit in her Las Vegas show, sparked a trend in eye patches, and publicly declared that she was "better

Figure 29: Zsa Zsa Gabor and Porfirio Rubirosa at the Orly Airport in Paris, France, May 2, 1955. (AP Photo)

off than Barbara, even with a black eye."[51] After the Hutton-Rubirosa wedding, however, the lovers scandalized newspaper readers when stories of Rubirosa's visit to Gabor on the set of *Three Ring Circus* in Phoenix were made public. Rubirosa used Hutton's private plane to visit Gabor, and they spent forty-eight hours together; Hopper again got the scoop.[52]

Public fascination with Gabor and Rubirosa lasted as long as their affair. A 1955 Hearst newsreel included footage of their Paris reunion after both their divorces were finalized. As a montage of the lovers admiring Rubirosa's sports car, choosing horses in a stable, and riding through the Bois de Boulogne played, the voice-over explained, "The season is spring, the scene is Paris, and romance is obviously the main item on the agenda as actress Zsa Zsa Gabor arrives for a reunion with Porfirio Rubirosa."[53] The two are very intimate in public; given their reputations, it is clear that they are sexually involved. That their romance was noteworthy enough to be featured in a newsreel demonstrates the level of public interest in the pair.

Importantly, Gabor's sexuality, though often figured within marriage, was not reproductive; that is, despite the evidence of her daughter, Francesca Hilton, Gabor never presented herself as a mother. As Adrienne L. McLean argues in *Being Rita Hayworth*, female Hollywood stars are understood as being mothers first and actresses second: "As is well known, very few Hollywood babies have *not* been the apple of their mothers' eyes, the center of their households, the thing they rush home to be with after studio work is done (the litany is fairly standard). As is also well known, virtually all Hollywood women with young children are characterized as devoted mothers."[54] Though Gabor was occasionally photographed with Francesca, and their relationship is mentioned in Gabor's 1960 autobiography, she generally eschewed the role of mother. Gabor's publicity rarely references Francesca, motherhood in general, or the supposed fulfillment that caring for children can bring. Gabor suggested instead that a woman's duty was to please men in their bedrooms rather than care for their children in their nurseries. Markedly different from both traditional models of femininity as well as most celebrity personifications of those models, Gabor's persona offered a glamorous if ambivalent alternative to postwar ideologies of contained feminine sexuality, one that she made seem especially natural.

In the 1970s, when she was clearly old enough to be a grandmother (even if she increasingly fudged her birth date and continued to dress as she had twenty years earlier), Gabor's flexible persona absorbed other understandings of the feminine, incorporating postmenopausal sexuality into her earlier bombshell image. In the 1970s, postmenopausal women were rarely seen on television: frumpy, nagging Edith Bunker is their primary representative, and conventional understandings of menopause suggested women lost their sex drives and their sex appeal. Gabor made multiple appearances on *The Tonight Show*, *The Merv Griffin Show*, *The Mike Douglas Show*, and *The David Frost Show* in the 1970s and 1980s. In all, she discussed her current marriage, her sisters and mother, and her most recent flirtations. Always dressed in décolletage, covered in diamonds, pearls, or colored jewels that matched her gown, her cotton candy hair fluffed about her face, she presented herself as still desirable and desiring. One famous anecdote, which both Gabor and Johnny Carson denied, is especially shocking.[55] According to the story, during a 1972 *Tonight Show* appearance, Gabor brought one of her Persian cats onstage. She asked the famously womanizing Carson if he'd like to pet her pussy; Carson suggested she "move the damn cat." Though this incident probably never happened (Gabor hated cats but often brought her tiny lapdogs with her), its circulation in popular culture suggests that audiences were willing to believe in her rapacious desires and provocative sensuality.

Insisting on her continued desire and desirability, Gabor personified the tradition of older women who welcome the "change of life" for its freedom from pregnancy and remain both erotically experienced and erotically charged enough to attract men (see figure 30).[56] Even in 1991, visiting *The Late Show with David Letterman* to promote her latest autobiography, *One Lifetime Is Not Enough*, she remained flirtatious. She accused Letterman of being a "pervert," obsessed with stories about her time in jail and the "gun-toting lesbians" she met there. She tells Letterman that he's her type, and Letterman says he's both flattered and scared.[57] He should be; despite the fact that Gabor is likely in her seventies, her face is

Figure 30: Zsa Zsa Gabor on August 15, 1986, the day of her wedding to Frederic Prinz von Anhalt. (AP Photo/File)

smooth, her figure is lush, and her manner is charming. She's still a compelling guest, and the audience roars with laughter at their banter.

Gabor's success in 1991 led to another *Letterman* appearance. On October 15, 1993, on one of his regular visits to Los Angeles, Letterman premiered a short film of the two friends (Letterman called her one of his "all-time favorite people"). They ate fast food in several Los Angeles restaurants, including McDonald's, Jack in the Box, Wendy's, Burger King, KFC, Taco Bell, and local favorites In-N-Out and Fatburger.[58] The segment, about five minutes long, begins with Letterman picking up Gabor in a convertible at her enormous Bel Air mansion, her husband Prinz van Anhalt gruffly waving good-bye. Gabor is wearing a yellow pantsuit, a white shirt with a man's tie, and large sunglasses, looking casual and chic. Her fluffy blond hair blows in the breeze, and she's relaxed and laughing throughout. At McDonald's, their first stop, Letterman orders her a Filet-O-Fish and asks to see the wine list; Gabor bellows with laughter. Throughout the segment, Gabor and Letterman send up her aristocratic pretensions (they entwine their arms to sip soda and carelessly toss food wrappers into the backseat), her sexual proclivities (at In-N-Out Letterman tells the audience to "make up your own jokes," and she playfully bites at his finger when he feeds her a very long french fry), and her age (Letterman asks an employee if he has "seen that Jurassic Park movie" and explains that "she used to keep those animals as pets"). Gabor is relaxed and funny and seems very comfortable with Letterman, the fast-food employees, and the smorgasbord of food. Their montage frequently cuts back to Prinz von Anhalt sitting on the porch and clearly waiting for her return, smoking a giant cigar. Though the jokes are generally on her, she's clearly in on them, an active and willing participant in the parody of her persona, and the shots of Prinz von Anhalt remind the audience that she's a real person, with a real husband, house, and life outside of Letterman's parodic frame.

Gabor's willingness to mock her persona wasn't a late-life invention, however. For example, in 1964 she hosted an episode of *Shindig!*[59] In addition to introducing several of the musical acts, charming host Jimmy O'Neill, and telling a few jokes, Gabor sang the program's most elaborate musical number, a cover of Chris Smither's "High Heel Sneakers." Gabor's song, though clearly played for laughs (nearly forty young male and female dancers go-go around her as she swings her satin-clad hips, toys with her feather boa, and adjusts her opera gloves until she knocks out the three principal male dances with a blown kiss), is integrated into her entire guest-hosting stint: this program is built around the incongruity of the Hungarian glamour girl "rocking" with the kids. The teenage audience seems genuinely amused by Gabor's antics, and she is relaxed and loose as she flirts with O'Neill. In every way, Gabor is part of the show, and there's nothing mean-spirited about it. Her song, though especially elaborate and genuinely bizarre, is not the only novelty song. The musical guests included Willie Nelson, Marianne Faithfull, and the Animals playing their recent hits relatively straight, but the house band also performed "Sea Cruise" on an obviously fake "ocean liner" and with their tongues firmly in cheek. Thirty years before cruising LA fast-food joints with a cynical talk-show host, Gabor exploited the incongruity of her image and the signs of popular culture (first rock music, then french fries) for her own benefit and on her own terms.

Even so, after her arrest in 1989, Gabor's persona was largely reduced to that incident. For example, in 1996 she joined other famously temperamental celebrities in a series of NutraSweet television commercials, "showing her sweeter side" by throwing a party for Los Angeles policemen. In 1996's *A Very Brady Sequel* (as in 1991's *The Naked Gun 2½* and 1993's *Beverly Hillbillies* and *The Naked Truth*), she revisited the Kramer slap.[60] In the Brady film, after Roy Martin (Tim

Matheson), Carol Brady's first husband, outbids her at a charity auction, Gabor nearly attacks him. Her friend Rosie O'Donnell stops her, reminding her of all the trouble she got into the last time. Gabor agrees—she got in so much trouble she was invited "on Letterman, on Leno, on Larry King." Choosing to grow old in the spotlight but refusing to modify her sex symbol image (into, say a devoted mother and grandmother like Sophia Loren, an AIDS activist like Elizabeth Taylor, or a PETA crusader like Brigitte Bardot), Gabor seemed trapped in a parody of the persona she'd constructed and occupied for over four decades.

Despite its restrictiveness in later years, Gabor's persona always included an awareness of her performance and a parodic citation of feminine norms. In her first autobiography, she explained that she "saw things not as they were but as a play within a play," understanding her life as a performance.[61] Thus, Gabor's persona can be understood as subversive if not actively feminist, not least because it can be understood as a performance of femininity. In 2001, Cindy Adams described her appeal: "Was she blonde? No. Did she have that nose? No. But you knew it. That was the difference. You weren't *looking* for the truth. You knew there *was* none."[62]

Mary Ann Doane suggests that the female performance of feminine behavior can illuminate the constructed nature of gender;[63] Judith Butler delineates the conditions of that performance. "Performativity," she argues, "is neither free play nor theatrical self-presentation" but is instead activated within constraint and legible only so far as it cites previous performances.[64] Gabor's obviously false nose and hair, combined with her obviously playful descriptions of female behavior and belief, suggest that both she and her audience understood femininity as a role to be performed rather than an immutable identity. Following from Butler (who is following Foucault), repeated and reiterated performances, compelled by the very forces that constrain their play, inevitably produce a slip between the sign (turned-up nose and golden-blond hair) and referent (femininity). Gabor's persona drew on conservative domestic ideology for its constitutive elements, incorporating an understanding of women as objects of desire who needed a man for emotional and financial security. If her performance was less than absolutely emancipatory, it did point toward transgressive possibility. As Alan Sinfield reminds us, "dissident potential derives ultimately . . . from conflict and contradiction that the social order inevitably produces within itself, even as it attempts to sustain itself."[65] Thus, Gabor's performance of femininity, though imbricated within patriarchal understandings of female sexuality, has subversive qualities. This is especially evident through her presence on television situation comedies.

Naturalism on Television

When Zsa Zsa Gabor first appeared on television in 1951, the medium was still relatively new but had already established conventions of performance and presentation. In 1950, for example, Rudy Bretz (who had been working in television since 1940, joining CBS's original staff) characterized television as immediate, spontaneous, and actual. Its immediacy, Bretz explains, "refers to the feeling the viewer has that what he is watching is at that very moment occurring at some distant place." Although immediacy characterizes radio as well, television is even more immediate because it includes visuals as well as sound. Movies, as a recording of past (fictional or real) events, can never be immediate. The "feeling that the action being watched has never happened before" gives television its spontaneous quality. Actuality, which "refers to the feeling that what is being seen is real," continues Bretz, "enhances the feelings of immediacy and spontaneity." He asserts that television viewers are most interested in those programs that highlight all three characteristics, singling out parades, sports broadcasts, audience participation shows, and variety programs as especially "natural" fits for television.[66]

Explicit in Bretz's and other early analyses of television are comparisons with theater, radio, and film. Edward Padula enthusiastically compared the "magic world of television" to theater ("television is one continuous, live performance"), film (it "is produced through the medium of the camera and photographed"), and radio ("television is electronically picked up and sent out by air waves.")[67] The director, writer, and producer Carl Beier Jr. admitted that "much of [television's] material and its technique have been borrowed from allied arts" but promised that its own "peculiar potentialities" would be quickly explored and exploited. For Beier, the speed at which television moved, both in terms of its broadcast simultaneity and the "unbroken continuity" of television narrative, was its chief strength. Further, like music, television was an "art in time as well as in space and sound." For these and other early analysts, television's liveness was "exalted as a way to conquer time and distance" and promised to transmit real events to real people in real time.[68] Only radio could offer such simultaneity, but without visual material it was limited. Film and theater, on the other hand, were respectively a recording of past events or an obvious representation of fictional narratives.

Other early television analysts, like Edward Padula, foregrounded intimacy as the chief "communicative power of this new medium of sight and sound." Using close-ups and projecting those close-ups into viewers' own homes gave television "the ability to delve down into the inner personality of the actor . . . and expose the innate nature of man."[69] For the director Irving Pichel, the most salient difference between film and television was "the fact that the theater screen enlarges while the television receiver reduces." The effect of this seemed to signal a greater connection between the television program's narrative, characters, and themes as well as a focus on confined actions and small settings. Landscapes and crowd scenes, Pichel explains, "are ineffective," but constrained spaces, such as the interior of a submarine, are ideal.[70] What Christine Becker terms the "living room intimacy of television" offered a unique experience of narrative, setting, and character that neither film nor theater could equal.[71]

Television's ability to aggregate earlier representational forms like radio, theater, and film reached its apotheosis in the drama anthologies that dominated prime-time schedules in the 1950s. According to Becker, in the 1955–56 season, there were twenty-nine different anthology series. About half were "helmed" by "established Hollywood talent," recorded rather than broadcast live, and ran a half hour. The more prestigious shows, such as *Kraft Television Theatre, Goodyear Television Playhouse,* and *Studio One,* Becker explains, did not have a host, were filmed and broadcast live in New York City, and ran a full hour. Both kinds of programs, however, were crucial for the networks' financial and critical success. Live shows in particular helped "burnish [the] corporate image" of sponsors, but "the more mundane filmed shows . . . steadily climbed in the ratings and satisfied consumer products sponsors" who needed to turn a profit as well as garner critical acclaim.[72] For many television historians, such as Elana Levine, live drama anthologies distinguish television's so-called Golden Age, when the medium seemed to surpass both theater and film.[73]

As William Boddy points out, these programs helped reinforce a hierarchy that favored the networks' live programs over shorter, filmed programs: "The complex criteria—live versus film, the drama of character versus that of plot, an aesthetic of theatrical naturalism versus Hollywood genre and spectacle, . . . the television writer as legitimate playwright versus motion picture studio employee—all operated to reinforce the opposition between the networks and Hollywood."[74] Not surprisingly, Zsa Zsa Gabor's many appearances on anthology programs—including *Playhouse 90, Matinee Theatre, Lux Playhouse, GE True Theater,* and *Climax!,* a mystery series—were all half-hour telefilms.

"A Man of Taste," produced for *Climax!* in 1955, demonstrates many of Boddy's characteristics.[75] The swiftly moving plot introduces Charles Martin Westling (Michael Rennie) and his lover, Madame Florizel (Gabor) in Charles's office. The lovers both enjoy the finer things in life, will do anything (even murder) to get them, and have experience with blackmailers: Florizel murdered her first husband in order to inherit his wealth; Charles murdered a talented artist in order to drive up the value of his paintings. Werner Klemperer plays the blackmailer hot on Charles's trail. Charles and Florizel plot to murder Klemperer, as well as the artist Matt Sloane (John Kerr), with poison mushrooms (but leave Sloane's pregnant wife alive). Sloane's death will ensure that his remaining paintings will be worth a fortune. Florizel convinces Charles that the police will never suspect him, because no one would be so foolish as to commit the same crime twice. In Switzerland at Sloane's cabin studio, Florizel cooks an omelet with a poison mushroom sauce, but Klemperer knows about her husband's "accidental" death by mushrooms. Sloane is saved, and Klemperer sends Charles to prison. The telefilm ends where it began, with Charles awaiting execution, Florizel watching pitilessly through the bars of his prison cell.

This program, like most of the *Climax!* mysteries, favors plot over character, includes several different locations, and features ham-fisted acting. As Boddy suggests, the "theatrical naturalism" of prestige programs like *Studio One* is replaced by thin characterizations suggested by the performers' personalities rather than their acting techniques. Gabor is particularly unconvincing, whether as a murderer or a cook. Her dialogue is stilted, her body stiff and uncomfortable, and she delivers most of her lines directly to the camera rather than to her fellow actors. The qualities that made her such an engaging presence on variety programs like *The Steve Allen Show* and *Bachelor's Haven* hamper her dramatic performance. At the same time, however, Gabor's lovely and expressive face, captured in close-up, nearly makes up for her mannered acting. *Climax!* is a television program that exploits the medium's conventions and depends on the personalities of the performers.

Not surprisingly, the unique qualities of television, especially its immediacy and intimacy, required a specific type of acting. Padula explained that television needed "a new type of performer who has the combined abilities of the theatre actor, the personability of the screen player, and the mechanical technique of the radio performer." He warned budding thespians that television performers, unlike live theater or radio actors, had to have a "photogenic personality" that took advantage of the medium's reliance on "the medium-close and close-up technique of production." In television, actors needed more than a good voice or a strong talent; they also needed an especially "sensitive" face.[76] Pichel, too, delineated the differences between stage and screen acting. In short, film and television actors must do less (no projection, no physical improvisation), but they must do it within greater technical constraints (shooting out of order, hitting their marks). Television actors must "sustain [their] performance not only dramatically, but technically as well." Pichel admits that though the lack of a live audience limits actors because they have no immediate feedback, it also allows for retakes. The shorter rehearsal period for film and television, though difficult for actors to adjust to, is offset by film and television's opportunities to finesse a scene through subsequent takes, all of which might incorporate a director's feedback.[77] At the same time, of course, multiple short takes limit actors from creating long emotional arcs; further, they might perform only their lines for the camera rather than playing a scene with a partner. In many ways, then, television performance was built from within, dependent on the performers' ability to ignore outside distractions and to develop nuanced character without feedback from the audience or other performers.

What Rudy Bretz defines as actuality underscores the importance of realism, and therefore naturalist acting, to television. For Edward Padula, television demands "a more naturalistic school of acting" than either theater or film; Irving Pichel suggests that the actor "wears the clothes of the character and lives in sets so realistic" that the creation of natural and authentic characters is supported to a much greater extent than in theatrical performances; Melvin R. White argues that television actors must create people who seem to think, talk, and move as real human beings rather than exaggerated theatrical characters who must be legible to the back rows of the auditorium.[78] As I've demonstrated throughout, privileging "naturalist" performance is a complex negotiation between theories of acting, the challenges of the film or television medium, and institutional pressures to connect performer with role. Though contemporary analysts suggest that the technology of television demanded a specific kind of acting, and that television audiences insisted on naturalism, this critique equally demonstrates the influence of the naturalist paradigm on early television performance.

The naturalist paradigm that structured television and film performance was definitely familiar to Cold War audiences. Cynthia Baron asserts that "in the 1950s, the popular press contributed and responded to the public's interest in Lee Strasberg's top secret invention, 'the Method.'"[79] Strasberg argued that Method actors need to be protected "from the gaze of observers while they experimented with their art" while simultaneously inviting privileged observers into classes, giving newspaper interviews, and publishing books and essays defining "the Method." His closed-door policies "generated intrigue" and fed public curiosity about his techniques.[80] Conflating the Method with naturalism, audiences looked for authenticity and realism in television as well as film performance.

Though many critics affirmed that "a kind of emotional realism [was] eminently possible" on television,[81] suggesting that it might engender truly great performances, others suggested that personality was paramount. As early as 1946, Irving Pichel reminded readers that "a constant appears through all" of a performer's characters. "That constant," he continued, "is the actor's personality. . . . It is made up of his voice, stature, typical movement, of the range and depth of his human sympathies, of his intellectual perceptiveness." Television performers were especially able to develop their personalities through repeated performances of the same character, as when James Arness played Marshal Matt Dillon for twenty years on *Gunsmoke*. In this example as well as countless others, television seems to depend on personality for its success. In his influential 1981 essay, John Langer reviewed four decades of television performance in order to define televisual stardom. He opposed film stars to television personalities, suggesting that television's "intimate vision" privileging "the ordinary" and "'the exceptional' is "the exception rather than the rule." Langer points out that "news, current affairs, talk shows, variety, game and quiz shows"—the kinds of programs Rudy Bretz championed decades earlier—"are all significantly structured in and around various manifestations of the television personality." Even fictional forms, such as soap operas, detective shows, domestic situation comedies, "are similarly structured around personalities," though these personalities are not based on the performer but on character types "through whom the narrative is generated." According to Langer, good film performance seems to submerge the actor within a role, while good television performance exploits authentic personality.[82]

For Langer and a generation of television scholars, television performers are familiar and ordinary, seen every week or even every day, and therefore lack the charismatic presence of screen stars. Further, as John Ellis points out, "the performer's image is equated with that of the fictional role (rather than vice versa)."[83] The television role creates a particular personality, rather than a star persona that informs character as when Esther Williams plays a "bathing beauty" or Carmen Miranda represents *Latinidad.* In the case of Zsa Zsa Gabor, however, Ellis's formation does not hold. As the readings of *December Bride, Mr. Ed,* and *The Joey Bishop Show* demonstrate below, Gabor's persona informed her roles, whether or not she explicitly played herself. Further, as Deborah Jermyn points out in her work on Sarah Jessica Parker, some television performers achieve the kind of intertextual coverage generally assumed to be the exclusive domain of film stars.[84] Though Jermyn argues that Parker is a new kind of television star, Gabor's own intertextuality suggests that television personality and stardom have never been mutually exclusive.

Like a Natural (Television) Woman

Zsa Zsa Gabor guest-starred on several family sitcoms in the late 1950s and early 1960s. Significantly, Gabor played herself on these programs, and the series regulars interact with her as "Zsa Zsa Gabor, Hollywood bombshell." Gabor thus tests the limits of naturalism, both because she's playing herself, eliding her persona with her character, and also because her performance of self points up the naturalist fiction of television programming. Like Williams and Miranda before her, Gabor uses the naturalist paradigm for subversive ends—if not intentionally, then certainly with that effect. Further, Gabor's supreme awareness of herself as a performer, her long-standing parodic performances, and her careful crafting of persona suggest that she was at least partly conscious of her subversive presence on the domestic sitcom.

In the 1955 Gabor episode of *December Bride* (CBS 1954–1959), Lily (Spring Byington) and her friend Hilda (Verna Felton) are organizing a campaign for accident prevention when her daughter, Ruth (Frances Rafferty), returns home after having smashed the family car—again.[85] Her husband, Matt, and neighbor Pete denigrate women drivers and vow they'll aggressively prosecute whoever caused the accident. The doorbell rings—it's Zsa Zsa Gabor![86] Both Matt and Pete are tongue-tied and blame Ruth for the accident. Lily decides Zsa Zsa would be perfect to speak at her televised accident-prevention dinner. The night of the dinner, Zsa Zsa works late on the film she's currently starring in and wears a black satin coat over her sexy showgirl costume—in which she is forced to give her speech when the coat gets torn. The (male) audience and waiters are so distracted by her gorgeously displayed body that they suffer numerous accidents (see figure 31).

In her 1962 episode of *Mr. Ed* (syndicated 1961; CBS 1961–1964), Zsa Zsa moves next door to Mr. Ed and his human owners, Carol (Connie Hines) and Wilbur Post (Alan Young). As they talk about having a celebrity as a neighbor, the doorbell rings—it's Zsa Zsa Gabor! Gabor confides in Wilbur that she'd really like to do a new movie, but it's a Western and she's terrified of horses.[87] Wilbur suggests that she get to know Mr. Ed. Zsa Zsa agrees to the plan and spends several days sitting on Mr. Ed's back, learning that horses are gentle, friendly creatures. Ultimately, she agrees to do the film, but only if Mr. Ed can play her horse. Since the movie's being shot in Australia, the producers have to buy rather than borrow Mr. Ed. Of course Wilbur refuses, but Mr. Ed overhears Wilbur's regret that he can't afford to buy Carol a fur coat and runs away with Zsa Zsa. Carol tells Wilbur that Mr. Ed means more than a mink, and Wilbur rushes to catch the boat. Zsa Zsa announces that she doesn't need Mr. Ed, kisses him good-bye, and sails for Australia.

Figure 31: Zsa Zsa Gabor looking anything but bridal in a publicity photo for her 1955 appearance on CBS's *December Bride*.

Her episode of *The Joey Bishop Show* (NBC 1960–1964; CBS 1965) opens with Zsa Zsa's appearance on Joey Barnes's (Bishop) program in January 1964 and then quickly segues to Joey's home.[88] Joey's assistant Larry (Corbett Monica) arrives, still dazed from the friendly kiss Zsa Zsa gave him the night before. He's fallen madly in love and vows to ask Zsa Zsa for a date. The doorbell rings—it's Zsa Zsa Gabor! Wearing a sable coat, leather opera gloves, and a diamond bracelet, she presents Joey Jr. with a rattle filled with diamonds. When Ellie (Abby Dalton) and Joey bring her into the newly decorated nursery, Zsa Zsa announces it's not manly enough. She offers to redecorate the nursery herself and pay for everything. Joey agrees, but his wife is furious. Ellie changes her opinion of Zsa Zsa's ostentatious taste and aristocratic manner when Zsa Zsa agrees to give a speech at her women's club. Before she can tell Joey, he orders Zsa Zsa to return the nursery to its original state. Though Zsa Zsa is insulted, she agrees, and again pays for everything. The episode concludes as Zsa Zsa and Larry set off on their date.

On all three programs, Gabor's persona, built by decades' worth of glimpses of her "real" self in tabloids and legitimate newspapers, on television talk shows and variety programs, and in newsreels, introduces ideologically subversive notions. Using the constituent elements of her persona—sexual desire and desirability, Hungarianness, and self-parody—Gabor's "characters" rupture the generic naturalism of the television programs. Just as Carmen Miranda contrasts with her US co-stars, Gabor counterpoints the more subdued housewives, and her hyberbolic performance style makes the domestic sitcom conventions of the laugh track and double takes seem more "natural." Gabor's natural *hyper*femininity highlights the more appropriate maternal, middle-class gender impersonations of the program's female stars. Even so, and even though Gabor is revealed at program's end to be more "down-to-earth" and less adversarial than originally assumed, her persona highlights the tensions inherent in the domestic sitcom and domestic ideology itself.

Mary Beth Haralovich suggests that "the durability of the suburban family sit-com indicates the degree of institutional as well as popular support for ideologies that naturalize class and gender identities."[89] Though it's risky to generalize about such a varied genre, Nina Leibman identifies several characteristics of the domestic sitcom: the suburban, middle-class family; the wise and benevolent father at the center of the household; and the containment of social problems within the confines of family. Further, the production process virtually guaranteed seamless narratives: sponsors, who expected their products to be viewed in the best possible light, had a great deal of control; the laugh-track reinforced the humorous and pleasant experience; and network standards-and-practices departments ensured that the programs were morally correct. Leibman suggests these programs solidified the idea that family was more powerful than church, state, or business, "interacting with these institutions yet continually establishing itself as more important to the formation of the individual and as the supplier of solutions."[90] Of course, it's riskier still to generalize from mass media to the lives of real men and women; however, most historians grant that 1950s–1960s television reflected Cold War ideologies if not realities, agreeing with Elaine Tyler May that the family was "a source of meaning and security in a world run amok."[91]

Focusing on the family, the domestic sitcom naturalized white, bourgeois US identity. Defenders of a "traditional" Christian, white United States recognized the burgeoning civil rights movement and the specter of Eastern European communism as challenges to the status quo. Not surprisingly, television families remained suburban, middle-class, and overwhelmingly WASP, providing a broadcast bulwark against infiltration by nonwhite, non-Protestant, and noncapitalist interlopers. This racially and politically whitewashed image seemed desirable, even to those who could never achieve it. As Herman Gray reminisces in the 1991 documentary *Color Adjustment*, white culture seemed "so good, so wholesome" that even he, a black child, longed to belong to TV families and imagined himself inside the representational frame.[92]

Gabor, of course, challenged the all-American television ideal. Though Gabor professed her loyalty to the United States, and proudly became a citizen in 1949, she simultaneously identified as Hungarian. Perhaps because Gabor's ethnic identity was associated at least as much with communism as with European aristocracy, her excessive consumption on the domestic sitcom grounded her within capitalist rather than socialist narratives of the immigrant experience. Further, Gabor was excessively and nearly exclusively sexual, avoiding other markers of femininity and contrasting representations of everyday and Hollywood women of the fifties and sixties. She rarely mentioned Francesca in interviews and never references her own family life on the family sitcoms. Her interactions with the children on these sitcoms is equally limited; she offers to decorate a nursery, but not to interact with the child. Gabor is completely different from the television mothers, offering an option to middle-class maternal devotion and reproductive female sexuality.

In the domestic sitcom, Gabor's persona was used as a foil for more conventional female protagonists.[93] Playing herself, she offers a natural alternative to the ideologically stable Ruth, Carol, and Ellie. According to Denise Mann, the guest star's presence on television is always already excessive, bringing luxury, independence, and glamour to the "homogenizing tendencies" of the domestic sitcom.[94] Audiences primarily knew Gabor from the massive publicity surrounding her romances, her wealth, and her wit rather than her film and television roles. Her excess on these programs, then, seems part of her natural personality and makes it particularly potent. Zsa Zsa disrupts the households of the protagonist families, most notably by introducing working women, overt sexuality, and ostentatious European wealth into middle-class, suburban homes, opening a space to consider nonreproductive, consuming femininity, distinguished from middle-class maternity and appropriate consumption.

Gabor's performance style is equally different from her costars', and she doesn't work within the conversational conventions of the domestic sitcom. Thus, not only on the level of plot and narrative but also in terms of style and convention, her performance introduces significant ruptures within the domestic realm. Obviously, Spring Byington, Mr. Ed, and Joey Bishop are also performers, but they are "in character" while Gabor is not. Because audiences are made aware that Gabor is an actress, they may also be reminded that the protagonists are acting. Gabor's excessive celebrity lays bare the conventions of television naturalism, illuminating the domestic sitcom as a performance of ideology as dependent on the naturalist paradigm as contemporary films.

Because she is playing herself, Gabor's status as a performer and working woman is highlighted. All episodes revolve around her show business career. Though many middle-class women worked in the postwar era,[95] television mothers usually stayed at home. In contrast, Gabor's career drives the narratives; she enters the suburbs because she's a star. In general, the sitcom families use her celebrity to resolve their own crises. Although this suggests that Gabor's natural personality is managed and contained by the sitcom's narrative, it resists total incorporation. Though Zsa Zsa can interact with and even assist everyday families, she is never made ordinary. Importantly, the protagonists (and thus the audience) continue to see her as a star, whose value depends on a successful public career rather than private, domestic labor.

In *December Bride*, Gabor's status as actress enables her spectacular presentation. When she first visits the Henshaw home, she is exquisitely dressed in a wool coat with a silver fox scarf and huge fox cuffs, coordinating form-fitting sheath, elbow-length leather gloves, pearl and diamond earrings, and long pearls knotted and nestled between her breasts. She glows in this scene, and men and women alike are awed by her presence. It's hard not to be: she is stunning, and she manipulates her clothes, her jewelry, and the room to set herself off. At one point, she slowly takes off each glove, places them in her matching leather pocketbook, opens her coat and drapes it off her shoulders so that the fur frames her face, crosses to the lowest sofa, sits, and gracefully winds her legs around each other: she is effortlessly and naturally glamorous. Hilda, Lily, and Ruth, on the other hand, are dressed in cotton day dresses with little jewelry, never touch their clothing, and sit unremarkably if neatly on the other, less striking sofa and armchair. In all these programs, Gabor is extraordinarily self-possessed, and the camera draws the audience's eye to the constant adjustments of her clothes, her body, and her relationship to the other actors and the furniture in the room. If her appearance represents an unorthodox version of "acting," she's certainly performing, supremely aware of herself, but never self-conscious or fidgety. Importantly, this self-presentation had been a hallmark of her performance style since her start on *Bachelor's Haven*, as I discuss above.

Gabor especially mobilizes her persona in scenes at the movie studio, high-lighting both her sexuality and her ethnic heritage. Trying to convince her director that she can play Annie Oakley, she insists that she's been practicing her Western "drool" and that she's ready to move on to more dramatic, realistic roles. When she reads her new lines, her Hungarian accent is thicker and more humorously deployed than in any other scene; thus, she is too foreign to play an American heroine. Her nationality limits her acting ability but increases her appeal. The audience's laughter at her accent suggests, and the director's state-ments prove, that her authentic self is more interesting than any character she might play: her excessive foreignness compels the audience. The director orders her into costume, and she gets into a low-cut black bodice with silver sequins and illusion netting, black feather train and black feather boa, fishnet hose, and silver, high-heeled sandals. She emerges from the dressing room, one hand on her hip, the other on the door frame, and the audience applauds. Like Esther Williams's, her "natural" body and its sexual promise suggest their own narrative, one that skirts the edges of good taste and network standards and practices. Next, she and her young, naive costar practice their love scene. He tries to kiss her but can't figure out where to put his hands. Finally, he drapes his arms around her shoul-ders and kisses her gently. Zsa Zsa puts her arms around him; he embraces her passionately, kisses her hotly, and staggers out for a drink of water.

Throughout this scene, the audience is teased with the delayed spectacle of Gabor's sexuality. Will she dress as the saloon girl or remain in chaste "cowgirl" clothes? Will the cowboy ever kiss her? Will their kiss be passionate? (The teasing resonates with Zsa Zsa's removal of her gloves in the first scene and is echoed in the final scene, when it initially seems she will perform in her coat rather than the showgirl costume.) This delay renders the ultimate exposure of her hidden, authentic body even more spectacular. The focus on her physical attributes and their presumed sexuality suggests that Zsa Zsa's natural self (sexy and sexual) is revealed. This revelation calls attention to how Gabor's character troubles the domestic narrative, where women are housewives instead of movie stars, moth-ers instead of lovers, and wear flowered dresses instead of sequins and feathers.

Denise Mann suggests that "the Hollywood star's association with consumer excess and ostentatious behavior ran counter to fifties ideals of homogeneity and equal opportunity for all."[96] Though Mann is specifically referring to Hollywood stars on musical and other variety programs, her comments illuminate the ten-sions inherent in celebrity performances of self within any televisual context. In the case of Gabor, her conspicuous consumption is overlaid with her ethnic identity. Because she's an aristocratic Hungarian, not only her celebrity status but her "true" self counters "fifties ideals" of economic equality. *Mr. Ed* opposes Gabor's luxury, glamour, and wealth against the Posts' middle-class thrift. When Wilbur asks Zsa Zsa if she'll lose money if she doesn't make the film, she shrugs and smiles, as though finances don't affect her. In order to get used to Mr. Ed, she is helped onto his back by three white-coated attendants (her secretary, a manicurist, and a male lackey) and a French maid. Sitting regally, she dictates a letter to a jeweler ("Last week, a gentleman gave me a diamond necklace for my birthday. Please make a pair of matching earrings for my next birthday, which will be in two weeks"), rejects an offer of marriage from the Duke of Moravia ("Have him call me back when he's a king"), eats cucumber sandwiches from a silver tray, and spritzes herself and "Mr. Eddy" with expensive French perfume.

Carol's clothes, attitude, and desire for luxury are contrasted with Zsa Zsa's. When Carol is with Mr. Ed, she treats him like a horse rather than a glorified armchair. She wears regular clothes rather than Zsa Zsa's ornate costumes; in the barn, for example, Zsa Zsa wears a hat, gloves, a mink coat, a lace dress, stockings, pumps, a diamond bracelet, and large pearl earrings, while Carol is suitably dressed in slacks and a gingham blouse. Though Carol admires Zsa Zsa's mink and clearly wants one of her own, she defers her desire so that her husband can get Mr. Ed back, telling him that his friendship with the horse is more important than a fur coat. Connie is sensible about money, while Zsa Zsa apparently believes that luxury is worth any price. Gabor's signifying Old World extravagance is consciously compared to the Posts' American prudence.

The Joey Bishop Show constructs Zsa Zsa as a parodic performer. When Joey introduces her on his program, the audience goes crazy, and Joey tells his wife the next morning that she's his favorite guest, a sentiment he repeats throughout the program. Larry is so overcome by her beauty that he can't speak, walk, or eat in her presence. When Ellie complains to her friend Susan that Zsa Zsa is too glamorous for their decorating style, Susan refuses to sympathize, as she's awed by Zsa Zsa's Hollywood aura. Even Ellie has to admit that having Zsa Zsa speak at the women's club will help her win the upcoming president's election; the other housewives will be impressed that she's friends with a celebrity. Over and over, the characters comment on Zsa Zsa's "natural" celebrity, but the effect is to expose its construction and Zsa Zsa's performative excess and hyperfemininity.

Clearly, on *The Joey Bishop Show*, Gabor's persona is reflexively marked. Even in the fifties and sixties, popular culture texts such as gossip columns and talk shows—as well as Gabor's own performances—highlighted her gold-digging, predatory sexuality. Zsa Zsa delivers several jokes about the relationship between love and money; for example, she thinks Joey Jr. would be better off with her version of Joey's favorite nursery rhyme: "Peter Peter Pumpkin Eater had a wife and couldn't keep her. Put her in the Ritz Hotel and there he kept her very well." Though Zsa Zsa seems truly excessive in this program, she is also carefully recuperated. For example, she worries that Larry's passion for her is a joke; Ellie and Joey assure her that he's totally sincere, and Zsa Zsa seems to be genuinely interested in dating a "regular guy." Zsa Zsa's fear that her romantic reputation has made her an easy target coupled with her attraction to sweet, sensitive Larry thwarts any negative judgments of her character or attractiveness.

The acknowledgments of Gabor's persona also participate in the recuperative projects of all three programs. Though Zsa Zsa's beauty, sexuality, wealth, wit, and passion are all too much for "real" life, her excess is also reframed as generosity. Her feelings are hurt when Joey doesn't like her nursery, but she immediately agrees to return it to its original state and pay for everything. In *Mr. Ed*, when Wilbur tries to return the payment and reclaim his horse, the producer refuses. As Wilbur goes to say a final, genuinely heartfelt good-bye to Mr. Ed, Zsa Zsa announces that she can ride "any horse in Australia, and if you pester me, I'll ride a kangaroo." She bids a warm farewell to Wilbur and Mr. Ed and swans onto the boat. Because Zsa Zsa realizes that friendship is more important than the things that money can buy, her excess is partially contained by the program's more conservative messages. On the other hand, her fur-trimmed and jewel-bedecked traveling costume (her natural clothes, after all), as well as her numerous suitcases and expectation of luxury accommodations, refuses absolute incorporation.

Gabor is partially stabilized by the end of *December Bride* as well. By showing her earning the respect of Lily, Ruth, and Hilda, the episode makes it clear that Zsa Zsa, despite her seeming difference, would be welcome in the domestic community. Further, in a notably reflexive moment, Hilda worries that the speech's television audience will be scandalized by Zsa Zsa's costume and by the men's obvious sexual interest in her. Of course, the station confirms that audiences enjoyed her performance (of the five hundred calls it received, the only complaint was about a riot at a television store when the salesman tried to change the channel), and Zsa Zsa agrees to do it again next year. Obviously, her celebrity is valuable, and her sexual excess is exciting for both the television audiences inside the narratives and those watching the programs.

Zsa Zsa Gabor's performances of self on the domestic sitcom demonstrate how naturalism influenced performance on television, just as it did in the movie musical. Recovering how the discourses of naturalism flex across genre and across performer indicate its paradigmatic status while also demonstrating how naturalism may incorporate a variety of performance styles. In the case of Gabor, naturalist discourse helps finesse the relationships among notions of playing the self, television personality, celebrity persona, and authenticity. Though these notions are certainly not synonymic, they are clearly linked together by the naturalist paradigm. Zsa Zsa Gabor is a key antecedent for contemporary celebrity performances of self, demonstrating the labor constructing a flexible and enduring persona requires, and the complicated meanings of authenticity that inhere in celebrity performance.

Further, as is the case with all the spectacular women I consider, Gabor's performances can be both naturalist and subversive, despite feminist critiques of naturalism as a performance technique and generic convention. Critics such as Laura Mulvey in film and Jill Dolan in theater have decried naturalism for encouraging identification:[97] if the onstage and onscreen representations seem authentic, then so too will the ideologies they present. By identifying with conservative characters, audience members embrace hegemonic notions of sex, race, ethnicity, class, and gender. "Unless form *and* content converge," as Tracy C. Davis asserts in an argument embraced by many, conventional dramaturgy can perpetuate and replicate the ideology of domination."[98] As I hope to have demonstrated throughout, however, naturalism and feminism may coexist, at least in some women's spectacular film and television performances. Naturalist performance, at least, both supports and challenges an ideological status quo that erases the agency of female performers as well as the characters they play.

Of course, as these case studies also demonstrate, there are limits to audience readings of any performance, and subversive potential is constrained by social and cultural context as well as industrial structures. Even so, Russell, Williams, Horne, Miranda, and Gabor indicate how playing oneself enables a kind of agency for performers otherwise imbricated within representational and institutional systems of domination. When Jane Russell mobilizes pieces of the "authentic" biography created by Howard Hughes's massive publicity campaigns in the films she produces herself, she comments on how women—and female sexuality—are positioned within the film industry. Esther Williams's "natural" body enables recognizably feminist narratives even within her formulaic and heteronormative musical comedies. Lena Horne's presentation of "authentic" blackness, drawing on minstrel tropes of the tragic mulatto, nonetheless offers alternatives to rapacious black female sexuality as well as providing necessary and welcomed models of ideal middle-class black femininity, challenging cinematic portrayals to such an extent that she was quickly rendered illegible for mass audiences and her film career was cut short. As a symbol of the Good Neighbor policy and *Latinidad*, Carmen Miranda seems especially unnatural. At the same time, however, her dancing body disrupted the narratives of her films, and her spectacular performances called into question the "natural" femininity of her Anglo costars by presenting its carnivalesque inversion. Finally, Zsa Zsa Gabor, famous for being famous, tested the limits of intelligible female sexuality on television screens, bringing overconsumption, hypersexuality, and decadence into 1950s and 1960s living rooms. Naturalism is often blamed for a host of antifeminist, antimulticultural, antiprogressive textual politics. But these spectacular women illuminate the limitations in this familiar account. The naturalist paradigm, which explicitly depends on casting according to physical type, merging biography with character, and professionalizing performance, allows actresses' bodies, personal histories, and labor to communicate meaning in excess of and counter to the narratives within which they're contained.

NOTES

INTRODUCTION   PLAYING HERSELF: THE NATURALIST
PARADIGM AND THE SPECTACLE OF FEMALE SEXUALITY

1. *There's No Business like Show Business*, directed by Walter Lang (1954; Los Angeles: Twentieth Century–Fox, 2002), DVD.

2. Rick Altman, *The American Film Musical* (Bloomington and Indianapolis: Indiana University Press, 1989), 200, 211, 250.

3. David Bordwell, Janet Staiger, and Kristin Thompson, *The Classical Hollywood Cinema: Film Style and Mode of Production to 1960* (New York: Columbia University Press, 1985), 3.

4. Steven Cohan, "Introduction: Musicals of the Studio Era," in *Hollywood Musicals: The Film Reader*, ed. Steven Cohan (London and New York: Routledge, 2002), 12.

5. Ed Sullivan quoted in Randall Riese and Neal Hitchens, *The Unabridged Marilyn: Her Life from A to Z* (New York: Congdon and Weed, 1988), 338.

6. Marilyn Monroe quoted in Susan Strasberg, *Marilyn and Me: Sisters, Rivals, Friends* (New York: Warner Books, 1992), 43.

7. Ibid., 137, 123, 85, 101.

8. Ibid., 85.

9. Lee Strasberg, "View from the Studio: 'Iceman' Passes Its One Hundredth Performance," *New York Times*, September 2, 1956.

10. Cynthia Baron, "The Method Moment: Situating the Rise of Method Acting," *Popular Culture Review* 9, no. 2 (1998): 99.

11. Sharon Marie Carnicke, "Lee Strasberg's Paradox of the Actor," in *Screen Acting*, ed. Alan Lovell and Peter Krämer (London and New York: Routledge, 1999), 78.

12. Baron, "The Method Moment," 94.

13. Bruce McConachie, "Method Acting and the Cold War," *Theatre Survey* 41, no. 1 (May 2000): 53.

14. Baron, "The Method Moment," 101.

15. Michael Trask, "Patricia Highsmith's Method," *American Literary History* 22, no. 3 (Fall 2010): 587. Of course, Baron, Carnicke, and McConachie also consider the interplay between the popularity of Method acting and the popularity of Freudian psychology and its various incarnations.

16. Colin Counsell, *Signs of Performance: An Introduction to Twentieth-Century Theatre* (London and New York: Routledge, 1997), 62, 66.

17. Trask, "Patricia Highsmith's Method," 587, 589, 596.

18. Bruce McConachie, *American Theater in the Culture of the Cold War: Producing and Contesting Containment, 1947–1962* (Iowa City: University of Iowa Press, 2003), 99.

19. Lee Strasberg in Sharon Marie Carnicke, *Stanislavsky in Focus: An Acting Master for the Twenty-First Century*, 3rd ed. (Oxon: Routledge, 2009), 10.

20. Alexander Knox, "Acting and Behaving," *Hollywood Quarterly* 1, no. 3 (April 1946): 262, 263, emphasis in original; Alexander Knox, "Performance under Pressure," *Hollywood Quarterly* 3, no. 2 (Winter 1947–48): 159.

21. Fredric Jameson in James Naremore, *Acting in the Cinema* (Berkeley, Los Angeles, and London: University of California Press, 1988), 201.

22. Theodore Hoffman in Steve Vineberg, *Method Actors: Three Generations of an American Acting Style* (New York: Schirmer Books, 1991), 102–103.

23. See, for example, Naremore, *Acting in the Cinema*; Lucy Fischer, "The Lives of Performers: The Actress as Signifier in the Cinema," in *Making Visible the Invisible: An Anthology of Original Essays on Film Acting*, ed. Carole Zucker (Metuchen, NJ, and London: Scarecrow Press, 1990); Barry King, "Articulating Stardom," in *Star Texts: Image and Performance in Film and Television*, ed. Jeremy Butler (Detroit: Wayne State University Press, 1991); Richard de Cordova, "Genre and Performance: An Overview," in *The Film Genre Reader III*, ed. Barry Keith Grant (Austin: University of Texas Press, 2003); John O. Thompson, "Screen Acting and the Commutation Test," in *Movie Acting: The Film Reader*, ed. Pamela Robertson Wojcik (New York and London: Routledge, 2004); and Richard Dyer, *Stars* (London: BFI, 1992).

24. Laura Mulvey, *Visual and Other Pleasures* (Bloomington: Indiana University Press, 1989).

25. Sue Harper, "Film History: Beyond the Archive?" *Journal of Contemporary History* 39, no. 3 (July 2004): 453.

26. Paul MacDonald, "Why Study Film Acting? Some Opening Reflections," in *More than a Method: Trends and Traditions in Contemporary Film Performance*, ed. Cynthia Baron, Diane Carson, and Frank P. Tomasulo (Detroit: Wayne State University Press, 2004), 23.

27. Alan Lovell and Peter Krämer, introduction to *Screen Acting*, ed. Alan Lovell and Peter Krämer (London and New York: Routledge, 1999), 2–5.

28. Barry King, "Articulating Stardom," in *Star Texts: Image and Performance in Film and Television*, ed. Jeremy Butler (Detroit: Wayne State University Press, 1991), 127.

29. Dyer, *Stars*, 162.

30. Naremore, *Acting in the Cinema*, 23, 1, 4.

31. Cynthia Baron, Diane Carson, and Frank P. Tomasulo, introduction to *More than a Method: Trends and Traditions in Contemporary Film Performance*, ed. Cynthia Baron, Diane Carson, and Frank P. Tomasulo (Detroit: Wayne State University Press, 2004), 2.

32. Carole Zucker, introduction to *Making the Visible Invisible: An Anthology of Original Essays on Film Acting*, ed. Carole Zucker (Metuchen, NJ: Scarecrow, 1990), vii.

33. Lev Kuleshov, *Kuleshov on Film: Writings by Lev Kuleshov*, trans. Ronald Levaco (Berkeley and Los Angeles: University of California Press, 1975), 67.

34. Martin Barker and Thomas Austin, eds., *Contemporary Hollywood Stardom* (New York and London: Oxford University Press, 2003), 255.

35. Lovell and Krämer, *Screen Acting*, 6.

36. Jeremy G. Butler, introduction to *Star Texts: Image and Performance in Film and Television*, ed. Jeremy G. Butler (Detroit: Wayne State University Press, 1991), 8–9.

37. Richard de Cordova, "Genre and Performance: An Overview," in *Film Genre Reader II*, ed. Barry Keith Grant (Austin: University of Texas Press, 2003), 131–136, 139.

38. Jerome Delamater, "Ritual, Realism and Abstraction: Performance in the Musical," in *Making the Visible Invisible*, ed. Carole Zucker (Metuchen, NJ, and London: Scarecrow Press, 1990), 45, 61. Delamater borrows the distinction between aggregate and integrated

musicals from Martin Rubin's seminal *Busby Berkeley and the Tradition of Spectacle* (New York: Columbia University Press, 1993); see especially 41–44 in Rubin for the original discussion.

39. Cavan Sieczkowski, "Lindsay Lohan, Marilyn Monroe Compared for 'Talent Slipping Away,'" *Huffington Post*, January 15, 2013, http://www.huffingtonpost.com/2013/01/15/ indsay-lohan-marilyn-monroe-new-york-times-talent-slipping-away-_n_2479818.html (April 2, 2013).

40. Neil Genzlinger, "There's a Word for a Movie like This," *New York Times*, March 23, 2013.

41. Nancy Jo Sales, "Adrift . . . ," *Vanity Fair*, October 2010, http://www.vanityfair.com/ hollywood/features/2010/10/lindsay-lohan-201010.

42. Janet Maslin, "Sisters, Sisters, So Cute and So Well-Dressed," *New York Times*, July 29, 1998.

43. Caryn James, "Portrait of the Party Girl as a Serious Young Artist," *New York Times*, May 9, 2006.

44. Meryl Streep in Sales, "Adrift."

45. Josh Grossberg, "Lindsay Lohan: A Timeline of All Her Arrests (and Boy, There Are a Lot of 'Em)," *E! Online*, November 29, 2012, http://www.eonline.com/news/367020/lindsay -lohan-a-timeline-of-all-her-arrests-and-boy-there-are-a-lot-of-em (April 2, 2013).

46. Amy Bittinger Kunkle, "Lindsay Lohan: List of Lohan's Criminal and Rehab History," *Examiner.com*, November 7, 2011, http://www.examiner.com/article/lindsay-lohan-list-of -lohan-s-criminal-and-rehab-history (April 2, 2013); Steve DiCarlo, "Lindsay Lohan's Lovers! A Look Back at Her Steamy Hook-Ups," *Celebuzz.com*, Apr. 2011, http://www.celebuzz .com/2011-09-29/lindsay-lohans-lovers-a-look-back-at-her-steamy-hook-ups-photos/ (April 2, 2013).

47. Adrienne L. McLean, introduction to *Headline Hollywood: A Century of Film Scandal*, ed. Adrienne L. McLean and David Cook (New Brunswick and London: Rutgers University Press, 2001), 1.

48. Jeanine Basinger, *The Star Machine* (New York: Alfred A. Knopf, 2007), 74.

49. Carnicke, *Stanislavsky in Focus*, 152. Carnicke explains Strasberg's versions of these two exercises. In the private moment, "actors recreate behavior they would normally never do in front of others, like taking a shower," in order to break down inhibitions (64). Affective memory, which Strasberg explained his students "used . . . in our way, for own results" (quoted on 66), is generally understood as the instantaneous recall of emotionally charged events from the actor's life. The actor shapes these authentically experienced emotions into the character's response. Affective memory (sometimes called sense memory or emotional recall) is perhaps the most controversial aspect of Strasberg's Method. For more, see Carnicke's excellent exegesis of Strasberg's development of affective memory in *Stanislavsky in Focus*, especially 63–69 and 150–167.

50. Richard de Cordova, *Picture Personalities: The Emergence of the Star System in America* (Urbana and Chicago: University of Illinois Press, 1990), 140.

51. Moya Luckett, "Toxic: The Implosion of Britney Spears' Star Image," *Velvet Light Trap* 65 (Spring 2010): 41.

52. Julie A. Wilson, "Star Testing: The Emerging Politics of Celebrity Gossip," *Velvet Light Trap* 65 (Spring 2010): 26.

53. Joshua Gamson, *Claims to Fame: Celebrity in Contemporary America* (Berkeley: University of California Press, 1994), 137.

54. Elizabeth Podnieks, "Celebrity Bio Blogs: Hagiography, Pathography, and Perez Hilton," *Auto/Biography Studies* 24, no. 1 (Summer 2009): 68, 60.

55. Steven Gaines, "Bad Behavior in Boldface," *New York*, April 9, 2012.

56. "Cruise Rescues Woman Stuck in Snow," *Contactmusic.com*, January 10, 2008, http://www.contactmusic.com/news/cruise-rescues-woman-stuck-in-snow_1055720; Pam

Lambert, "Tom Terrific," *People*, August 26, 1996, http://www.people.com/people/archive/article/0,,20142095,00.html; Natalie Finn and Bruna Nessif, "Ryan Gosling and Eight More Real-Deal Celebrity Heroes," *E! Online*, April 4, 2012, http://www.eonline.com/news/205736/ryan-gosling-and-eight-more-real-deal-celebrity-heroes; "St. Tom's Ambulance," *Mirror*, June 19, 2012, http://www.questia.com/library/1G1–293571360/st-tom-s-ambulance-cruise-in-real-life-rescue-mission (all April 5, 2013).

57. Mark Morford. "The Great Tom Cruise Backlash," *SFgate*, July 6, 2005, http://www.sfgate.com/entertainment/morford/article/The-Great-Tom-Cruise-Backlash-Will-this-2657320.php (April 5, 2013).

58. Brooks Barnes, "Tom Cruise Doesn't Need Your Pity. Here's Some Anyway," *New York Times*, June 25, 2010, http://mediadecoder.blogs.nytimes.com/2010/06/25/tom-cruise-doesnt-need-your-pity-heres-some-anyway/.

59. Maureen Orth, "What Katie Didn't Know," *Vanity Fair*, October 2012, 186ff.

60. Kim Masters and Daniel Miller, "How Tom Cruise Plans to Fight Scientology Backlash," *Hollywood Reporter*, September 9, 2012, http://www.hollywoodreporter.com/news/tom-cruise-scientology-jack-reacher-katie-holmes-371459.

61. "Rupert Everett Advises Gay Actors Not to Come Out in Hollywood Again," *Huffington Post*, Jan. 14, 2013, http://www.huffingtonpost.com/2013/01/14/rupert-everett-hollywood-gay-actors-coming-out_n_2471872.html (April 5, 2013).

62. Ramin Setoodeah, "Straight Jacket," *Newsweek*, May 10, 2010.

63. Aaron Sorkin, "Now That You Mention It, Rock Hudson Did Seem Gay," *Huffington Post*, May 12, 2010, http://www.huffingtonpost.com/aaron-sorkin/now-that-you-mention-it-r_b_574210.html (April 5, 2013).

64. Sharon Waxman, "You've Read the Gossip; Still Want to See the Movie?" *New York Times*, June 27, 2005.

65. Stephen Holden, "Lord Love a VW Bug That Knows Its Mind," *New York Times*, June 22, 2005.

66. Manohla Dargis, "The Cellphone Gets Its Close-Up," *New York Times*, August 1, 2013, http://www.nytimes.com/2013/08/02/movies/the-canyons-is-an-erotic-thriller-with-lindsay-lohan.html?partner=rss&emc=rss&_r=1&; Claudine Zap, "'The Canyons' Adds Up to an Abysmal Box Office Abyss," *Yahoo Movies*, August 27, 2013, http://movies.yahoo.com/blogs/movie-talk/canyons-adds-abysmal-box-office-abyss-000855351.html.

67. Stephen Rodrick, "The Misfits," *New York Times Magazine*, January 13, 2013.

68. John Huston in George Kouvaros, *Famous Faces yet Not Themselves: "The Misfits" and Icons of Postwar America* (Minneapolis: University of Minnesota Press, 2007), 109.

69. Richard Dyer, with a supplementary chapter by Paul McDonald, *Stars*, new ed. (London: BFI, 1998), 8.

70. Thomas R. Bates, "Gramsci and the Theory of Hegemony," *Journal of the History of Ideas* 36, no. 2 (April–June 1975): 351.

71. John Fiske, "British Cultural Studies and Television," in *Channels of Discourse, Reassembled: Television and Contemporary Criticism*, ed. Robert C. Allen (London: Routledge, 1992), 219.

72. Dyer, *Stars*, 30, 47, 31.

73. Ibid., 60.

74. Alan Sinfield, *Faultlines: Cultural Materialism and the Politics of Dissident Reading* (Berkeley and Los Angeles: University of California Press, 1992), 41.

75. *Bus Stop*, directed by Joshua Logan (1956; Los Angeles: Twentieth Century–Fox, 2001), DVD.

76. John Huston in Kouvaros, *Famous Faces yet Not Themselves*, 109.

1   Engineered for Stardom: Publicity, Performance, and Jane Russell

1. Ashton Reid, "Jane Does a Movie," *Collier's*, January 13, 1945, 70.

2. Controversy over *The Outlaw*'s content and publicity campaign delayed its national release for several years. In February 1943, Howard Hughes bought out a San Francisco cinema for six weeks in order to release the film there. In part because of his publicity efforts, the run was extended to nine weeks, as I discuss below. *The Outlaw* had limited runs in Detroit, San Francisco, and New York City between 1946 and 1949 but was not released nationally until 1950. Russell was filming *Young Widow* at the time of Reid's interview; it was released in March 1946 without controversy.

3. This number is based on my own undoubtedly incomplete research of Russell citations, augmented by the work of my research assistant, Evleen Nasir, in June 2012. As another hallmark of her publicity popularity, Russell was featured in *Life* magazine six times in 1941–1945.

4. Reid, "Jane Does a Movie," 71.

5. "Jane Russell, a Howard Hughes Find, Is 1941's Best New Prospect," *Life*, January 10, 1945, 42. The photos discussed in this section were not available for this book. They may be viewed at http://books.google.com/books?id=8kgEAAAAMBAJ&pg=PA42&dq=jane +russell&hl=en&sa=X&ei=FD-FUuigOIKi2QWv_IG4Ag&ved=0CDEQ6AEwAA#v =onepage&q=jane%20russell&f=false.

6. George Kouvaros, *Famous Faces yet Not Themselves: "The Misfits" and Icons of Postwar America* (Minneapolis: University of Minnesota Press, 2007), 5.

7. *The Outlaw*, directed by John Huston (1943; Los Angeles: Legend Films, 2009), DVD. This is how Rio is generally described in the film itself, which points out several times that she is the orphan of an Irish father and Mexican mother. Both ethnic identities are presumably meant to signal her "tempestuous" nature.

8. "Jane Russell, a Howard Hughes Find," 44–45.

9. Laura Mulvey, "Visual Pleasure and Narrative Cinema," in *Issues in Feminist Film Criticism*, ed. Patricia Erens (Bloomington and Indianapolis: Indiana University Press, 1990), 33.

10. Michael Kirby, "On Acting and Not-Acting," in *Acting (Re)Considered: A Theoretical and Practical Guide*, ed. Phillip B. Zarrilli (New York and London: Routledge, 1995), 41. Kirby generally differentiates between nonmatrixed acting, where the actor is understood by the audience to be in a performance through contextual clues rather than performance choices, and matrixed acting, where the actor actively creates a performance and character through a series of specific choices. His continuum is more nuanced than this brief definition suggests.

11. Kouvaros, *Famous Faces yet Not Themselves*, 102, 34.

12. Ibid., 34.

13. Jeanine Basinger, *The Star Machine* (New York: Alfred A. Knopf, 2007), 73–75.

14. Anita Gates, "Jane Russell, Sultry Star of 1940s and '50s, Dies at 89," *New York Times*, February 28, 2011, http://www.nytimes.com/2011/03/01/movies/01russell.html?_r=0.

15. Jane Russell, *Jane Russell: My Path and My Detours: An Autobiography* (New York, London, Toronto, and Sydney: Franklin Watts, 1985), 63.

16. All biographical details in this paragraph come from the obituary "Jane Russell," *Economist*, March 10, 2011, http://www.economist.com/node/18329456.

17. Kate Stables, "Jane Russell," *Sight and Sound* 22, no. 3 (March 2012): http://old.bfi.org .uk/sightandsound/newsandviews/obituaries/jane-russell.php.

18. Hedda Hopper, "Jane Has No Worries—at Least for 20 Years," *Los Angeles Times*, October 30, 1955. Hopper's feature on Russell is notable for its familiar insistence that Russell was always divided in half, torn between her movie career and her desire to be a good wife and mother.

19. Russell, *Jane Russell*, 67.

20. Joshua Gamson, "The Assembly Line of Greatness: Celebrity in Twentieth-Century America," *Critical Studies in Mass Communication* 9 (1992): 2.

21. Thomas Harris, "The Building of Popular Images: Grace Kelly and Marilyn Monroe," in *Stardom: Industry of Desire*, ed. Christine Gledhill (London and New York: Routledge, 1991), 40.

22. Leonard J. Leff, "Star Struck: Guy Madison and David Selznick in Postwar Hollywood," *Film History: An International Journal* 23, no. 4 (2011): 85.

23. Anthony Slide, *Inside the Hollywood Fan Magazine: A History of Star Makers, Fabricators, and Gossip Mongers* (Jackson: University of Mississippi Press, 2010), 7, 3.

24. Richard de Cordova, *Picture Personalities: The Emergence of the Star System in America* (Urbana and Chicago: University of Illinois Press, 1990), quotations from 145, 140, 142.

25. Nick Muntean and Anne Petersen, "Celebrity Twitter: Strategies of Intrusion and Disclosure in the Age of Technoculture," *M/C Journal* 12, no. 5 (December 2009), http://journal.media-culture.org.au/index.php/mcjournal/article/view/194.

26. Walter Seltzer, interview by Ronald L. Davis, August 25, 1986, OHC 392, transcript, Ronald Davis Oral History Collection, Southern Methodist University DeGolyer Library, Dallas, TX, 3.

27. Janet Leigh, interview by Ronald L. Davis, July 25, 1984, OHC 308, transcript, Ronald Davis Oral History Collection, Southern Methodist University DeGolyer Library, Dallas, TX, 9.

28. E. J. Fleming, *The Fixers: Eddie Mannix, Howard Strickling, and the MGM Publicity Machine* (Jefferson, NC: McFarlane, 2005), 118.

29. Seltzer, interview, 6.

30. Muntean and Petersen, "Celebrity Twitter."

31. Bill Hendricks, interview by Ronald L. Davis, July 26, 1979, OHC 185, transcript, Ronald Davis Oral History Collection, Southern Methodist University DeGolyer Library, Dallas, TX, 9.

32. Slide, *Inside the Hollywood Fan Magazine*, 8.

33. Esmé Chandlee, interview by Ronald L. Davis, May 23, 1985, OHC 328, transcript, Ronald Davis Oral History Collection, Southern Methodist University DeGolyer Library, Dallas, TX, 4.

34. Seltzer, interview, 10.

35. Ann Straus, interview by Ronald L. Davis, May 20, 1985, OHC 332, transcript, Ronald Davis Oral History Collection, Southern Methodist University DeGolyer Library, Dallas, TX, 35.

36. David Karnes, "The Glamorous Crowd: Hollywood Movie Premieres between the Wars," *American Quarterly* 38, no. 4 (Autumn 1986): 554–555.

37. Ann Doran, interview by Ronald L. Davis, August 10 and 15, 1983, OHC 277, transcript, Ronald Davis Oral History Collection, Southern Methodist University DeGolyer Library, Dallas, TX, 26.

38. For more on this process, see Ronald L. Davis, *The Glamour Factory: Inside Hollywood's Big Studio System* (Dallas: SMU Press, 1993), 90.

39. Simon Dixon, "Ambiguous Ecologies: Stardom's Domestic Mise-en-Scène," *Cinema Journal* 42, no. 2 (Winter 2003): 82.

40. Davis, *The Glamour Factory*, 152, 144.

41. Russell, *Jane Russell*, 69, 71, 91.

42. Davis, *The Glamour Factory*, 147.

43. Russell, *Jane Russell*, 16.

44. Emily Torchia, interview by Ronald L. Davis, July 16, 1984, OHC 306, transcript, Ronald Davis Oral History Collection, Southern Methodist University DeGolyer Library, Dallas, TX, 6; Davis, *The Glamour Factory*, 88.

45. Basinger, *The Star Machine*, 18.

46. Douglas W. Churchill, "Screen News Here and in Hollywood," *New York Times*, December 13, 1940; Douglas W. Churchill, "Hollywood Legend," *New York Times*, December 15, 1940.

47. "Life of Howard Hughes Was Marked by a Series of Bizarre and Dramatic Events," *New York Times*, April 6, 1976; Donald L. Bartlett, and James B. Steele, *Howard Hughes: His Life and Madness* (New York: W. W. Norton, 2004), 148.

48. Davis, *The Glamour Factory*, 152.

49. Thomas M. Pryor, "Film News and Comment," *New York Times*, May 11, 1941; Thomas M. Pryor, "By Way of Report: Howard Hughes Buys Theatre to Show 'The Outlaw'—Other Film Matters," *New York Times*, April 25, 1943.

50. Peter Dart, "Breaking the Code: A Historical Footnote," *Cinema Journal* 8 no. 1 (Autumn 1968): 40.

51. Ibid.

52. Lydia Lane, "Eye Make-Up Is Important to Glamor Says Jane Russell," *Miami News*, July 6, 1952, http://news.google.com/newspapers?nid=2206&dat=19520706&id=AmEo AAAAIBAJ&sjid=vusFAAAAIBAJ&pg=4583,2303276.

53. Basinger, *The Star Machine*, 59.

54. Harris, "The Building of Popular Images," 41.

55. "Jane Russell and John Payne," http://www.flickr.com/photos/35255697@N03/ 5487702409/ (June 5, 2012).

56. "Services Set for Hollywood Publicist Russell Birdwell," *Los Angeles Times*, December 20, 1977. As an example of the coincidences that marked my research and strengthened my belief that these spectacular actresses formed a cohort: Birdwell directed Zsa Zsa Gabor in *The Girl in the Kremlin* in 1957.

57. "Speaking of Pictures," *Life*, April 13, 1949, http://books.google.com/books?id =_1AEAAAAMBAJ&pg=PA8&dq=%22jane+russell%22+life+archive&hl=en&sa =X&ei=o_jYT6XmMOq26QGlvqG4Aw&sqi=2&ved=0CEUQ6AEwAw#v=onepage&q =%22jane%20russell%22%20life%20archive&f=false (June 13, 2012). This photo essay includes seven pictures of Russell in two pages, five of them with servicemen or equipment, one in a bathing suit on a rocky beach, and another of her looking over her shoulder to show off her seamed-stockinged legs.

58. Philip K. Scheuer, "Pin-up Girl Has Hollywood Abuzz," *Los Angeles Times*, May 6, 1945.

59. Mark Borkowski, "I'm Sorry Simon Cowell, You Are about 75 Years behind the Times," *Independent*, April 27, 2009, http://www.independent.co.uk/news/media/advertising/ irsquom-sorry-simon-cowell-you-are-about-75-years-behind-the-times-1674692.html.

60. "Speaking of Pictures."

61. Robert B. Westbrook, "'I Want a Girl, Just like the Girl That Married Harry James': American Women and the Problem of Political Obligation in World War II," *American Quarterly* 42, no. 4 (December 1990): 592–596.

62. Borkowski, "I'm Sorry Simon Cowell."

63. "For Memorial Day, Some Starry-Eyed Military," *Carole & Co. Blog*, May 28, 2012, http://carole-and-co.livejournal.com (June 4, 2012); *New York Journal-American* Photographic Morgue, Harry Ransom Center, University of Texas, http://norman.hrc.utexas.edu/ NYJAdc/ItemDetails.cfm?id=888 (June 5, 2012); Associated Press Images Archive, http:// www.apimages.com/search.aspx?st=k&cfas=person_featured_name&person_featured _name=%22jane%20russell%22&id=491672&showact=results&sort=date&sh=10&kwstyle =or&dbm=panorama&adte=1322974156&ish=x&dah=-1&pagez=60&cfasstyle=and&# (June 5, 2012); "Don't Chatter!" *Life*, January 26, 1942, http://books.google.com/books?id =PE4EAAAAMBAJ&pg=PA23&dq=%22jane+russell%22+life+archive&hl=en&sa=X&ei=o _jYT6XmMOq26QGlvqG4Aw&sqi=2&ved=0CEkQ6AEwBA#v=onepage&q=%22jane%20 russell%22%20life%20archive&f=false (June 13, 2012).

64. Slide, *Inside the Hollywood Fan Magazine*, 86.

65. See the Associated Press Image Archive, http://www.apimages.com/OneUp.aspx?st=k&kw=%22jane%20russell%22%20and%20army&showact=results&sort=relevance&intv=None&sh=10&kwstyle=or&adte=1341856032&pagez=60&cfasstyle=AND&rids=fd26ad13428441fdac09b632104a1ad6&dbm=PY2000&page=1&xslt=1&mediatype=Photo (June 2, 2012).

66. Westbrook, "'I Want a Girl, Just like the Girl That Married Harry James,'" 605.

67. "Gold at Your Disposal," *Pic*, November 11, 1941, 10–11.

68. "Chilly Glamour," *Life*, January 29, 1945, 94–96.

69. Kouvaros, *Famous Faces yet Not Themselves*, 102.

70. *Gentlemen Prefer Blondes*, directed by Howard Hawks (1953; Los Angeles: Twentieth Century Fox, 2006), DVD; *The French Line*, directed by Lloyd Bacon (1953; Los Angeles: RKO, 2012), DVD.

71. Kouvaros, *Famous Faces yet Not Themselves*, 7.

72. *Gentlemen Prefer Blondes*, of course, opens with the duet "Two Little Girls from Little Rock." *The French Line* inexplicably includes Russell and McCarty participating in an onboard nightclub act (McCarty is a fashion designer, and Russell is impersonating her house model, neither of whom would necessarily be tapped to star in a cabaret). Dressed in red sequined leotards (skimpier than the red sequined evening dresses Monroe and Russell sport), the two complain about meager French fare and insist that "Any Gal from Texas" would prefer a giant steak—and a handsome cowboy to go along with it. It's a lavishly costumed number, but it trades on the sexiness of Russell and McCarty, who bump and grind through the musically simple song with little of its predecessor's charm.

73. Bosley Crowther, "French Line Anchors; Jane Russell and Oil Aboard at Criterion, Gang Warfare Erupts at the Paramount," *New York Times*, May 15, 1954; Philip K. Schueuer, "Russell's Dancing Heats Up 'French Line,'" *Los Angeles Times*, February 25, 1954.

74. Brog, "The French Line," *Variety*, January 6, 1954, *VarietyUltimate.com* (June 17, 2012).

75. Leonard J. Leff and Jerold Simmons, *The Dame in the Kimono: Hollywood, Censorship, and the Production Code* (Lexington: University of Kentucky Press, 2001), 213.

76. Susan Doll, "Marilyn Monroe in 'Gentlemen Prefer Blondes,'" *How Stuff Works*, http://entertainment.howstuffworks.com/marilyn-monroe-early-career14.htm (June 12, 2012).

77. "Marilyn Takes Over as Lorelei," *Life*, May 25, 1953, 79ff., http://books.google.com/books?id=gUYEAAAAMBAJ&source=gbs_all_issues_r&cad=1.

78. For more on *Life* magazine's relationship with Hollywood film production, see *Life Goes to the Movies* (New York: Time-Life Books, 1975).

79. A slide show of over a dozen photographs from Clark's shoot is available on the *Life* magazine website: http://life.time.com/icons/marilyn-monroe-jane-russell-on-the-set-of-gentlemen-prefer-blondes/#1.

80. Florence Jacobowitz and Richard Lippe, "Performance and the Still Photograph: Marilyn Monroe," *CineAction* 44 (1994): 12–19, 16 quoted.

81. Danae Clark, *Negotiating Hollywood: The Cultural Politics of Actors' Labor* (Minneapolis and London: University of Minnesota Press, 1995), 22.

82. See, for example the online catalog for "Star Power: Edward Steichen in the Condé Nast Studio," available at http://www.fep-photo.org/exhibition/edward-steichen-star-power/, and "Sundance 2012: Exclusive EW Portraits, Day 1," *Entertainment Weekly*, January 29, 2012, http://www.ew.com/ew/gallery/0,,20469830_20563687,00.html

83. Charles Wolfe, "The Return of Jimmy Stewart: The Publicity Photograph as Text," in *Stardom: Industry of Desire*, ed. Christine Gledhill (London: Routledge, 1991), 92.

84. See, for example, the Katie Holmes Tumblr accessed July 12, 2012, http://www.tumblr.com/tagged/katieholmes?before=1341275757, featuring photographs read multiple ways both before and after her July 2012 divorce from Tom Cruise.

85. Richard Corliss, "Remembering Jane Russell: Brunette Bombshell," *Time*, March 4, 2011, http://entertainment.time.com/2011/03/04/remembering-jane-russell-brunette-bombshell/.

86. "Fuss over Ladies and a Ladies Man," *Life*, January 11, 1954, 24.

87. The costume in question is actually a low-cut, sequined one-piece, with cutouts on her belly and pelvis, rather than the kind of two-piece more traditionally called a bikini. Contemporary commentary refers to it as a bikini, however, and I've used that nomenclature here. There are several images of Russell in the bikini available on the Web, such as http://www.thetimes.co.uk/tto/multimedia/archive/00125/FRE014AA_125795j.jpg.

88. Charles Samuels, "Hollywood's Censorship Rebellion," *Exposed* 1, no. 1 (1955): 29, 32.

89. "Hot Stuff!" *Movie Life*, April 1954, 21.

90. "Russell Uncensored," *Movie Play*, (January 1955, 27).

91. "Designing Women," *Movie Life*, April 1954, 46.

92. Dixon, "Ambiguous Ecologies," 82.

93. Slide, *Inside the Hollywood Fan Magazine*, 7.

94. "Russell Uncensored," 27.

95. Jonathan Rosenbaum, *Placing Movies: The Practice of Film Criticism* (Berkeley and Los Angeles: University of California Press, 1995), 98–99.

96. Hopper, "Jane Has No Worries—at Least for 20 Years."

97. *Gentlemen Marry Brunettes*, directed by Richard Sale (1955; Paris: Russ-Field Productions, 2012), DVD; *The Fuzzy Pink Nightgown*, directed by Norman Taurog (1957; Los Angeles: Russ-Field Productions, 2012), DVD.

98. Kouvaros, *Famous Faces yet Not Themselves*, 63.

99. Denise Mann, *Hollywood Independents: The Postwar Talent Takeover* (Minneapolis: University of Minnesota Press, 2008), 1.

100. Mark Cousins, "Jane Russell Obituary," *Guardian*, March 1, 2011, http://www.guardian.co.uk/film/2011/mar/01/jane-russell-obituary.

101. "Columbia to Film Adventure Drama," *New York Times*, July 11, 1953; Thomas M. Pryor, "New Film in View for Jane Russell," *New York Times*, June 15, 1954.

102. Thomas Pryor, "Britain's Censors Bar Movie Dance: Back Production Code Move to Cut Gwen Verdon," *New York Times*, June 6, 1955. As far as I can tell, the footage in question is unavailable.

103. Russell sang with the Kay Kyser Orchestra in the mid-1940s and released *Let's Put Out the Lights* for Columbia. In 1954, she began singing gospel music with Connie Haines and Beryl Davis. The single "Do Lord" from *The Magic of Believing* for Capitol Records was certified gold by the Recording Industry Association of America, selling two million copies. For more on her recording career, see the Jane Russell page at AllMusic.com: http://www.allmusic.com/artist/jane-russell-mn0000810994.

104. Maureen Turim, "Gentlemen Consume Blondes," in *Issues in Feminist Film Criticism*, ed. Patricia Erens (Bloomington: Indiana University Press, 1990), 104.

105. "Film Review: Gentlemen Marry Brunettes," *Variety*, September 14, 1955, VarietyUltimate.com (June 21, 2012); Richard Griffith, "'Brunettes' Regarded as 'Almost a Bore,'" *Los Angeles Times*, November 8, 1955; A. H. Weiler, "Screen: Charleston Era: Mayfair Has 'Gentlemen Marry Brunettes,'" *New York Times*, October 31, 1955.

106. "Film Review: Gentlemen Marry Brunettes."

107. Frank Deford, "Jane Russell," *People*, October 28, 1985, http://www.people.com/people/archive/article/0,,20092046,00.html. The title is taken from the modest garment the kidnappers provide her with so that she doesn't tempt them with her beauty.

108. "'The Fuzzy Pink Nightgown' on View," *New York Times*, October 31, 1957; "Orpheum Has New Farce: Jane Stars in Pink Nightie," *Daily Boston Globe*, October 12, 1957; John L. Scott, "'Fuzzy Pink Nightgown' Light Comedy Offering," *Los Angeles Times*, August 22, 1957.

109. "'The Fuzzy Pink Nightgown' on View," 41.

110. Kirby, "On Acting and Not-Acting," 40.

111. Matthew H. Wikander, *Fangs of Malice: Hypocrisy, Sincerity, and Acting* (Iowa City: University of Iowa Press, 2002), xi–xii, xvii, 195.

112. David Krasner, "I Hate Strasberg: Method Bashing in the Academy," in *Method Acting Reconsidered: Theory, Practice, Future*, ed. David Krasner (New York: St. Martin's Press, 2000), 5.

113. Morris Carnovsky, "Design for Acting: The Quest of Technique," *Tulane Drama Review* 5, no. 3 (March 1961): 69.

114. Vernon Scott, "Jane Russell Ready to Give Up Movies," *Washington Post and Times Herald*, August 10, 1959.

2   MORE THAN A MERMAID: ESTHER WILLIAMS, PERFORMANCE, AND THE BODY

1. Esther Williams, *The Million Dollar Mermaid* (New York: Harcourt, 1999), 166.

2. Williams's films are obviously provocative texts for queer scholars, and the camp address of her films is undeniable. I refer interested readers to Steven Cohan, *Incongruous Entertainment: Camp, Cultural Values, and the MGM Musical* (Durham, NC: Duke University Press, 2005), which provides a representative reading of *Bathing Beauty*.

3. Ibid., 68.

4. Catherine Williamson, "Swimming Pools, Movie Stars: The Celebrity Body in the Post-War Marketplace," *Camera Obscura* 13, no. 2 38 (1996): 5, 8–9.

5. *Easy to Love*, directed by Charles Walters (1953; Los Angeles: MGM, 1992), VHS.

6. "Film Review: Easy to Love," *Daily Variety*, November 11, 1953, 3.

7. Aagje Swinnen and John Stotesbury, *Aging, Performance, and Stardom: Doing Age on the Stage of Consumerist Culture* (Berlin and London: LIT Verlag, 2012), 100.

8. Williams, *The Million Dollar Mermaid*, 45.

9. Other actresses were not so fortunate. For example, in an interview with Ronald Davis, Lucille Ball described her 1951 pregnancy with her first child, Lucie Arnaz. She was "elated" to be pregnant (and had suffered several previous miscarriages) but had to hide her expanding belly from Harry Cohn, who was reluctantly starring her in *The Magic Carpet* (1951). When that project finished filming, Ball and her "pot-belly" told Cecil B. DeMille that she was unable to do *The Greatest Show on Earth*, even though all she "ever wanted in [her] life [was] to be directed by a great director like yourself." DeMille responded: "Get rid of it!" Ball refused after explaining that it was too late (and that she desperately wanted the child) because she'd hidden the pregnancy in order to finish *The Magic Carpet*. DeMille retorted, "Lucille, . . . you're the only one I know who screwed Desi Arnaz, Harry Cohn, Paramount Pictures, and Cecil B. DeMille all at the same time." Lucille Ball, interview by Ronald L. Davis, August 21, 2980, OHC 197, transcript, Ronald Davis Oral History Collection, Southern Methodist University DeGolyer Library, Dallas, TX, 41–42.

10. Williams, *The Million Dollar Mermaid*, 250–251.

11. Ibid., 245.

12. Ibid., 24–49, 56.

13. See, for example, "Esther's Reward," *Movie Play*, January 1955, 23, and Lee Cordner, "How Esther Has Changed," *Modern Screen*, September 1956, 47ff., which told readers that "Hollywood had long since learned . . . that the three Gage kids come first" (47).

14. Hedda Hopper, "Esther Williams . . . Glamorous Mother of Three," *Los Angeles Times*, May 30, 1954.

15. Williams, *The Million Dollar Mermaid*, 243–244.

16. Ibid., 22.

17. Bosley Crowther, "Island Paradise; 'Raw Wind in Eden' Bows at Loew's State," *New York Times*, September 20, 1958.

18. Williams, *The Million Dollar Mermaid*, 298–300.

19. Ibid., 395.

20. Williams, *The Million Dollar Mermaid*, 386–393.

21. Eleanor Powell is another Classical Hollywood star whose powerful body dictated narrative, often posing similar problems for her romance plots. For more, see Adrienne L. McLean, "Putting 'Em Down like a Man: Eleanor Powell and the Spectacle of Competence," in *Hetero: Queering Representations of Straightness*, ed. Sean Griffin (Albany: SUNY Press, 2009).

22. *Million Dollar Mermaid*, directed by Mervyn LeRoy (1952; Los Angeles: MGM, 1992) VHS; *Skirts Ahoy!*, directed by Sidney Lanfield (1952; Los Angeles: MGM, 1992), VHS; *Dangerous When Wet*, directed by Charles Walters (1953; Los Angeles: MGM, 1992), VHS.

23. Williams, *The Million Dollar Mermaid*, 73.

24. Cynthia Baron, "Crafting Film Performances: Acting in the Hollywood Studio Era," in *Screen Acting*, ed. Alan Lovell and Peter Krämer (London and New York: Routledge, 1999), 34. For more on actor training, see also Cynthia Baron and Sharon Marie Carnicke, *Reframing Screen Performance* (Ann Arbor: University of Michigan Press, 2008), especially chapter 1.

25. Baron, "Crafting Film Performances," 34; Estelle Harman, interview by Ronald L. Davis, July 16, 1997, OHC 404, transcript, Ronald Davis Oral History Collection, Southern Methodist University DeGolyer Library, Dallas, TX, 4.

26. Lillian Burns Sidney. interview by Ronald L. Davis, Aug. 17, 1986, OHC 370, transcript, Ronald Davis Oral History Collection, Southern Methodist University DeGolyer Library, Dallas, TX, 2; Jamie Lee Curtis, "Lillian," in *Projections 7: Film-makers on Filmmaking, in Association with "Cahiers du Cinéma"* (1997): 147.

27. Harman, interview, 7.

28. Baron, "Crafting Film Performances," 34–35.

29. Al Trescony, interview by Ronald L. Davis, August 20, 1976, OHC 376, transcript, Ronald Davis Oral History Collection, Southern Methodist University DeGolyer Library, Dallas, TX, 8.

30. Phyllis Loughton Seaton, interview by Ronald L. Davis, July 23, 1979, OHC 180, transcript, Ronald Davis Oral History Collection, Southern Methodist University DeGolyer Library, Dallas, TX, 14.

31. Hugh O'Brian, interview by Ronald L. Davis, August 17, 1988, OHC 434, transcript, Ronald Davis Oral History Collection, Southern Methodist University DeGolyer Library, Dallas, TX, 23.

32. Harman, interview, 4.

33. Burns Sidney, interview, 9.

34. Trescony, interview, 6–7.

35. Seaton, interview, 16.

36. Joan Leslie, interview by Ronald L. Davis, August 13, 1981, OHC 229, transcript, Ronald Davis Oral History Collection, Southern Methodist University DeGolyer Library, Dallas, TX, 9.

37. Seaton, interview, 16–17.

38. Baron, "Crafting Film Performances," 31.

39. Morris Carnovsky quoted in James Barron, "Morris Carnovsky Is Dead at 94; Acting Career Spanned 60 Years," *New York Times*, September 2 1992, http://www.nytimes.com/1992/09/02/arts/morris-carnovsky-is-dead-at-94-acting-career-spanned-60-years.html.

40. Norman Lloyd, interview by Ronald L. Davis, July 23–24, 1979, and August 14, 1980, OHC 179, transcript, Ronald Davis Oral History Collection, Southern Methodist University DeGolyer Library, Dallas, TX, 17.

41. For more on the Group Theatre, see Wendy Smith, *Real Life Drama: The Group Theatre and America, 1931–1940* (New York: Grove Press, 1994).

42. Barron, "Morris Carnovsky Is Dead at 94."

43. The Hollywood Blacklist killed the careers of many of these actors and directors, including Carnovsky, one of the notorious Hollywood Ten. For more, see Patrick McGilligan and Paul Buhle, *Tender Comrades: The Backstory of the Hollywood Blacklist* (Minneapolis: University of Minnesota Press, 1997) and Milly S. Barranger, *Unfriendly Witnesses: Gender, Theater, and Film in the McCarthy Era* (Carbondale: University of Illinois Press, 2008).

44. Baron, "Crafting Film Performances," 36.

45. Naturalist acting is a complicated, often contested subject for theater historians and practitioners. Though now most associated with Lee Strasberg's Method, it is not a monolithic style. For more about naturalist acting in the US theater and film context, see David Krasner, ed., *Method Acting Reconsidered: Theory, Practice, Future* (New York: St. Martin's Press, 2000); Baron, Carson, and Tomasulo, *More than a Method*; Baron and Carnicke, *Reframing Screen Performance*; and Steve Vineberg, *Method Actors: Three Generations of an American Acting Style* (New York: Schirmer Books, 1991).

46. Janet Leigh, interview by Ronald L. Davis, July 25, 1984, OHC 308, transcript, Ronald Davis Oral History Collection, Southern Methodist University DeGolyer Library, Dallas, TX, 6.

47. Leslie, interview, 47.

48. Harman, interview, 7.

49. James Naremore, *Acting in the Cinema* (Berkeley and Los Angeles: University of California Press, 1988), 18.

50. Jean Porter, interview by Ronald L. Davis, April 18, 1980, and April 4, 1981, OHC 194, transcript, Ronald Davis Oral History Collection, Southern Methodist University DeGolyer Library, Dallas, TX, 47.

51. Williams, *The Million Dollar Mermaid*, 84.

52. Lillian Burns Sidney, quoted in Baron, "Crafting Film Performances," 37.

53. Ibid., 40.

54. Ibid., 38.

55. Hedda Hopper, "Hannibal Will Be Esther Williams's Suitor in Her Next Splashy Picture," *Los Angeles Times*, January 9, 1954.

56. Edward R. Murrow, "Esther Williams," disc 2, *The Best of Person to Person* (1955; Los Angeles: Koch Vision, 2006), DVD.

57. *Esther Williams at Cypress Gardens*, directed by Alan Handley and Roy Montgomery, NBC-TV, 1960, Netflix Streaming Video.

58. Both these examples demonstrate how the naturalist paradigm transfers to television performance, a point I take up in the final chapter, on Zsa Zsa Gabor.

59. Baron and Carnicke, *Reframing Screen Performance*, 22–23, 18.

60. "M-G-Mythology," *Newsweek*, June 13, 1949, 8, quoted in Williamson, "Swimming Pools, Movie Stars," 10.

61. Williams, *The Million Dollar Mermaid*, 75.

62. Lillian Burns Sidney quoted in Curtis, "Lillian," 141.

63. Esther Williams quoted in Williamson, "Swimming Pools, Movie Stars," 6.

64. Williams, *The Million Dollar Mermaid*, 77.

65. Ibid. Sidney was married to Lillian Burns at the time. According to her autobiography, Williams found him a more sympathetic and useful mentor.

66. Ibid., 86–87.

67. In *Acting in the Cinema*, James Naremore reminds us that the famous footage no longer exists, and that Kuleshov and his collaborator Pudovkin disagreed about both its content and effect; even so, he points out on page 24 that "movies have always proved Kuleshov's point."

68. Williams, *The Million Dollar Mermaid*, 76.

69. Cohan, *Incongruous Entertainment*, 71.

70. Williams, *The Million Dollar Mermaid*, 169.

71. Naremore, *Acting for the Cinema*, 40.

72. David Thomson, *A Biographical Dictionary of the Cinema* (London: Andre Deutsch, 1994), 29.

73. Williams, *The Million Dollar Mermaid*, 98.

74. Marvin Carlson, *Performance: A Critical Introduction*, 2nd ed. (London and New York: Routledge, 2004), 5, 110.

75. Sharon Marie Carnicke, "Screen Performance and Directors' Visions," in *More than a Method: Trends and Traditions in Contemporary Film Performance*, ed. Cynthia Baron, Diane Carson, and Frank P. Tomasulo (Detroit: Wayne State University Press, 2004), 67.

76. Williams, *The Million Dollar Mermaid*, 222.

77. Williamson, "Swimming Pools, Movie Stars," 9.

78. Steven Cohan, "Introduction: Musicals of the Studio Era," in *Hollywood Musicals: The Film Reader*, ed. Steven Cohan (London and New York: Routledge, 2002), 11.

79. Rick Altman, "The American Film Musical and the Myth of Entertainment," in *Hollywood Musicals: The Film Reader*, ed. Steven Cohan (London and New York: Routledge, 2002), 42, 48.

80. Williams, *The Million Dollar Mermaid*, 215.

81. Carnicke, "Screen Performance and Directors' Visions," 42.

82. Cohan, *Incongruous Entertainment*, 45.

83. Williams, *The Million Dollar Mermaid*, 217, 220–221.

84. Ibid., 219, 221.

85. Danae Clark, *Negotiating Hollywood: The Cultural Politics of Actors' Labor* (Minneapolis and London: University of Minnesota Press, 1995), 9.

86. Ibid., 121.

87. Cohan, *Incongruous Entertainment*, 87.

88. Their swimming is intercut with the family back at the hotel. Katie's mother, played by the vaudevillian Charlotte Greenwood, wows the crowd with her high kicks, splits, and windmill arms. Greenwood's film roles generally capitalized on her elastic limbs; a very tall woman, she could kick over her own head. She is another actress whose body determined her performance style, and her athleticism provides an interesting counterpoint to Williams's ballet with Lamas. By including this zany scene between segments of their love song, the film undercuts what might have been its romantic highlight. For more on Greenwood, see chapter 4 below.

89. Adrienne L. McLean, *Being Rita Hayworth: Labor, Identity, and Hollywood Stardom* (New Brunswick, NJ, and London: Rutgers University Press, 2004), 127.

90. Susan Knobloch, "Helen Shaver: Resistance through Artistry," in *Screen Acting*, ed. Allan Lovell and Peter Krämer (London: Routledge, 1999), 106–107.

91. Judith Butler, *Bodies That Matter: On the Discursive Limits of "Sex"* (New York and London: Routledge, 1993), 2.

92. Susan Leigh Foster, "Choreographies of Gender," in *Performance Studies*, ed. Erin Striff (New York: Palgrave, 2003), 169, 171.

93. Of course, *Skirts Ahoy!* is equally available to a queer reading (as are many of Williams's other films). Here, I read the relationship between the women as nonsexual in order to advance the idea of female community and in order to focus specifically on Williams's embodiment of Whitney Young as a feminist role model. Further, setting aside the queer potentials of the text offers an equally radical critique: even heterosexual women can privilege other women over men.

94. Williams, *The Million Dollar Mermaid*, 205–206. I recognize the dangers of relying too heavily on Williams's autobiography, and don't mean to suggest that this is an unimpeachably "true" source for the events of her life; I insist, however, that Williams chose to present her life and her career in a specific way.

95. Lucie Arbuthnot and Gail Seneca, "Pre-text and Text in *Gentlemen Prefer Blondes*," in *Hollywood Musicals: The Film Reader*, ed. Steven Cohan (London and New York: Routledge, 2002), 77–78.

96. Williams generally executes a modified Australian crawl, always keeping her head out of the water and facing the camera, or an underwater sidestroke, crossing the camera frame horizontally. The race in *Skirts Ahoy!*, though obviously not a competition among equals, nonetheless highlights Williams's impressive athletic ability.

97. Paul MacDonald, "Why Study Film Acting? Some Opening Reflections," in *More than a Method: Trends and Traditions in Contemporary Film Performance*, ed. Cynthia Baron, Diane Carson, and Frank P. Tomasulo (Detroit: Wayne State University Press, 2004), 32.

3 Light Egyptian: Lena Horne and the
Representation of Black Femininity

1. Peter B. Flint, "Ava Gardner Is Dead at 67; Often Played Femme Fatale," *New York Times*, January 28, 1990, http://www.nytimes.com/1990/01/26/obituaries/ava-gardner-is -dead-at-67-often-played-femme-fatale.html?pagewanted=all&src=pm.

2. James Gavin, *Stormy Weather: The Life of Lena Horne* (New York, London, Toronto, and Sydney: Atria Books, 2009), 214.

3. Judith Butler, *Bodies That Matter: On the Discursive Limits of "Sex"* (New York and London: Routledge, 1993), 2.

4. Gavin, *Stormy Weather*, 10–12. This is Gavin's explanation of her racial lineage; accounts vary. Unless otherwise specified, all biographical details in this section of the chapter come from Gavin's biography.

5. Jayna Brown, *Babylon Girls: Black Women Performers and the Shaping of the Modern* (Durham, NC: Duke University Press, 2008), 200–201.

6. Quoted in Brown, *Babylon Girls*, 201.

7. Kristin McGee, *Some Liked It Hot: Jazz Women in Film and Television, 1928–1959* (Middletown, CT: Wesleyan University Press, 2009), 239. This clause also kept her away from relatively nuanced roles like the mother of a mixed-race child in the 1934 version of *Imitation of Life*, played by Louise Beavers. Fredi Washington, a green-eyed mixed-race actress, played Beavers's mulatto daughter and was one of the only light-skinned black actresses to precede Horne in Hollywood.

8. Arthur Knight, *Disintegrating the Musical: Black Performance and American Musical Film* (Durham, NC: Duke University Press, 2002). 148.

9. Aljean Harmetz, "Lena Horne, Singer and Actress, Dies at 92," *New York Times*, May 10, 2010, http://www.nytimes.com/2010/05/10/arts/music/10horne.html. Despite her recollection, no such exchange exists in the DVD version of the film.

10. Megan E. Williams, "'Meet the Real Lena Horne': Representations of Lena Horne in *Ebony* Magazine, 1945–49," *Journal of American Studies* 43, no. 1 (2009): 122.

11. Gavin, *Stormy Weather*, 13, 220, 315, 329, 473.

12. Ibid., 290–291.

13. John Andrews, "Lena Horne, 1917–2010," *World Socialist Web Site*, May 13, 2010, http:// wsws.org/articles/2010/may2010/horn-m13.shtml (July 27, 2012).

14. Harmetz, "Lena Horne, Singer and Actress, Dies at 92."

15. John Fordham, "Lena Horne Obituary," *Guardian*, May 10, 2010, http://www.guardian .co.uk/music/2010/may/10/lena-horne-obituary; Gavin, *Stormy Weather*, 188, 275, 425.

16. Harmetz, "Lena Horne, Singer and Actress, Dies at 92." The obituary clarifies that Nina Mae McKinney signed a five-year contract with MGM in 1929.

17. Ibid.

18. Shane Vogel, "Performing 'Stormy Weather': Ethel Waters, Lena Horne, and Katherine Dunham," *South Central Review* 25 no. 1 (Spring 2008): 96.

19. Ibid., 93.

20. *Stormy Weather*, directed by Andrew Stone (1943; Los Angeles: MGM, 2005), DVD.

21. Abel, "Stormy Weather," *Variety*, June 2, 1943, http://www.varietyultimate.com/archive/issue/WV-06–02–1943–8.

22. T.M.P. "'Stormy Weather,' Negro Musical with Bill Robinson at the Roxy—'Hers to Hold' Opens at Criterion," *New York Times*, July 22, 1943.

23. Gavin, *Stormy Weather*, 132.

24. Ibid., 180.

25. Shari Roberts, "Seeing Stars: Feminine Spectacle, Female Spectators, and World War II Hollywood Musicals" (PhD diss., University of Chicago, 1993), 136–141.

26. See, for example, Jackie Ormes, "Lena Horne Sets a New Box Office Record," *Chicago Defender*, October 21, 1944.

27. *Lena Horne: The Lady and Her Music*, directed by Paddy Sampson (1984; New York: RKO Home Video, 1985), VHS.

28. Vogel, "Performing 'Stormy Weather,'" 96–97.

29. Frank Rich, review of *Lena Horne: The Lady and Her Music*, directed by Arthur Faria, Nederlander Theatre, New York, *New York Times*, May 13, 1981, http://www.nytimes.com/1981/05/13/arts/theater-lena-horne-the-lady-and-her-music.html?&pagewanted=1.

30. This clip is available at http://www.youtube.com/watch?v=EMf0Z7EPdLo (August 6, 2012). Despite the interruption of riotous applause, Horne immediately segues into "If You Believe" from *The Wiz*.

31. Scott McMillin, *The Musical as Drama: A Study of the Principles and Conventions behind Musical Shows from Kern to Sondheim* (Princeton, NJ: Princeton University Press, 2006), 25.

32. Raymond Knapp, *The American Musical and the Formation of National Identity* (Princeton, NJ: Princeton University Press, 2005), 8.

33. Jane Feuer, *The Hollywood Musical*, 2nd ed. (Bloomington and Indianapolis: Indiana University Press, 1993), 31, 3.

34. Richard Dyer, *Only Entertainment*, 2nd ed. (London and New York: Routledge, 2002), 39.

35. Knapp, *The American Musical and the Formation of National Identity*, 10.

36. For more on links between minstrelsy and nineteenth-century burlesque, see my *Actresses and Whores: On Stage and in Society* (Cambridge; Cambridge University Press, 2005), 114–115.

37. Knapp, *The American Musical and the Formation of National Identity*, 56.

38. Eric Lott, *Love and Theft: Blackface Minstrelsy and the American Working Class* (Oxford: Oxford University Press, 1995), 267.

39. Knapp, *The American Musical and the Formation of National Identity*, 56.

40. Martin Rubin, *Busby Berkeley and the Tradition of Spectacle* (New York: Columbia University Press, 1993), 16.

41. Though nearly all blackface minstrels in the antebellum United States were Anglo immigrant men, William Lane, who called himself Master Juba, was a freeborn black dancer on the minstrel circuit until his death at age twenty-seven in 1852. Knapp, *The American Musical and the Formation of National Identity*, 49–51.

42. Lott, *Love and Theft*, 5.

43. Robert C. Toll, *Blacking Up: The Minstrel Show in Nineteenth-Century America* (New York and Oxford: Oxford University Press, 1974), 51–57.

44. Jennifer Fuller, "The Smell of Flak in the Morning: *Tropic Thunder*'s Talk Show Tour," *Flow TV* 8, no. 6 (August 21, 2008), http://flowtv.org/?p=1615 (March 15, 2010).

45. Lott, *Love and Theft*, 18–20. Lott demonstrates how this narrative is more important for the ways it mobilizes tropes of blackness and authenticity than for its accuracy describing minstrel's originary performance.

46. Ibid., 20.

47. Ibid., 53.

48. Annemarie Bean, "Transgressing the Gender Divide: The Female Impersonator in Nineteenth-Century Blackface Minstrelsy," in *Inside the Minstrel Mask: Readings in Nineteenth-Century Blackface Minstrelsy*, ed. Annemarie Bean, James V. Hatch, and Brooks McNamara (Wesleyan CT: Wesleyan University Press), 250.

49. Peter Stanfield, "An Excursion into the Lower Depths: Hollywood, Urban Primitivism, and *St. Louis Blues*, 1929–1937," *Cinema Journal* 41, no. 2 (Winter 2002): 90.

50. Bean, "Transgressing the Gender Divide," 247.

51. Donald Bogle, *Toms, Coons, Mulattoes, Mammies, and Bucks: An Interpretive History of Blacks in American Films*, 4th ed. (New York and London: Continuum Press, 2001), 9.

52. William J. Mahar, *Behind the Burnt Cork Mask: Early Blackface Minstrelsy and Antebellum American Popular Culture* (Urbana and Chicago: University of Illinois Press, 1999), 18, 307–308.

53. Bean, "Transgressing the Gender Divide," 247. The homoerotics of such representations are clear; for more, see in particular Lott, *Love and Theft*, 161–168.

54. Mahar, *Behind the Burnt Cork Mask*, 269.

55. Ibid., 305–306.

56. Ibid., 327.

57. Lott, *Love and Theft*, 165.

58. Mahar, *Behind the Burnt Cork Mask*, 152.

59. Toll, *Blacking Up*, 76.

60. Heather May, "Middle-Class Morality and Blackwashed Beauties: Francis Leon and the Rise of the Prima Donna in the Post-War Minstrel Show" (PhD diss., Indiana University, 2007), 123, 134.

61. Ibid., 22.

62. Lynn Abbott and Doug Seroff, *Ragged but Right: Black Traveling Shows, "Coon Songs," and the Dark Pathway* (Jackson: University of Mississippi Press, 2007), 39, 82, 107.

63. Brown, *Babylon Girls*, 214–215.

64. Sean Griffin, "The Gang's All Here: Generic versus Racial Integration in the 1940s Musical," *Cinema Journal* 42 no. 1 (Fall 2002): 23.

65. In Griffin, "The Gang's All Here," 29.

66. McMillin, *The Musical as Drama*, 103.

67. Martin Rubin points out that though the plots and characters of most integrated musicals are realistic, many contain several numbers that are "impossible from the standpoint of the realistic discourse of the narrative" because their motivations, performance, mise-en-scène, and cinematography contradict the films' diegesis. Quoted in the introduction to *Hollywood Musicals: The Film Reader*, ed. Steven Cohan (New York and London: Routledge, 2002), 2.

68. Richard Dyer, "Entertainment and Utopia," in *Genre: The Musical*, ed. Rick Altman (London: Routledge, 1981), 183.

69. Rick Altman, *The American Film Musical* (Bloomington and Indianapolis: Indiana University Press, 1987), 306, 286–287.

70. See Steven Cohan, *Incongruous Entertainment: Camp, Cultural Value, and the MGM Musical* (Durham, NC: Duke University Press, 2005), 27.

71. Altman, *The American Film Musical*, 151.

72. McMillin, *The Musical as Drama*, 55.

73. Knight, *Disintegrating the Musical*, 15.

74. Steve Vineberg, *Method Actors: Three Generations of an American Acting Style* (New York: Schirmer Books, 1991), 45, 195.

75. Jerome Delamater, "Ritual, Realism and Abstraction: Performance in the Musical," in *Making the Visible Invisible*, ed. Carole Zucker (Methuen, NJ: Scarecrow Press, 1990), 61.

76. Sumiko Higashi, "Movies and the Paradox of Female Stardom," in *American Cinema of the 1950s: Themes and Variations*, ed. Murray Pomerance (New Brunswick, NJ: Rutgers University Press, 2005), 70; Carol Clover, "Dancing in the Rain," in *Hollywood Musicals: The Film Reader*, ed. Steven Cohan (London and New York: Routledge, 2002), 158.

77. Steven Cohan, "Introduction: Musicals of the Studio Era," in *Hollywood Musicals: The Film Reader*, ed. Steven Cohan (London and New York: Routledge, 2002), 13.

78. Dyer, *Only Entertainment*, 20–27.

79. Ibid., 39.

80. *Cabin in the Sky*, directed by Vincente Minnelli (1943; Los Angeles: MGM, 2006), DVD.

81. Hugh Fordin, *MGM's Greatest Musicals: The Freed Unit* (New York: Da Capo Press, 1996), 73; Ibid., 75.

82. M.P., "'Cabin in the Sky,' a Musical Fantasy, with Ethel Waters, at Loew's," *New York Times*, May 28, 1943; Lewis quoted in James Naremore, "Uptown Folk: Blackness and Entertainment in *Cabin in the Sky*," in *Representing Jazz*, ed. Krin Gabbard (Durham, NC: Duke University Press, 1995), 176.

83. Naremore, "Uptown Folk," 177.

84. Richard Dyer, *Heavenly Bodies: Film Stars and Society* (New York: St. Martin's Press, 1986), 44.

85. In Shane Vogel, "Lena Horne's Impersona," *Camera Obscura* 67, no. 23 1 (2008): 18.

86. Gavin, *Stormy Weather*, 151.

87. *Till the Clouds Roll By*, directed by Richard Whorf (1946; Los Angeles: MGM), Amazon.com Instant Video.

88. Horne in Sam Irvin, *Kay Thompson: From Funny Face to Eloise* (New York: Simon and Schuster, 2010), 97.

89. *The Ziegfeld Follies*, directed by Lemuel Ayers, Roy Del Ruth, Robert Lewis, Vincente Minnelli, and George Sidney (1945; Los Angeles: MGM), Amazon.com Instant Video.

90. *Broadway Rhythm*, directed by Roy Del Ruth (1944; Los Angeles: MGM, 2009), DVD. It's not coincidental that both these numbers, as well as Horne's MGM debut in *Panama Hattie* (1942) with "The Sping," are Latin numbers. As I discuss in the following chapter, Hollywood representations of Latinos and Latinas are always racially ambiguous, and "Latin" rhythms are appropriated by white characters to signal their freedom and sensuality. Horne's frequent salsas, sambas, and cha-chas overlap both these tropes.

91. *The Duchess of Idaho*, directed by Robert Z. Leonard (1950; Los Angeles: MGM, 1995), VHS.

92. Megan E. Williams, "The *Crisis* Cover Girl: Lena Horne, the NAACP, and Representations of African American Femininity, 1941–1945," *American Periodicals: A Journal of History, Criticism, and Bibliography* 16, no. 2 (2006): 201–203.

93. Emily Torchia, interview by Ronald L. Davis, July 16, 1984, OHC 306, transcript, Ronald Davis Oral History Collection, Southern Methodist University DeGolyer Library, Dallas, TX, 48.

94. Williams, "'Meet the Real Lena Horne,'" 121, 123.

95. Gavin, *Stormy Weather*, 113, 149.

96. Ibid., 259, 113, 262, 149, 173.

97. McGee, *Some Liked It Hot*, 243.

98. Gavin, *Stormy Weather*, 261.

99. Ibid., 204.

100. Vogel, "Lena Horne's Impersona," 12–13.

101. Ibid., 15.

102. Lee Strasberg, *Strasberg at the Actors Studio: Tape-Recorded Sessions*, ed. Robert H. Hethmon (New York: Theatre Communications Group, 1991), 15.

103. See George Kouvaros, *Famous Faces Yet Not Themselves: "The Misfits" and Icons of Postwar America* (Minneapolis: University of Minnesota Press, 2007), 53, as well as the discussion in the previous chapter.

4   CARNIVAL!: CARMEN MIRANDA AND THE SPECTACLE OF AUTHENTICITY

1. "Carmen Miranda—Querida Adão," YouTube video, posted by Doni Sacramento on April 5, 2007, http://www.youtube.com/watch?v=L2IK-Y3–2CE.

2. José Ligiéro Coelho, "Carmen Miranda: An Afro-Brazilian Paradox" (PhD diss., New York University, 1998), 75.

3. *The Gang's All Here*, directed by Busby Berkeley (1943; Los Angeles: Twentieth Century–Fox, 2008), DVD; *Doll Face*, directed by Lewis Seller (1945; Los Angeles: Twentieth Century–Fox, 2008), DVD.

4. I discuss Miranda's costume in detail below. *Baiana* is the name given to the traditional dress of enslaved and formerly enslaved women in the Bahia region of Brazil; these women are sometimes also Baianas. Others use the spelling "Bahianas," which I've adopted here in order to differentiate the women and their clothes.

5. Coelho, "Carmen Miranda," 75.

6. Because the *chanchada*'s style and narratives were similar to those of US movie musicals, Miranda's Brazilian film work prepared her to join the Fox studio, though she spoke little English and had no formal acting training. In fact, her US debut, *Down Argentine Way*, used her in much the same way as *Alô Alô Carnaval* and the earlier *Alô Alô Brasil*. Miranda filmed her songs on a soundstage, and they were edited into the final version. In *Down Argentine Way*, her songs serve as a prologue (the film opens with Miranda singing her hit "South American Way") and offer local color in Buenos Aires (star Betty Grable visits the El Tigre nightclub to hear "Miss Carmen Miranda" sing her Brazilian samba hits "*Mamãe Eu Quero*/Mama, I Want" and "*Bambu Bambu*").

7. Robert Stam, *Tropical Multiculturalism: A Comparative History of Race in Brazilian Cinema and Culture* (Durham, NC: Duke University Press, 1997), 83; Robert Stam, *Subversive Pleasures: Bakhtin, Cultural Criticism, and Film* (Baltimore and London: Johns Hopkins University Press, 1989), 92.

8. Mary Beltrán, *Latina/o Stars in U.S. Eyes: The Makings and Meanings of Film and TV Stardom* (Urbana and Chicago: University of Illinois Press, 2009), 3.

9. *Something for the Boys*, directed by Lewis Seiler (1944; Los Angeles: Twentieth-Century Fox, 2008), DVD.

10. Shari Roberts, "'The Lady in the Tutti-Frutti Hat': Carmen Miranda, a Spectacle of Ethnicity," *Cinema Journal* 32, no. 3 (Spring 1993): 19.

11. Mikhail Bakhtin, *Rabelais and His World*, trans. Helene Iswolsky (Bloomington: Indiana University Press, 1984), 316.

12. Lizabeth Paravisini-Gebert, "'Writers Playin' Mas': Carnival and the Grotesque in the Contemporary Caribbean Novel," in *A History of Literature in the Caribbean*, vol. 3, ed. A. James Arnold with Julio Rodríguez-Luis and J. Michael Dash (Amsterdam and Philadelphia, John Benjamins Publishing Co., 1984), 216–217.

13. Priscilla Peña Ovalle, *Dance and the Hollywood Latina: Race, Sex, and Stardom.* (New Brunswick and London: Rutgers University Press, 2011), 49.

14. *Springtime in the Rockies*, directed by Irving Cummings (1942; Los Angeles: Twentieth Century–Fox, 1998), VHS.

15. Peña Ovallle, *Dance and the Hollywood Latina*, 51.

16. *Down Argentine Way*, directed by Irving Cummings (1940; Los Angeles: Twentieth Century–Fox, 2006), DVD.

17. In English, full-length biographies are limited to Coelho's dissertation and Martha Gil-Montero's authorized biography (see below), as well as biographical sketches in Peña Ovalle's and Roberts's essays and material in the documentary *Carmen Miranda: The Girl from Rio*, included in the DVD of *Something for the Boys*. There are a few Brazilian biographies that have not been translated into English. Because I focus on Miranda's position vis-à-vis discourses of naturalism rather than her Brazilian reception, I did not have these biographies translated for my research.

18. Peña Ovalle, *Dance and the Hollywood Latina*, 56.

19. For "raucous," see Gil-Montero, *Brazilian Bombshell: The Biography of Carmen Miranda* (New York: Donald I. Fine, Inc., 1989), 14; Coelho, "Carmen Miranda," 25.

20. Gil-Montero, *Brazilian Bombshell*, 15–19.

21. Ibid., 40–43.

22. Ibid., 21.

23. Coelho, "Carmen Miranda," 42; for a detailed account of Miranda's Brazilian career, see 39–63. All the material in this and the next paragraph comes from this dissertation.

24. Peña Ovalle, *Dance and the Hollywood Latina*, 56–59.

25. Coelho, "Carmen Miranda," 7; Stam, *Tropical Multiculturalism*, 80.

26. Gil-Montero, *Brazilian Bombshell*, 70.

27. Brooks Atkinson, "The Play: 'The Streets of Paris' Moves to Broadway—Paul Robeson in 'The Emperor Jones,'" *New York Times*, June 2, 1939.

28. Coelho, "Carmen Miranda," 185–188. All translations of Miranda's lyrics come from Coelho unless otherwise specified.

29. Gil-Montero, *Brazilian Bombshell*, 130–132, 154.

30. Peña Ovalle, *Dance and the Hollywood Latina*, 68.

31. Gil-Montero, *Brazilian Bombshell*, 179, 195–197, 217, 229, 244, 258.

32. Ibid., 6, 10.

33. Gil-Montero, *Brazilian Bombshell*, 7.

34. Charles A. Perrone, "Performing São Paulo: Vanguard Representations of a Brazilian Cosmopolis," *Latin American Music Review* 23, no. 1 (Spring/Summer 2002): 60; Veloso, "Caricature and Conqueror, Pride and Shame."

35. Caetano Veloso, "Caricature and Conqueror, Pride and Shame," *New York Times*, October 20, 1991.

36. Michael T. Luongo, "Rio Remembers Carmen Miranda; A Tiny Museum's Big Party Honors Brazilian Legend," *Chicago Tribune*, July 10, 2005.

37. Roberts, "'The Lady in the Tutti-Frutti Hat,'" 14.

38. James Mandrell, "Carmen Miranda Betwixt and Between, or Neither Here nor There," *Latin American Literary Review* 29 (January 2001): 27.

39. Gil-Montero, *Brazilian Bombshell*, 52–54. The performance can be viewed on YouTube at http://www.youtube.com/watch?v=0j03I59Gn6c, posted by Doni Sacramento, April 2, 2007.

40. Coelho, "Carmen Miranda," 94.

41. Toyin Falola and Matt D. Childs, *The Yoruba Diaspora in the Atlantic World* (Bloomington: Indiana University Press, 2004), 80, 87–88.

42. Coelho, "Carmen Miranda," 30–31.

43. Ibid., 1, 97.

44. Mandrell, "Carmen Miranda Betwixt and Between," 31–32.

45. Roberts, "'The Lady in the Tutti-Frutti Hat,'" 12.

46. Gil-Montero, *Brazilian Bombshell*, 134.

47. *Week-End in Havana*, directed by Walter Lang (1941; Los Angeles: Twentieth Century–Fox, 2005), DVD.

48. Gil-Montero, *Brazilian Bombshell*, 134–135.

49. Peña Ovalle, *Dance and the Hollywood Latina*, 2.

50. Gil-Montero, *Brazilian Bombshell*, 135–136.

51. See, for example, Ana M. López, "Are All Latins from Manhattan? Hollywood, Ethnography, and Cultural Colonialism," in *Unspeakable Images: Ethnicity and the American Cinema*, ed. Lester D. Friedman (Urbana and Chicago: University of Illinois Press, 1991), 404–424; Mandrell, "Carmen Miranda Betwixt and Between"; and Roberts, "'The Lady in the Tutti-Frutti Hat.'"

52. Gil-Montero, *Brazilian Bombshell*, 64, 71.

53. Cynthia H. Enloe, *Bananas, Beaches and Bases: Making Feminist Sense of International Politics* (Berkeley and Los Angeles: University of California Press, 1990), 126.

54. Philip Swanson, "Going Down on Good Neighbours: Imagining *América* in Hollywood Movies of the 1930s and 1940s (*Flying Down to Rio* and *Down Argentine Way*)," *Bulletin of Latin American Research* 29, no. 1 (2010): 72.

55. Clara E. Rodríguez, *Heroes, Lovers, and Others: The Story of Latinos in Hollywood* (Washington, DC: Smithsonian Books, 2004), 82.

56. Swanson, "Going Down on Good Neighbours," 76.

57. López, "Are All Latins from Manhattan?" 407.

58. Brian O'Neil, "The Demands of Authenticity: Addison Durland and Hollywood's Latin Images during World War II," in *Classic Hollywood, Classic Whiteness*, ed. Daniel Bernardi (Minneapolis and London: University of Minneapolis Press, 2001), 360, 361. Obviously, these representational tropes echo those of black Americans in the movie musical, as Dyer and others point out.

59. Hedda Hopper, "Learning Their Latin," *Washington Post*, July 10, 1941. This is the only reference I've found to Miranda playing her own nationality rather than a Cuban entertainer, and the film offers no clarification.

60. Roberts, "The Lady in the Tutti-Frutti Hat." 7.

61. It is not coincidental, of course, that Ameche appears in both these films, nor that Miranda is paired with Faye and Grable, the "Fox Blondes." I discuss Miranda and her cohort in more detail below.

62. Swanson, "Going Down on Good Neighbours," 81.

63. It's doubtful that Harold and Fayard Nicholas actually occupied the same soundstage as Grable, Greenwood, Ameche, and the rest of the principals. Their very short sequence is abruptly cut to, and the lighting is different between it and the other sections of the finale.

64. O'Neil, "The Demands of Authenticity," 367.

65. Esther Williams, *The Million Dollar Mermaid* (New York: Harcourt, 1999), 139.

66. O'Neil, "The Demands of Authenticity," 367–368.

67. Ibid., 370. Of Miranda's films, *Springtime in the Rockies* is a notable exception. In the cabaret at Lake Louise, there are three Natives in "traditional" tribal dress; two are working as waiters, and one is enjoying the floor show.

68. Coelho, "Carmen Miranda," 16, 49.

69. Ibid., 56, 134–138, 141.

70. Constance Valis Hill, *Brotherhood in Rhythm: The Jazz Tap Dancing of the Nicholas Brothers* (New York: Oxford University Press, 2000), 32.

71. Susan Manning, *Modern Dance, Negro Dance: Race in Motion* (Minneapolis: University of Minnesota Press, 2004), 149–150.

72. An earlier number, "She Was Always True to the Navy," was cut from the film. According to Gil-Montero, the navy objected to the number, though she doesn't give a reason. The song implies that "she" was a prostitute beloved by all branches of the armed forces, a particularly negative image of US fighting men. Miranda's costume, including a lighthouse hat, is relatively revealing as well. The *baiana* covers her navel but dips below that level on the right side, she wears an especially low-cut halter top, and her slit skirt reveals more than a flash of upper thigh. Given the PCA's preoccupation with costuming for dances, I assume that the number was cut because of the racy costume in combination with the racy lyrics. For more, see Gil-Montero, *Brazilian Bombshell*, 154–155, and

"Doll Face (1945)—"She Was Always True to the Navy," YouTube video, posted by Gregory May, June 30, 2011, https://www.youtube.com/watch?v=hULPVluqtvY&playnext=1&list =PL0AA87245823C66A1&feature=results_video.

73. Gil-Montero, *Brazilian Bombshell*, 130.

74. Coelho, "Carmen Miranda," 116.

75. "GI Movie Weekly: Sing with the Stars," *Army-Navy Screen Magazine* 72, UCLA Film and Television Archive.

76. Steven Cohan, "Introduction: Musicals of the Studio Era," in *Hollywood Musicals: The Film Reader*, ed. Steven Cohan (London and New York: Routledge, 2002), 12.

77. Don Ameche, interview by Ronald L. Davis, March 1, 1977, OHC 113, transcript, Ronald Davis Oral History Collection, Southern Methodist University DeGolyer Library, Dallas, TX, 30.

78. Roberts, "'The Lady in the Tutti-Frutti Hat,'" 4.

79. Dave Kehr, "New DVDs: Carmen Miranda," *New York Times*, June 17, 2008.

80. Sheldon Wigod, "The Iconography of the American Musical: *The Gang's All Here*," in *Varieties of Filmic Expression: Proceedings of the Seventh Annual International Film Conference of Kent State University*, ed. Douglas Radcliff-Umstead (Kent, OH: Romance Languages Department, Kent State University, 1989), 31.

81. Stam, *Subversive Pleasures*, 93.

82. Review of *The Gang's All Here*, *Variety*, December 1, 1943, *VarietyUltimate.com*, emphasis added.

83. The dance is identified in the credits as the jitterbug, but it is equally identifiable as the Lindy Hop. I suspect it's named as the jitterbug for the reasons just discussed rather than for its choreographic properties. For more on the evolution of the Lindy Hop, see Anthea Kraut, "'Stealing Steps' and Signature Moves: Embodied Theories of Dance as Intellectual Property," *Theatre Journal* 62, no. 2 (May 2010): 173–189.

84. Faye was pregnant during filming, and in fact this was her last film with Fox. Her condition may have required more modest dress. Miranda's dress, however, is a tight black skirt and chartreuse bolero jacket with heavily fringed black epaulets. Her chartreuse hat, complete with pom-pommed veil, sits jauntily on her head, and her gold platform shoes are visible as she dances. As always, the lines of her street clothing echo the *baiana*, marking her off from the other characters.

85. Wigod, "The Iconography of the American Musical," 34.

86. Philip K. Scheuer, "Three Theaters Present 'Something for the Boys,'" *Los Angeles Times*, November 24, 1944; Bosley Crowther, "'Something for the Boys,' a Girl-Packed Musical, at Roxy—'Bowery to Broadway' at Criterion," *New York Times*, November 30, 1944.

87. Marjory Adams, "New Films Metropolitan: 'Something for the Boys,'" *Daily Boston Globe*, December 15, 1944.

88. John Docker, *Postmodernism and Popular Culture: A Cultural History* (Cambridge: Cambridge University Press, 1995), 187.

89. I'm not sure how this costume made it past the censors; the sides and good portions of the backs and torsos of the dancers are covered by nude-colored mesh, definitely suggesting nudity.

90. Nadine Wills, "'110 per cent Woman': The Crotch Shot in the Hollywood Musical," *Screen* 42, no. 2 (Summer 2001): 121, 134.

91. Clark, "Doing the Samba on Sunset Boulevard," 258.

92. Ibid., 259.

93. Stam, *Subversive Pleasures*, 86.

5   FAMOUS FOR BEING FAMOUS: PERSONA, PERFORMANCE,
AND THE CASE FOR ZSA ZSA GABOR

1. *Touch of Evil,* directed by Orson Welles (1958; Universal City, CA: Universal Studios, 2000), DVD.

2. See, for example, Sheila Marikar, "How Zsa Zsa and the Gabor Girls Paved the Way for Today's Starlets," *ABC News Online,* August 17, 2010, http://abcnews.go.com/Entertainment/zsa-zsa-gabor-gave-paris-hilton-kim-kardashian/story?id=11410727#.UMIpw4UZ8iM.

3. Neal Gabler, *Life: The Movie: How Entertainment Conquered Reality* (New York: Vintage Books, 2000), 163.

4. Don Ameche, interview by Ronald L. Davis, March 1, 1977, OHC 113, transcript, Ronald Davis Oral History Collection, Southern Methodist University DeGolyer Library, Dallas, TX, 30.

5. Peter Harry Brown, *Such Devoted Sisters: Those Fabulous Gabors* (New York: St. Martin's Press, 1985), 100.

6. UCLA Film and Television Archive 04-AAA-5462, VHS.

7. "Life's Cover," *Life,* October 15, 1951, 11.

8. "Another Gabor," *Life,* October 15, 1951, 103–104.

9. "Emmy Countdown: Red Carpet Out at Nokia Theatre," *Seattle Times,* September 16, 2009, http://seattletimes.com/html/entertainment/2009878775_apustvemmycountdown.html.

10. Gabler, *Life: The Movie,* 163.

11. Gabor's birth year is difficult to determine. Neither of her autobiographies makes it clear, and most of her biographers agree that the true date is impossible to pin down. In her first autobiography, *Zsa Zsa Gabor: My Story Written for Me by Gerold Frank* (New York: Crest Books, 1960), she claims that she married her first husband, the Turkish diplomat Burhan Belge, when she was fifteen or sixteen years old (45). Sources date this marriage to 1937, which suggests that Gabor was born in 1921 or 1922. In 1989, when she was tried and convicted for driving without a license, with an open container of alcohol in her car, and for assaulting a police officer, "so skillfully did she dodge questions about her age that the judge finally gave up and assigned her one; he picked 66" (Diane Lade, "The Age-Old Lie: Nancy Reagan Does It and Zsa Zsa Gabor Used to before She Was Found Out," *Sun Sentinel,* January 15, 1990, http://articles.sun-sentinel.com/1990-01-15/features/9001190471_1_zsa-zsa-gabor-brandt-age), which puts her birthday in 1923. When she married her current husband, Frédéric Prinz von Anhalt, in 1986, she listed her birth year as 1930, a completely impossible date (Leslie Bennetts, "It's a Mad, Mad, Zsa Zsa World," *Vanity Fair Online,* September 7, 2007, http://www.vanityfair.com/culture/features/2007/10/zsazsa200710). Most sources, however, name February 6, 1917, a date that seems sanctioned by Prinz von Anhalt, who hosted a lavish ninety-fifth birthday party for her in 2012, as well as by the Hungarian consulate, which "sincerely congratulate[d] Zsa Zsa Gabor on the occasion of her 95th birthday" (Derrick J. Lang, "Zsa Zsa Gabor Spends 95th Birthday Behind Closed Doors," *Huffington Post,* February 7, 2012, http://www.huffingtonpost.com/2012/02/07/zsa-zsa-gabors-95th-birthday_n_1260296.html). Gabor has always explained the discrepancies as the result of her and Eva's decision to pretend to be older when they first arrived in the United States (see, for example, Bennetts, "It's a Mad, Mad Zsa Zsa World").

12. Brown, *Such Devoted Sisters,* 6–7.

13. Zsa Zsa Gabor and Gerold Frank, *Zsa Zsa Gabor: My Story, Written for Me by Gerold Frank* (Cleveland: Cleveland World Publishing Company, 1960), 19, 31, 33.

14. Ibid., 32–47.

15. Zsa Zsa Gabor and Wendy Leigh, *One Lifetime Is Not Enough* (New York: Bantam Doubleday Dell Publishing Group, 1991), 24.

16. Ibid., 30.

17. "Turkish Official's Wife Here, Lauds Absence of Oppression," *Los Angeles Times*, June 21, 1941.

18. "Timeline: The Love Life of Zsa Zsa Gabor," *Los Angeles Times*, May 20, 2011, http://timelines.latimes.com/zsa-zsa-gabor/.

19. Gabor and Frank, *Zsa Zsa Gabor*, 127, 153.

20. "George Sanders Sues Zsa Zsa for Divorce," *Los Angeles Times*, November 3, 1953.

21. Hedda Hopper, "Eye Trouble," *Los Angeles Times*, December 31, 1953.

22. Art Ryon, "Industrialist Weds Zsa Zsa in New York," *Los Angeles Times*, November 6, 1962; the reporter was attempting to reproduce Gabor's accent.

23. "Zsa Zsa Gabor Gets License to Wed No. 5," *Los Angeles Times*, March 5, 1966.

24. "Timeline: The Love Life of Zsa Zsa Gabor."

25. James Marnell, "Navy's 'Grand Old Lady' Jumps Ship after 43 Years," *Los Angeles Times*, August 15, 1986, http://articles.latimes.com/1986–08–15/news/mn-3713_1_zsa-zsa -gabor.

26. Nikki Finke, "Boasts, Not Bucks for Zsa Zsa? The Marketing of a Misdemeanor Loses Steam," *Los Angeles Times*, December 1, 1989, http://articles.latimes.com/1989–12–01/news/ vw-302_1_zsa-zsa.

27. "Zsa Zsa Gabor Doing Better, Should Be Released from Hospital Soon," *Los Angeles Times*, August 2, 2010, http://latimesblogs.latimes.com/lanow/2010/08/zsa-zsa-gabor-hip -replacement.html.

28. Robin Hindery, "Prince Frederic von Anhalt, Zsa Zsa's Flamboyant Husband, Joins Race for Governor," *Huffington Post*, February 17, 2010, http://www.huffingtonpost.com/ 2010/02/17/prince-frederic-von-anhal_n_466434.html; Anthony McCartney, "Constance Francesca Hilton, Zsa Zsa Gabor's Daughter, Files for Conservatorship," *Huffington Post*, March 20, 2012, http://www.huffingtonpost.com/2012/03/20/constance-francesca-hilton -conservatorship_n_1367984.html.

29. "Freedom's Choice," *Time*, January 7, 1957, 20ff. It wasn't economically possible to reproduce the cover image for this book, but it's easily available at http://content.time .com/time/covers/0,16641,19570107,00.html.

30. Edwin Schallert, "Foreign Press Film Fete May Become Other Events' Rival," *Los Angeles Times*, January 13, 1952.

31. Lydia Lane, "Zsa Zsa Gabor Tells Beauty, Success Secrets," *Los Angeles Times*, May 25, 1952.

32. Hedda Hopper, "Deep Drama Next Goal of Zsa Zsa," *Los Angeles Times*, February 17, 1953.

33. Hedda Hopper, "Wald to Produce 'David' for Adler," *Los Angeles Times*, March 6, 1958.

34. *The Steve Allen Show*, January 16, 1964, UCLA Film and Television Archive 04-AAL-9141, VHS.

35. All quotes and information from Endre Marton, "Papa Gabor's Poor Now but He's Still Rich in Memories," *Los Angeles Times*, January 3, 1954. The second, much shorter, article summarizes the first article and mentions Magda and Zsa Zsa's intellectual accomplishments and beauty; it is unattributed: "Ailing Hungarian Proud," *Los Angeles Times*, July 18, 1954.

36. Walter Ames, "Zsa Zsa Puts Americanism Thoughts in Congressional Record on Her Anniversary," *Los Angeles Times*, March 26, 1952.

37. Hedda Hopper, "Hope to Head Alaska Junket in December," *Los Angeles Times*, November 14, 1956.

38. "Film Stars Entertain at Hungarian Relief Rally," *Los Angeles Times*, December 1, 1956.

39. Gabor and Frank, *Zsa Zsa Gabor*, 132–133.

40. Regarding the nose job see, for example, Jacob Bernstein, "Zsa Zsa's Family Circus," *Daily Beast*, August 19, 2010, www.thedailybeast.com/articles/2010/08/19/zsa-zsa-gabor-is -dying-or-is-she.html.

41. Bennetts, "It's a Mad, Mad, Zsa Zsa World."

42. Ibid.

43. Richard de Cordova, *Picture Personalities: The Emergence of the Star System in America* (Urbana and Chicago: University of Illinois Press, 1990), 141.

44. Paul O'Neil, "Great Tell-It-All," *Life*, June 29, 1959, 129–139, quotations from 130, 139.

45. These reviews are quoted inside the front cover of Gabor and Frank, *Zsa Zsa Gabor*.

46. Ibid., 143.

47. "Porfirio Rubirosa Is Killed as Auto Crashes in Paris," *New York Times*, July 6, 1965.

48. In Shawn Levy, *The Last Playboy: The High Life of Porfirio Rubirosa* (New York: Harper Perennial, 2005), 126–127.

49. Hopper, "Eye Trouble." For most real victims of domestic violence, of course, Gabor's reaction would seem insulting; for most women it is at least outrageous.

50. "Barbara Hutton Wed to Rubirosa; Snubs Zsa Zsa," *Los Angeles Times*, December 30, 1953.

51. "Eye Blacked by Rubirosa, Zsa Zsa Says," *Los Angeles Times*, December 29, 1953.

52. Gabor and Frank, *Zsa Zsa Gabor*, 246.

53. Hearst Newsreel Footage, "Trujillo, Rubirosa, CS1393 [19—]," UCLA Film and Television Archive 04-AAF-0092.

54. Adrienne McLean, *Being Rita Hayworth: Labor, Identity and Hollywood Stardom* (New Brunswick, NJ, and London: Rutgers University Press, 2004), 80.

55. See "Jane Fonda Asks Johnny Carson About Zsa Zsa Gabor," YouTube video, from *The Johnny Carson Show*, 1989, posted by RustyShackleford965 on August 25, 2012, http://www.youtube.com/watch?v=m3IuPsY5CTE.

56. Lois Banner, *In Full Flower: Aging Women, Power, and Sexuality* (New York: Vintage Books, 1993), especially 281, 294.

57. "Zsa Zsa Gabor in that Green Dress Part 2 'One Lifetime Is Not Enough,'" YouTube Video, 5:27, from *The David Letterman Show*, Nov. 27, 1991, posted by srfup on Oct. 31, 2008, http://www.youtube.com/watch?v=gOhH0xF5F2w.

58. "Dave Letterman and Zsa Zsa's Fast Food Car Trip," YouTube video, from *The David Letterman Show*, 1994, posted by Henrybwalthall on November 19, 2012, http://www.youtube.com/watch?v=3F6ihYOgruY.

59. *Shindig!*, October 10, 1965, UCLA Film and Television Archive, 04-AAL-4728, VHS. Hosted by LA disc jockey Jimmy O'Neill, *Shindig!* ran on ABC September 1964–January 1966. The program was broadcast live, and several top bands performed onstage rather than lip-synched their numbers as on its rival *American Bandstand*. *Shindig!* is perhaps most famous for debuting the Who to US television audiences.

60. *A Very Brady Sequel*, directed by Arlene Sanford (1993; Los Angeles: The Ladd Company and Paramount Pictures), Netflix Streaming Video.

61. Gabor and Frank, *Zsa Zsa Gabor*, 163.

62. Bruce Handy, "Glamour and Goulash," *Vanity Fair*, July 2001, 106.

63. Mary Ann Doane, "Film and the Masquerade: Theorising the Female Spectator," *Screen* 25, no. 3–4 (September–October 1982): 81.

64. Judith Butler, *Bodies That Matter: On the Discursive Limits of "Sex"* (New York and London: Routledge, 1993), 95.

65. Alan Sinfield, *Faultlines: Cultural Materialism and the Politics of Dissident Reading* (Berkeley and Los Angeles: University of California Press, 1992), 41.

66. Rudy Bretz, "TV as an Art Form," *Hollywood Quarterly* 5, no. 2 (Winter 1950): 153–154.

67. Edward Padula, "Acting in Television," *High School Thespian* 11, no. 6 (1940): 10.

68. Carl Beier Jr., "A New Way of Looking at Things," *Hollywood Quarterly* 2, no. 1 (October 1946): 1–2.

69. Padula, "Acting in Television," 13.

70. Irving Pichel, "Films for Television," *Hollywood Quarterly* 5, no. 4 (Summer 1951): 365.

71. Christine Becker, *It's the Pictures That Got Small: Hollywood Film Stars on 1950s Television* (Middletown, CT: Wesleyan University Press, 2008), 26.

72. Ibid., 106–107.

73. Elana Levine, "Distinguishing Television: The Changing Meanings of Television Liveness," *Media, Culture & Society* 30, no. 3 (2008): 394.

74. William Boddy, *Fifties Television: The Industry and Its Critics* (Urbana and Chicago: University of Illinois Press, 1992), 76.

75. "A Man of Taste," directed by Allen Reisner, *Climax!*, CBS, December 1, 1955, UCLA Film and Television Archive, 04-AAB-6186, VHS.

76. Padula, "Acting in Television," 10.

77. Irving Pichel, "Character, Personality, and Image: A Note on Screen Acting," *Hollywood Quarterly* 2, no. 1 (October 1946): 25.

78. Padula, "Acting in Television," 13; Pichel, "Character, Personality, and Image," 27; Melvin R. White, *Beginning Television Production* (Minneapolis: Northwestern Press, 1950), 80.

79. Cynthia Baron, "The Method Moment: Situating the Rise of Method Acting in the 1950s," *Popular Culture Review* 9, no. 2 (1998): 89.

80. Sharon Marie Carnicke, *Stanislavsky in Focus: An Acting Master for the Twenty-first Century*, 3rd ed. (Oxon: Routledge, 2009), 10; Baron, "The Method Moment," 100.

81. Beier, "A New Way of Looking at Things," 5.

82. John Langer, "Television's 'Personality System,'" *Media, Culture & Society* 4 (1981): 352–354.

83. John Ellis, "Stars as a Cinematic Phenomenon," in *Star Texts: Image and Performance in Film and Television*, ed. Jeremy G. Butler (Detroit: Wayne State University Press, 1991), 313.

84. See Deborah Jermyn, "Bringing Out the Star in You? SJP, Carrie Bradshaw, and the Evolution of Television Stardom," in *Framing Celebrity: New Directions in Celebrity Culture*, ed. Su Holmes and Sean Redmond (London: Routledge 2006), 96–117.

85. "The Zsa Zsa Gabor Show," directed by Parke Levy, *December Bride*, CBS, November 13, 1955, UCLA Film and Television Archive 04-AAD-1251, VHS. Not coincidentally, Gabor was honorary chairman of the Holiday Traffic Safety Campaign in 1958, a cause she supported throughout the 1950s.

86. Throughout the textual readings, "Zsa Zsa" signals the character and "Gabor" signals the persona.

87. "Zsa Zsa and Mr. Ed," directed by Arthur Lubin, *Mr. Ed*, CBS, January 1, 1962, UCLA Film and Television Archive 04-AAI-6703, VHS. This plotline is surprising. Audiences familiar with Gabor were also familiar with her reputation as a horsewoman. In fact, she wears the same jodhpurs, houndstooth jacket, silk blouse, diamond brooch, and riding boots in her scenes with Mr. Ed as she wore playing herself as a champion horsewoman in the 1958 film *Country Music Holiday* as well as riding on the Bois de Boulogne with Rubirosa in the 1955 newsreel. Gabor's willingness to use her own clothes as costumes signals her participation in the construction of her characters (whether a fictional rich widow in *Country Music Holiday* or Rubirosa's real-life lover). Further, this riding costume, undoubtedly made to order, was more luxurious and thus more authentic than the budgets of *Mr. Ed* or *Country Music Holiday* could afford.

88. "Zsa Zsa Redecorates," directed by James V. Kern, *The Joey Bishop Show*, NBC, January 1, 1964, UCLA Film and Television Archive 04-AAF-8367, VHS. Bishop played a fictionalized version of himself, and his show always opened on the set of his comedy broadcast program (much like *Seinfeld* in the 1990s).

89. Mary Beth Haralovich, "Sit-coms and Suburbs: Positioning the 1950s Homemaker," in *Private Screenings: Television and the Female Consumer*, ed. Lynn Spigel and Denise Mann (Minneapolis: University of Minnesota Press, 1993), 138.

90. Nina C. Leibman, *Living Room Lectures: The Fifties Family in Film and Television* (Austin: University of Texas Press 1995), 43–64, 118–136, 150.

91. Elaine Tyler May, *Homeward Bound: American Families in the Cold War Era* (New York: Basic Books, 1992), 13.

92. In Marlon Riggs, *Color Adjustment* (1991; Los Angeles: California Newsreel), VHS.

93. Though these programs span a six-year period, over which Gabor's celebrity persona was at least to some extent recalibrated, her representation is relatively stable.

94. Denise Mann, "The Spectacularization of Everyday Life: Recycling Hollywood Stars and Fans in Early Television Variety Shows," in *Private Screenings: Television and the Female Consumer*, ed. Lynn Spigel and Denise Mann (Minneapolis: University of Minnesota Press, 1992), 47.

95. Susan Hartmann, "Women's Employment and the Domestic Ideal in the Early Postwar Years," in *Not June Cleaver: Women and Gender in Postwar America, 1945–1960*, ed. Joanne Meyerowitz (Philadelphia: Temple University Press, 1994), 84–127. Women in the 1950s worked as much as their wartime counterparts: employment figures for married women rose throughout the period, and middle-class women worked outside the home in increasing numbers. Hartmann reports that women's employment, rather than being ignored or denigrated, was largely supported by the Cold War public, in particular through the childcare tax credit developed to help working mothers at both poor and middle-class economic levels. Further, the National Manpower Council, charged with developing new strategies to increase US market power, suggested that women were an important part of the labor force, and that rather than leading to juvenile delinquency and neurotic children, working mothers improved the standard of living for their families, encouraged the participation of fathers in child care, and were more satisfied with their lives and thus better able to parent (86–90). Of course, "implicit or explicit throughout the work of the NMC [and other groups] was the assumption that women's childbearing role was central" (93).

96. Mann, "The Spectacularization of Everyday Life," 42.

97. See, for example, Laura Mulvey, *Visual and Other Pleasures* (Bloomington: Indiana University Press, 1989) and Jill Dolan, *The Feminist Spectator as Critic* (Ann Arbor: University of Michigan Press, 1991).

98. Tracy C. Davis, "*Extremities* and *Masterpieces*: A Feminist Paradigm of Art and Politics," in *Feminist Theatre and Theory*, ed. Helene Keyssar (Basingstoke, Eng.: Palgrave Macmillan, 1995), 138.

INDEX

Note: Page numbers in *italics* indicate figures. Films are identified by year in parentheses; books by author in parentheses.

ABOUT THE AUTHOR

Kirsten Pullen, Ray A. Rothrock '77 Research Fellow, is an associate professor and the director of graduate studies in the Department of Performance Studies at Texas A&M University. She is also the director of TAMU's Academy of Visual and Performing Arts. She earned her PhD in theater from the University of Wisconsin in 2001 and taught at the University of Calgary before joining the TAMU faculty. Pullen has published books and articles on prostitution and performance, Internet fandom, theater audiences, and actresses; teaches courses in theater history and intercultural performance; and directs departmental productions.